PÂTISSERIE

Gluten Free

PÂTISSERIE
Gluten Free

The Art of French Pastry
Cookies, Tarts, Cakes, and Puff Pastries

PATRICIA AUSTIN

Foreword by Jeffrey Hamelman
Photography by Charlie Ritzo

Skyhorse Publishing

Skyhorse Publishing books may be purchased in bulk at special discounts for sales promotion, corporate gifts, fund-raising, or educational purposes. Special editions can also be created to specifications. For details, contact the Special Sales Department, Skyhorse Publishing, 307 West 36th Street, 11th Floor, New York, NY 10018 or info@skyhorsepublishing.com.

Skyhorse® and Skyhorse Publishing® are registered trademarks of Skyhorse Publishing, Inc.®, a Delaware corporation.

Visit our website at www.skyhorsepublishing.com.

10 9 8 7 6 5

Library of Congress Cataloging-in-Publication Data

Names: Austin, Patricia (Pastry chef) author.
Title: Pâtisserie gluten free: the art of French pastry: cookies, tarts,
    cakes and puff pastries / Patricia Austin; foreword by Jeffrey Hamelman;
    photography by Charlie Ritzo.
Description: New York, NY: Skyhorse Publishing, [2017]
Identifiers: LCCN 2016043176| ISBN 9781510712928 (hardback) | ISBN 9781510712966 (ebook)
Subjects: LCSH: Gluten-free diet—Recipes. | Pastry. | BISAC: COOKING / Methods / Baking.
Classification: LCC RM237.86 .A97 2017 | DDC 641.5/639311—dc23
LC record available at https://lccn.loc.gov/2016043176

Cover design by Margaret Shipman
Cover photo by Charlie Ritzo

Print ISBN: 978-1-5107-1292-8
Ebook ISBN: 978-1-5107-1296-6

Printed in China

To my spirit family
Chakwat mateguas

Contents

Foreword

Two decades ago the word "celiac" had not yet entered the common lexicon; today there are few people who are not familiar with the word. As awareness of celiac disease became more widespread, efforts were quickly underway to develop baked goods that could be tolerated by those afflicted with this terrible burden. Most of these early attempts were long on earnestness, but on the whole they were not particularly refined. Many if not most of the early recipes relied on various highly refined ingredients and assorted vegetable gums (so while the foods were in fact gluten-free, they were not necessarily good for you); others were just plain tasteless.

In all good things, evolution steadily unfolds, and this very much applies to the world of gluten-free baking. The collective initial work served to provide important stepping stones, laying the groundwork and bringing us to where we are today. And what we have today, in Patricia Austin's excellent *Pâtisserie Gluten Free*, is the apotheosis of that evolution.

Patricia has devoted over half her life to the pursuit of baking and pastry, and she truly is a baker's baker—organized, skilled, curious, ever in quest of more knowledge and more connection to the finer points of her chosen *métier*. I met Patricia more than thirty years ago, when she was still new to the trade. Her work was good, her attitude professional, her demeanor steady. Those attributes have served her well, and as she grew so too did they, and today she is a *pâtissier* of notable skill and refinement.

Pâtisserie Gluten Free is remarkable in many ways. First because it brings together in one place dozens of delectable cakes and pastries that have been painstakingly crafted by the hands of a dedicated chef (and thoroughly explained by her excellent and clear writing). Patricia presents us with an expansive array of flavors and textures, and in the aggregate these offer us the potential of months if not years of exploration in our kitchens as we savor the recipes. One very notable aspect of the book is the inclusion of a number of classic French pastries that have been part of the repertoire for decades, and that were developed without the inclusion of flour—they just happened to have used nuts instead. *Dacquoise* comes to mind, along with those incomparable *Macarons* (the *macaron* recipes themselves are worth the price of the book). Rubbing shoulders with these worthies are the newcomers that Patricia has developed, and these bring a ring of modernity to the book. Recipes like *Religieuses* and Pear Frangipane Tart, even in their gluten-free guise, can't help but elicit happy smiles and happy bellies. I consider myself a traditionalist, and from time to time worry that I am a rigid one. But when I first ate Patricia's *Canelé de Bordeaux* I was astonished at how good the gluten-free version was, and relieved that at least I'm not so rigid that I can't enjoy one!

Pâtisserie Gluten Free is a book to savor—for the warm tone of the writing, for the breadth and accuracy of the recipes, and for the evocative beauty of the photographs. There is meticulous artistry shining throughout these pages. Patricia's work has elevated the world of gluten-free baking to a sophisticated and distinguished level, and we readers and bakers are the fortunate beneficiaries of her excellent efforts.

—Jeffrey Hamelman

Preface

A Baker's Craft

As a child, I repeatedly found my way into the kitchen, where I would hang on to the cracked stoneware baking bowl for dear life, creaming the butter that ultimately turned into chocolate chip cookies or hermit bars. Here, in the world of baking, I disappeared into my senses, gazing deeply at luscious batters, breathing in the alluring aromas of rising cakes and caramelizing cookies, and enchanted with the hands-on, tactile connection of baking. In the end, the reward was magical: sweetness I could eat that filled me with tremendous pleasure and gratification. The act of baking gave me focus and kept me organized, while the kitchen became a place of love that held my young self.

Those early years set me squarely in the kitchen, so it naturally followed that my first jobs were in the food industry. At age seventeen, I became a croissant maker at a local business, Baguette French Bread. Mixing, pounding, folding, and gently rolling hundreds of croissants by hand was a great meditation in patience and physical endurance that reinforced my commitment to the craft.

Thousands of croissants later, in the early 1980s, a new bakery opened in Brattleboro, Vermont, that was the talk of the town. A close friend of mine had gotten a job there as a bread baker's apprentice and put in a good word for me. I brought whole wheat thumbprint cookies to the interview, professed my love of baking, and Jeffrey Hamelman (who is now a Certified Master Baker and director of the King Arthur Bakery) asked, "Can I see your hands?" Apparently they looked okay, because a week later I started as a pastry chef assistant at Hamelman's Bakery! Jeffrey introduced me to a new European style of baking that further fueled my passion and pushed me to work more efficiently and develop my work ethic. I learned about preparing *Feuilletées* (flaky pastries), *Génoise* (sponge cakes), yeasted breakfast pastries, delicate Swiss walnut tarts lined with jam and topped with tiny swirls of buttercream frosting, and many of the classics in French pastry. We would save all the "scraps" from a month's accumulation of leftover cakes, croissants, and buttercream and make the secret and deeply delicious rum cake that springs from the European sensibility of exacting minimum waste. In the early morning hours, I would stand on a milk crate at the double-burner stovetop, slowly and sleepily stirring poppy seed filling, and later hang over a five-gallon stainless steel pot bubbling with pastry cream as my whole body madly whipped with a gigantic hand whisk. Even my dreams were rich in pastry, including one featuring a giant chocolate croissant chasing me down an endless road!

In 1987, I committed to the enormous undertaking of opening a bakery in Keene, New Hampshire. The bakery thrived, and I continued to study European-style pastry making; from dawn to dusk I was wholly devoted to the art of baking and mastering techniques. However, even though the bakery was only twenty miles from Brattleboro, Vermont, I was truly homesick for my birthplace. I shed salty tears along the workbench and longed for the forest and rivers that had been my companions since early childhood. Eventually, I returned home to Vermont and sought a bakery model that would suit my free spirit.

Soon after, I fell in love with pâtisseries while in Paris in 2004, and this affair has since been the ardent force inspiring my work. From my *bon appartement* in the charming historical section of Île Saint-Louis, I devoted each day to French pastries, searching the city, speaking poor yet effortful French, and jubilantly collecting freshly prepared creations. Elegant ballotin pastry boxes from countless shops filled with exquisite delights would accompany me back home to be revealed, scrutinized, and swooned over. Then I'd take myself out for an afternoon tea ritual at the pâtisserie Ladurée on Rue Royale, where the golden, rosy cherub murals kept me company. There I would discreetly observe, sketch, and dissect the pastry creations, delighting in their visual presentation, textures, and flavors, determined to create them anew, and eventually gluten-free, while retaining their fabulous French pastry characteristics. That dream was waiting just around the corner.

In 2005, I began to offer gluten-free creations at the lively Brattleboro Area Farmers' Market, Vermont's oldest and most successful farmers' market. I now create pastries from my bakery, a cottage industry located at my home on a little mountain. I am fortunate to live in this beautiful part of the world and bake while the foxes trot by and the owls hoot in the evening. Raising hens and collecting fresh organic eggs for baking, keeping honeybees whose beeswax coats the canelé molds and honey sweetens the gingerbread, growing edible flowers for decorating, and tending the blueberry bushes and the *fraises de bois* (woodland strawberries) patch—these are the unique aspects of my baking world that I take pride in. Here, I have found my sweet spot, where I have honed in on recipe development and gluten-free French pastry making. After many years of baking, and more than a decade of baking gluten-free, I feel gratefully compelled to offer these recipes to you.

Introduction

French Pastries Made Gluten-Free

The long-held tradition of baking with wheat has a familiar, satisfying rhythm that is practiced by home and professional bakers alike. However, a new type of baking has settled in over the past decade, and that is gluten-free baking. Many of us are choosing to eat gluten-free for health reasons that range from general personal preferences to life-threatening allergies. Today we find gluten-free baking books that use multiple types of flour and gums with formulas set forth in good faith to make a delicious product. But gluten-free baking, with its scientific alteration of the standard baking process, has a steep learning curve, and turning out successful recipes is often difficult.

During my initial experimentation with gluten-free baking, I followed the trend of stashing large amounts of various gluten-free flours in my freezer and delving deep into the mixing bowl with what sometimes would feel like endless testing and retesting. My greatest success in gluten-free baking has resulted from using a gluten-free flour blend that most closely resembles baking with wheat flour, minus the use of gums. Many of us have a sensitivity to the commonly used xanthan gum and guar gum additives included in gluten-free flour blends, myself included. I was more than happy when I discovered a new flour blend that is free of gums. The recipes in this book have all been tested with a specific, revolutionary flour blend: Steve's Gluten Free Cake Flour from Authentic Foods, which is gluten-free, gum-free, and GMO-free. Using this blend means you'll sacrifice neither baking creativity nor quality. I've also included a recipe for a homemade gluten-free flour blend that will work in many of the recipes, plus further tips on the extensive variety of gluten-free blends on the market (see pages 1 to 3).

A return to the familiar rhythm of baking with outcomes that rival traditional recipes is what you will find in this book. The recipes were developed to highlight their distinctive French pastry characteristics: enticingly appetizing and memorably delicious. My sincere hope is that with this book home bakers and professional pastry chefs alike will feel the sweet desire to return to the kinship of the bakery, delve into the mixing bowl, and create delightful French pastries made gluten- and gum-free.

When I contemplate French pastry, the words that come to mind are *eating beauty*. Whether it's a rustic berry galette or an elegant chocolate gâteau, the complex flavor

Mise en Place: A French Culinary Term that Means "Setting in Place"

⌒

As a baker, the most common question I receive from my curious customers is "How long does it take to bake all these pastries?" I prepare for market day over the course of a few days so I can display and offer a generous selection of freshly made, visually inviting pastries. My love of baking keeps me on task, but the main reason my productivity is prolific and still delicious is rooted in the practice of mise en place.

In essence, mise en place means organizing ahead of time—preparing and arranging ingredients, tools, and the work area in anticipation of the actual baking process. Mise en place entails getting ready and taking each next step of preparation, one at a time, until the stage is set, all the props are in place, and the action is ready to begin. Performance relies largely on your organization and readiness as you move through the recipes.

Before mise en place begins, a thorough reading of the recipe is a must. I cannot emphasize this enough: read your recipe twice, from beginning to end. Then weigh and prep your ingredients and set them in the order of the recipe's ingredients list. Set out all the tools required so they are easily available. If you have one part of the recipe taking place on the stove and a simultaneous one at the work bench, make sure they are organized ahead of time with their respective tools and timers if needed. Keep your recipe nearby, don an apron, make sure your kitchen towels are at hand, and, voilà, you are ready to begin!

profiles, contrasting textures, and stunning finishes of French pastries are what set them apart in the world of baking. And French pastries are world renowned for their luxurious ingredients, especially butter; in France, bakers use a superior quality butter that contains a high percentage of butterfat, greatly contributing to the pastries' rich depth of full-bodied flavors. Flaky, tender pastries filled with lush creams, fresh fruits, nut pastes, and exceptional chocolate create a tempting feast for your eyes and mouth. As you bake your way through *Pâtisserie Gluten Free*, prepare to be eating beauty—with all your senses!

Baking with Your Five Senses, Plus One

What kind of baker are you? What are your strengths and challenges? The field of baking emphasizes the importance of science, which plays a fundamental role in successful baking. However, baking is equally about using your senses. Truthfully, I do not consider myself a scientific baker. My gut feeling says I am far from alone in this baker's bubble. Basics in baking, such as the evaporation of water, the subsequent forced elevation of the dough, and the use of leavenings, are generally familiar to me. However, after nearly forty years of professional baking, I still cannot explain the alchemy of baking. Over the years, I have made furtive attempts at greater comprehension, but it just does not stick. And while I'll pull out my trusty reference books for reminders, primarily I rely on the experience of my senses, including my intuition.

The world of baking captivates my senses; I am sensing and focusing, and doing so with intense curiosity and concentration. Mise en place keeps me steady, and my senses remain heightened and guide me through the process. When a baking failure occurs, and sometimes it does, I figure out what went wrong by using my five senses plus the mysterious sixth one: common sense.

Over time, as we develop our baking skills, we hone our senses and become more experienced and knowledgeable bakers. Baking gluten-free is, for many, a new challenge, and employing your five senses will help you to be successful. Remember that we all have our learning curves. Welcome to the fellowship of bakers!

Touch
The sense of touch provides tactile information about your baking throughout the various stages. We touch our ingredients, dough, and batter with our hands to discern the texture and integrity of the product. To determine when your baking is done, use your touch and trust your senses. Touch the pastries when they are fresh from the oven, warm, cool, and cold. This will help you learn the expected tactile characteristics of baked goods at different temperatures. Our sense of touch can be highly sensual, and this is an added pleasure in the experience of baking. You may need a firm or gentle hand, and stroking, smoothing, poking, pulling, squeezing, folding, slapping, and tapping are all essential and dynamic parts of the baking experience.

Sight
Look with your eyes to scan the work environment for tools, perceive ingredients for quality, and check measurements for accuracy. Sometimes we need to slow way down and stare intently into a bowl, searching perhaps for a stray piece of eggshell or a smidge of unwanted egg yolk in the egg whites that needs excavating. We observe the interactions of ingredients and resulting textural changes and watch for successful methodology of developing batter and dough. And we rely on our vision to help determine the timing for the next steps. Perceiving the transformative visual effect of textures, colors, and shapes is deeply gratifying and rousing to a baker. And the sight of your delicious pastries will activate your salivary glands!

Sound

When dough or batter is active in the mixer, various sounds signal the different stages of development and indicators for the next steps. These sounds may be the interaction between the ingredients or the ingredients and the tools involved. Listen to the creaming of butter and sugar against the mixing bowl, it will sound lighter and smoother as time passes. Eggs will often make a sloshing sound as they are added and before they're incorporated. The mixer will emit a new, more labored sound with the addition of flour as it slows down the mixer. When whole nuts are ground in a food processor, the sound starts out loud and grows quieter as the nuts become more finely ground. Sugar syrup will make different sounds at various stages of cooking as the size of the bubbles burst and the thickness of the syrup changes. The beeping or buzzing of the timer will guide your next assessment. Make a point to listen as you work and stroke, tap, rap, or squeeze your finished baked goods to know what they sound like.

Smell

Smell all your ingredients, in particular those that are perishable, as smell is a reliable indicator for freshness and quality of ingredients. Each recipe will emit characteristic smells as you put them together and place them in the oven to bake. When the sugars caramelize and emit deeper aromas, we know the baking is reaching its final stage in the oven. Bring a baked good as close to your nose as you desire; there is great pleasure when we inhale the aromas of our baking. Your sense of smell mingles with your sense of taste, offering you lasting pleasure.

Taste

Tasting, of course, can bring exquisite pleasure. It also provides tremendous information about simple concerns of freshness, quality, successful outcomes, and explorations of complex flavor combinations and nuances. Taste your ingredients, dough, and batter throughout the stages. Always taste for sugar, salt, flavoring, and leavening. Baking soda and baking powder will leave a mildly bitter, acidic taste in your mouth, especially when it is still in the form of a dry ingredient mixture. This flavor will lessen once moisture has been added. Learn to know what each pastry tastes like right from the oven, warm, cool, and cold. If there is a choice between eating with your fingers or a fork, remove the restriction of the utensil and opt for your touch-sensitive fingers. Fingers are meant for licking! If you feel slightly self-conscious, look for a private spot, if only briefly to lose yourself in the pleasure of the moment.

Common Sense

Common sense, the plus one of the senses, is an inherent basic awareness that includes your ability to perceive, comprehend, and judge situations as they arise. Simply put, this sense will add integrity to your skills as a baker. Be smart, use your mind, get organized, keep good notes, stay focused, and accept failures as learning opportunities. Embody your common sense as your best friend in the kitchen while you journey through your baking endeavors.

About the Recipes

Years ago, I had the good fortune to share an engaging dialogue about recipes with a lifelong passionate baker, Susanne Naegele. Susanne traveled from Germany to the United States carrying her sourdough culture and armed with a French pastry chef to open what would become a tremendous new baking enterprise in the town of Northampton, Massachusetts, in the mid-1970s. My first introduction to Susanne was at Hamelman's Bakery in Brattleboro, Vermont. While petite in stature, Susanne's presence was kindly formidable: her hair tucked into a tight bun, while her discerning eyes sharply scanned every action unfolding in the lively bakery. Decades later, Susanne imparted her wisdom with these words: "Recipes are suggestions." What you do with them is up to you. It can take time to develop a recipe to the point where you are wholly content with the outcome. There will always be those elusive recipes that keep us returning to resolve their nuances to our personal satisfaction.

Recipes and their origins can be the subject of great debate, particularly when it comes to French pastries. Throughout the history of baking, recipes are formed and transformed repeatedly. From fundamental recipes to great classics, bakers make alterations that range from subtle to extreme. New recipes can be creative amalgamations of existing recipes, and there are classics that remain predictable yet challenging in their production. In this book you will find both naturally gluten-free recipes and adaptations of traditional wheat-based recipes. As a lifelong baker, I have had the good fortune to be influenced by many chefs, friends, and acquaintances, and their inspirations are inevitably folded into my baking style and these recipes.

CHAPTER ONE

Ingredients, Equipment, Sources

Ingredients

Wherever you find yourself on the gluten-free continuum, I encourage you to seek out gluten-free ingredients that inspire your confidence and support your well-being. Some manufacturers of gluten-free products keep designated gluten-free facilities, while others process a variety of products that can or may contain traces of gluten. If you have a health condition such as celiac disease that involves severe gluten intolerance, be vigilant about sourcing your ingredients from designated gluten-free producers.

At the end of the day, your baking will only be as good as your ingredients. Whenever possible, buy the best! Hands down, choosing excellent ingredients will result in a higher-quality final product. Purchase local, organic produce when available; chances are, the closer to your region a product was grown and harvested, the fresher and better tasting it will be. I use GMO-free products; for example, organic cornstarch and organic confectioners' sugar (nonorganic confectioners' sugar contains cornstarch to reduce clumping, and nonorganic cornstarch is often genetically modified), and I swap out corn syrup for honey. Explore local shopping options, including farmers' markets, and review the Sources section on pages 14 and 15 when you set out to gather the ingredients on your recipe list. Recipe list ingredients should all be at room temperature unless otherwise noted. This includes the gluten-free flour blend, sugar, nuts, and eggs.

About the Gluten- and Gum-Free Flour Blend

Many people have a sensitivity and/or intolerance to the gums typically found in most gluten-free flour blends. The intent of this book is to offer less complicated gluten- and gum-free baking; this is best accomplished by using a blend I've found that most closely replicates wheat flour: Steve's Gluten Free Cake Flour from the Authentic Foods brand. This gluten-, gum-, and GMO-free flour blend saves you the fuss of creating your own blend and delivers consistently reliable results. The ingredients in the blend are white rice flour, potato starch, tapioca starch, and a proprietary fiber blend made from naturally occurring plant fibers, including psyllium and vegetable cellulose. All of the recipes in this book were tested using Steve's Gluten Free Cake Flour. You can find it online at authenticfoods.com as well as amazon.com.

You can also opt for another type of gluten-free flour blend that does or does not contain gums; look for brands that act as a cup-for-cup replacement for wheat flour. However, remember that each brand of gluten-free flour blend performs differently. They do not all contain the same ingredients or the same ratio of ingredients, which means that exchanging one gluten-free flour brand for another is not an exact science, and, therefore, your baking results will vary. For example, you may need to alter the liquid or flour measurements to obtain the correct texture of dough. In addition, the amount of fiber or protein will vary from brand to brand, resulting in varying degrees of ingredient reactions and performance.

As you bake your way through this book, I strongly suggest that you use the Authentic Foods brand of Steve's Gluten Free Cake Flour for all of the recipes (even when not specifically indicated) when possible for the most successful results. You'll see how happy it will make you!

If you'd prefer to make your own blend, you can use Patricia's Gluten- and Gum-Free Flour Blend, which is also GMO-free.

Patricia's Gluten- and Gum-Free Flour Blend

Makes 4½ cups (668 grams)

1¾ cups (280 grams) superfine white rice flour

½ cup (80 grams) superfine brown rice flour

¾ cup (120 grams) sweet rice flour

¾ cup (90 grams) tapioca starch

½ cup (80 grams) potato starch

3 tablespoons (18 grams) chia powder

Method

1 In a large bowl, combine all the ingredients and whisk together.

2 Sift the ingredients onto a large piece of parchment paper or into another bowl.

3 Pour the flour blend into a glass jar or plastic bag, label it, and store at room temperature or in the freezer.

Butter

All the recipes in this book use unsalted butter. The standard for unsalted butter in North America is regulated by the USDA, which states that unsalted butter must contain at least 80% butterfat, including milk fat, milk solids, and water. European-style butter has a reputation for producing richer tasting, more tender, and flakier baked goods because they are made with a higher butterfat content, ranging from 82 to 88%. These premium, higher fat butters are more costly, because fat is more expensive than water. Options for higher-fat butter are becoming more available in the United States. Many grocery and/or specialty stores now carry premium, high-fat, unsalted butter; Plugra is one commercially available brand. Though I encourage you to use a European-style high-fat butter in your baking, all of the recipes in this book can be made successfully using the butter that's commonly available in the United States, but it must be unsalted.

The recipes in this book call for butter in various states. Room temperature means the butter should be pliable enough for you to press your finger into it, leaving a soft but firm indentation. Softened butter is soft enough to easily scoop with a spoon and retain its shape. *Pommade* is a French term for butter that is very soft and creamy but not melted. Melted butter should be completely liquefied.

Cooking spray

Cooking spray is handy for recipes in which brushing or greasing just isn't practical. I like to use nonstick grapeseed oil or coconut oil spray and steer clear of canola oil, as it is a genetically modified oil.

Chocolate

The history of chocolate dates back to 400 B.C. Chocolate is as varied as wine, and its complex notes contribute significantly to the flavor profile of your baking. Unembellished chocolate melds with infinite ingredients, both savory and sweet, and offers a unique pleasure that delivers on its reputation as a food that promotes passion. Larger chocolate producers with widely available products that I recommend include Callebaut, Cacao Barry, Valrhona, El Rey, Scharffen Berger, and Ghirardelli. Keep chocolate well wrapped in a closed container and store in a cool, dry place.

Bittersweet chocolate is increasingly popular as a consumer treat and claims potential health benefits. The FDA's definition of bittersweet chocolate states that it must contain at least 35% chocolate liquor and can rise up to 80%. Bittersweet chocolate is made by grinding unsweetened chocolate with sugar, which results in a more palatable chocolate while retaining its bitter flavor. There are no regulations for how much sugar goes into bittersweet chocolate, so varieties of bittersweet chocolate may taste more or less sweet.

Couverture, a French word that means "a cover or blanket," is used to enrobe confections and is excellent to temper for chocolate work. Couverture is available in all types of chocolate varieties and has a high fat content, which provides a smooth, creamy texture, making it an upgrade in quality for some chocolate applications.

Milk chocolate contains cocoa butter, chocolate liquor, and some type of milk product. In the United States, milk chocolate is required to contain at least 10% chocolate liquor. Milk chocolate is much sweeter than dark chocolate and has a creamier texture, a lighter color, and a lower melting point temperature.

Semisweet chocolate falls into the same category as bittersweet chocolate, but it is generally assumed to be sweeter than bittersweet chocolate.

Unsweetened dark chocolate is known by many as "baking chocolate." Unsweetened chocolate is naturally unsweetened and is comprised of 50% cocoa beans and 50% cocoa butter with no added ingredients; it is not considered directly palatable. Unsweetened chocolate is the base ingredient for all other forms of chocolate (with the exception of white chocolate, which is not actually chocolate). There are no milk solids in dark chocolate. Despite its limited ingredients, the flavor profile of unsweetened chocolate varies significantly according to bean quality, varieties, and processing.

White chocolate does not contain chocolate liquor, but in the United States it is required to contain a minimum of 20% cocoa butter. So-called white chocolate products that contain vegetable fats instead of cocoa butter (which technically are not white chocolate) are inferior and are not recommended. White chocolate tastes sweeter than dark chocolate and takes well to infusion with other flavors.

Cocoa powder
Made from unsweetened chocolate, cocoa powder is the result of the extraction of cocoa butter from chocolate liquor. The leftover solids are ground to a fine powder that ranges in color from reddish brown to dark brown. Variations in color relate to the type of processing and acid/alkaline amounts. Dutch-processed cocoa is more alkaline, which results in a darker color. This type of cocoa is also associated with greater moisture and richer flavor. Natural cocoa is more acidic, will produce a red pigment in your product, and can result in a drier texture with less depth of flavor. I prefer to use Valrhona cocoa powder in my baking.

Cornstarch
Cornstarch is a thickener made from finely ground corn and must be fully cooked to eliminate its starchy taste. If possible, choose organic cornstarch, which will not contain GMOs.

Dairy
All of the dairy called for in the recipes are whole milk products. I recommend organic, local dairy products if you can source them.

Whole milk has more flavor than skim, low-fat, or fat-free milk. The recipes in this book call for whole milk.

Cream types are determined by the amount of milk fat they contain. Heavy cream and whipping cream are interchangeable terms; these generally contain between 36 and 40% milk fat. Either choice is acceptable to use in the recipes.

Eggs
A fundamentally common ingredient in baking, eggs contribute structure, flavor, and texture to baked products. In gluten-free baking, eggs play a particularly important role, assisting with structure and expansion during baking. When egg whites are fresh and at room

temperature, they will produce greater volume when whipped at high speed. Egg whites become thinner and less viscous as they age and will have reduced rising power. All the recipes in this book call for the use of large eggs. Shell included, large eggs weigh between 2 and 2¼ ounces (56 to 62 grams). A whole cracked large egg weighs a bit more than 1¾ ounces and up to 2 ounces (50 to 55 grams). I use local, organic eggs, which have a richly colored orange yolk that adds a deeper golden hue to baked goods.

Extracts/Oils/Flavorings
Choose high-quality, pure, all-natural extracts, oils, and flavorings to use in your baked goods. A huge assortment can be found online, in natural foods stores, and supermarkets. For coffee extract, I prefer to use the Italian brand Trablit (see Sources, pages 14 and 15).

Orange blossom water, also known as orange flower water, is a clear, floral distillation made from orange blossoms that has a sweet, distinctive scent of citrus with the perfume of orange blossom. Use it sparingly in sugar syrups, glazes, sweet breads, and pastries. Look for food-grade quality orange blossom water at Middle Eastern and European markets and specialty food shops (see Sources, pages 14 and 15).

Orange and lemon oils are cold-pressed citrus oils made from the rind of the fruit. They have a bright, intensely citrusy flavor that can be used to replace freshly grated orange or lemon zest in many recipes. Cooks love the convenience and purity of flavor that 100% citrus oil offers. Citrus oils are available at supermarkets and specialty food shops (see Sources, pages 14 and 15). I like to use the Boyajian brand.

Vanilla is used consistently in baking, so keep pure vanilla extract as a staple in your pantry. Buy real vanilla beans and store them in an airtight container at room temperature. Do not refrigerate the beans or they will dry out. To keep the beans soft and easy to scrape clean, snip off the stubby tips and place the beans upright in a Mason jar with their cut ends soaking in a few tablespoons of rum or brandy.

Food coloring
Opt for all-natural food colorings, available in liquid, paste, and powder form (see Sources, pages 14 and 15).

Leavenings
Yeast is a living fungus organism, and with the appropriate conditions it can grow and multiply. Fresh yeast can be challenging to source, but sometimes it is available from local bakeries and supermarkets. Working with fresh yeast is always my first choice; it requires

no activation by warm water and has more living yeast than other yeast options. Fresh yeast keeps in the refrigerator in an airtight container for one to two weeks and should crumble easily. When the texture of the yeast becomes spongy, it has begun to lose its potency.

My second choice is to use instant yeast, which can be added directly to dough without being hydrated first.

There is also active dry yeast (not instant), which is dehydrated and then vacuum packed to preserve freshness and shelf life. This type of yeast is dissolved in very warm water to become activated and generally contains the fewest number of living yeast cells.

Baking powder can be a single- or double-action leavener. The recipes in this book call for a double-acting baking powder, which means it activates when it is dissolved into a liquid or batter, and then again during the baking process.

Baking soda, known as sodium bicarbonate, is a single-action leavener. Baking soda's leavening relies on a batter or dough that contains an acidic ingredient, such as buttermilk, brown sugar, chocolate, or fruit, that it can react with.

Gluten-free flour
All of the recipes in this book were tested with Steve's Gluten Free Cake Flour, from the Authentic Foods brand. This gluten-free flour blend performs most similarly to wheat flour and is best for cookies, pastries, and cakes, but not yeasted breads. See pages 1 and 2 to learn more about it.

Fruit
High-quality produce will have a positive impact on the outcome of your recipe. Look for fresh, local, organic produce and choose it whenever possible; grab your basket and head to the farmers' market for the best berries to adorn your fresh fruit tarts. Bake with fruit that is ripe and ready for eating.

Nuts
Store nuts in the freezer if possible, kept in well-sealed freezer bags or heavy-duty plastic containers; either will help keep the nuts fresh longer. Always taste nuts before using them; nuts are subject to turning rancid, which results in an unpalatable bitter flavor and leaves them unsuitable for baking.

Nut pastes

Hazelnut, pistachio, and almond pastes are a few of the most common nut pastes used in French baking. Rich in flavor, these pastes are versatile in their uses for cakes, cookies, and creams. Cover well and refrigerate nut pastes after opening them; it is best to use them within six weeks of opening so they do not go rancid. Almond paste is an exception because of the high amount of sugar added during processing.

Salt

The recipes in this book primarily call for the use of finely ground, mineral-rich sea salt. You can use refined or unrefined sea salt. As an ingredient in baked goods, salt plays an important role in enhancing the flavor, strengthening dough structure, hindering yeast growth, and increasing browning. The salt market has grown significantly over the past decade, and there are now many salt types and flavors available. Salt can be found finely ground, coarse-grained, crystal, or in rock form.

Sugars

The culinary world, and baking in particular, makes use of an expansive list of sugars. Some types of sugar listed in this book are granulated sugar, brown sugar, confectioners' sugar, raw cane sugar, crystal sugar, coarse sugar, and pearl sugar. Liquid sugars include molasses, honey, and maple syrup.

Equipment

Aprons: Don an apron to protect your clothing from spills, splatters, and stains. Bib aprons and cross-back aprons are available online.

Bain-marie: A heatproof container that is set over (not in) another pan of hot water in order to keep a product hot or promote slow cooking over indirect heat. To set up a bain-marie, fill a medium saucepan one-third full with water and bring to a boil. Reduce the heat to medium and place a heatproof bowl over the top of the saucepan with the bottom over (not in) the water. Heat or cook the ingredients as directed in your recipe.

Baking sheets/pans: Also known as cookie sheets or sheet pans, the standard size is a 12½-by-17½-inch rectangle with ½-inch-high sides. Heavy-gauge baking pans will conduct heat more evenly and will not warp in the oven.

Bench brush: An elongated, rectangular brush that functions to sweep flour from large surfaces of dough, such as puff pastry, or to brush clean a workbench.

Bowls: An assortment of small, medium, and large mixing bowls is important. Stainless steel mixing bowls are indispensable. Keep a few glass or plastic bowls that are microwave-safe on hand for melting butter or chocolate.

Cake pans: Multiple sizes are available, and you'll need an 8- or 9-inch round cake pan as well as a 9-inch springform cake pan for the recipes in this book.

Cake turntable or lazy Susan: Assembling and decorating cakes and certain pastries is best accomplished on a cake turntable. You can also use a lazy Susan as an alternative.

Cheesecloth: This finely woven cotton cloth is used to strain liquids and sauces. You can also use it as a tool to hold ingredients for an infusion by creating a "purse" or sachet package. Simply set your ingredients in the center, then tie up the four corners with cooking twine.

Cherry pitter: A small handheld tool that pierces the cherry and pushes out the pit. You may reduce preparation time by using a cherry pitter, but keep close track so no stray pits get into your bowl of cherries.

Clothespins: The versatile clothespin is an excellent way to keep bags of dry products closed. Clothespins can also be handy for hanging up pastry bags to dry or pinch close the bottom part of a pastry bag (just above the tip) when refilling.

Cooling racks: An assortment of metal cooling racks in different shapes and sizes will come in handy for different baking needs. Include strong, tight-weave racks that will fit inside your baking sheets.

Culinary torch: A culinary or chef's torch is used for torching meringue or to caramelize sugar.

Cutters: Many shapes and sizes are available; for example, they can be round, fluted, scalloped, or theme shaped, including animals and nature styles. Cutters are available in stainless steel, Exoglass, tin, and plastic.

Cutting boards: Plastic or wood cutting boards are excellent for cutting fruit, nuts, and chocolate. Designate certain cutting boards for pastry items to eliminate the chance of absorbing odors or cross-contamination with raw foods.

Food processor: An invaluable electric kitchen appliance that can chop, puree, and blend dough. I recommend the Cuisinart 6- to 8-cup model.

Graters: Keep on hand the traditional stainless steel handheld box grater with four grating choices. I highly recommend getting a few different size microplanes for varying purposes. You can grate citrus zest, chocolate, and nuts, all with excellent consistency of texture.

Ice cream scoops: I keep an assortment of small, medium, and large ice cream scoops in my bakery. Use them to form consistent portions and uniform shapes for cookie dough and to scoop batter into smaller molds and pans with greater precision.

Immersion blender: An immersion blender will save you time and is excellent for reconstituting liquids and blending creams.

Knives: High-quality, sharp knives can add enjoyment and skill to your baking. You will need different knives for different purposes. They are a highly personal tool in the kitchen; choose carefully by trying out different knives. The handle should fit well in your hand and feel comfortable. You will need a serrated knife for slicing; a French knife for chopping and slicing (I recommend having two French knives, one large and one small); a paring knife for trimming, cutting, and releasing; and possibly an X-ACTO knife for templates and other baking prep work.

Ladles: I use stainless steel ladles for spooning chocolate onto cakes and serving sauces.

Measuring cups and spoons: These are tools you will use repeatedly when baking. Dry measuring cups are available in stainless steel or plastic. Use them specifically to measure dry goods. For liquids, use a liquid measuring cup that includes fluid ounces and has a spout for pouring. Measuring spoons generally come as a set; look for a stainless steel version that will not bend over time.

Metal spatulas: Metal spatulas have long handles and flat blades, which can be offset or straight, and come in many sizes. I suggest you keep at least one small, medium, and large spatula for different uses.

Mixers: KitchenAid makes excellent electric stand mixers that include whisk, paddle, and hook attachments, which all serve distinct purposes.

Molds: A vast selection of silicone, stainless steel, Exopan, copper, and nonstick molds are available for many types of baked products. Stainless steel ring molds of varying sizes are also available and are a good investment that will last a lifetime. Copper fluted canelé molds are the best choice for making authentic canelé pastries. Nonstick baba au rhum or timbale molds work well for the Bouchon recipe.

Oven: Whether you have a standard oven or a convection oven, you'll need to learn its temperament and performance. Keep an oven thermometer in your oven to discern accurate temperatures. All ovens have areas that brown more or less quickly. Convection ovens cause baked goods to brown and cook more quickly. If you are baking with a convection oven, the general rule of thumb is to lower the temperature by 25 to 50°F (4 to 10°C) when following a recipe intended for a standard oven.

Parchment paper: For lining baking sheets and rolling out dough. I like to use natural parchment that is chlorine-free. Parchment paper is available at most grocery stores, but you might check with your local bakery to see if you could purchase directly from them at a lower cost.

Pastry bags: Pastry bags, also called piping bags, are available in cloth, rubber, or plastic disposable bags, and all perform equally well. I prefer the reusable cloth or rubber bags, as they're a good choice from an environmental perspective. Plastic, disposable pastry bags are worth keeping on hand as a backup option.

Pastry brushes: Pastry brushes are used to apply egg wash, brush on glazes and syrups, and brush off excess flour. Keep a few different sizes on hand. I like having a bench brush for brushing flour from my work table.

Pastry docker: A handheld plastic or metal cylindrical tool with spiky nubs to pierce dough before baking; it's especially useful with puff pastry.

Peelers: Everyone has their favorite. Whether it's a Y shape or straight blade, you want at least one in your baking toolbox.

Pizza dough cutter: This tool comes in handy for cutting strips of raw dough or trimming the edges of pastry.

Plastic containers: I use plastic containers with lids to store prepped items and prepared batters. They are also good for storing unbaked batter in the freezer.

Rolling pins: There are many types and sizes of rolling pins. I recommend a wooden rolling pin that fits comfortably in your hands. A marble pin can be useful for bearing additional weight, and silicone and metal rolling pins are available options.

Rulers: Keep a 12-inch ruler and a yardstick that include imperial and metric measurements on hand. Metal rulers are a good choice because they can be easily cleaned.

Saucepans: An assortment of small, medium, and large saucepans with lids will be needed. Choose stainless steel for durability and heat tolerance.

Scale: The most important recommendation I can offer any baker is this: weigh your ingredients rather than measure them! The use of a digital scale will provide reliably consistent results and make you a better baker. Weighing ingredients also saves a lot of time. Purchase an electronic digital scale that includes ounces and grams. If you are a serious baker, keep a second scale and extra batteries on hand for backup.

Scissors: Kitchen scissors are a welcome tool when a knife just won't do the trick. I often use scissors for trimming raw dough, clipping the edges of baked items, and snipping small pieces of candied fruits. I also use them for snipping edible flowers.

Scrapers: Bench scrapers are a baker's friend. I have a little collection of various types: plastic with a rounded edge or flat sided, and metal scrapers with wooden or hard plastic handles. They come in various sizes, so look for scrapers that fit well in your hand. Scrapers assist in cutting dough, moving ingredients around, and cleaning the work table.

Sifter/Sieve: Sieves are available in different mesh grades to allow various degrees of product to pass through them. I keep tiny, small, medium, and large sieves on hand. They assist with tasks from sifting small amounts of baking powder to straining large portions of liquid.

Silicone baking mats: These clean up easily and are reusable. Silicone mats are excellent for particularly sticky items that may otherwise be difficult to remove from parchment paper.

Silicone spatulas: Silicone or rubber spatulas come in many sizes and styles and are useful for folding mixtures and scraping batter from bowls. Silicone spatulas tolerate high heat, whereas regular rubber spatulas do not.

Tart pans: Many options are available for tart pan shapes and sizes. I like to use stainless steel, straight-sided rings and fluted, nonstick tart pans with removable bottoms.

Thermometers: A digital candy thermometer is necessary to determine the stages of cooking sugar. You will need one for making macarons and buttercream. Keeping a backup is always a good idea.

Timers: I keep a few digital timers and spare batteries.

Sources

Amazon
amazon.com
(888) 280–4331
Steve's Gluten Free Cake Flour, baking equipment,
spices, extracts, flavorings, and other ingredients

Authentic Foods
authenticfoods.com
(800) 806–4737
Steve's Gluten Free Cake Flour and gluten-free products

Chai Wallah
www.chai-wallah.com
neil@chaiwallah.com
Chai spice

Chef Rubber
chefrubber.com
(702) 614–9350
Baking equipment and ingredients

Confection Crafts
confectioncrafts.com
(503) 505–0481
All-natural food colorants

Cuisinart
cuisinart.com
(800) 726–0190
Food processors, electric immersion blenders, and appliances

Culinary Cookware
culinarycookware.com
(800) 305–5415
French bakeware

iGourmet
igourmet.com
(877) 446–8763
Flavorings, nuts, and spices

J.B. Prince Company, Inc.
jbprince.com
(800) 473–0577
Baking equipment

Kerekes
bakedeco.com
(800) 525–5556
Baking equipment and tools

King Arthur Flour
kingarthurflour.com
(800) 827–6836
Baking equipment, flavorings, spices, and sweeteners

KitchenAid
kitchenaid.com
(800) 541–6390
Mixers and appliances

Pastry Chef Central
pastrychef.com
(888) 750-CHEF
Baking and pastry supplies

Red Stick Spice
redstickspice.com
(225) 930–9967
Gourmet spice shop and pure extracts

CHAPTER TWO

French Pastry Basic Recipes

The recipes in this chapter recur throughout the book. You will make many of them repeatedly, and your hands will move more fluently each time you practice a round of these pastry essentials.

Gluten-Free Flour Blends (see pages 1 to 3)

Egg Wash

Dorure au jaune d'oeuf

Makes 2 tablespoons
(60 grams)

1 large egg (55 grams)

1 teaspoon (5 grams) milk

Primarily used to glaze pastries before baking, egg wash is applied with a pastry brush in a thin layer. When baked, egg-washed pastries have increased browning and a shine to them.

Method

1 Whisk the egg and milk together in a small bowl.

2 Apply the wash using a pastry brush.

Simple Syrup

Sirop simple

Makes 1¼ cups (325 grams)

---

1 cup (200 grams) granulated sugar

⅔ cup (160 grams) water

Simple syrup takes well to many flavors, including coffee, rum, and lemon. The syrup is generally applied with a pastry brush to moisten layers of pastry or cake. Simple syrup keeps for up to 2 weeks in the refrigerator.

Method

1 In a medium saucepan, combine the sugar and water and stir with a wooden spoon or silicone spatula.

2 Place over medium heat and cook until the mixture comes to a full boil.

3 Set aside to cool completely, then transfer to a jar or plastic container, cover, and refrigerate until ready to use.

Apricot Glaze

Glaçage à l'abricot

Makes ¾ cup (200 grams)

---

1 cup (320 grams) apricot preserves

¼ cup (58 grams) water

This glaze is used to preserve cut fruit, seal the bottom of blind-baked tart shells, and add shine to baked fruit tarts. It is applied with a pastry brush.

Method

1 In a small saucepan, combine the apricot preserves and water and place over medium heat. Stir the mixture with a wooden spoon and bring just to a boil.

2 Pour the mixture through a fine-mesh strainer, cool, then refrigerate until ready to use. Reheat the glaze just before using.

3 You may thin the glaze with a teaspoon or more of water as needed.

Sugar Icing Glaze

Glaçage au sucre

Makes about ⅔ cup
(225 grams)

---

3 tablespoons (30 grams)
water

1 teaspoon (5 grams)
pure vanilla extract

1¾ cups (175 grams)
confectioners' sugar

For glazing pastries or cookies, this simple recipe can be adjusted to create different flavors, such as lemon, orange, or chocolate. Add a teaspoon of lemon juice or orange juice (or a bit more if you'd like more flavor) or a tablespoon of melted chocolate. You can increase or decrease the viscosity by adding more water or more confectioners' sugar.

Method

1 Pour the water and vanilla into a large measuring cup.

2 Sift the confectioners' sugar into a bowl, then add it to the water-vanilla mixture. Using a silicone spatula, gently press the sugar into the water, but do not stir. Allow the mixture to sit for 10 minutes, then whisk until smooth. If there are remaining lumps, strain the glaze through a fine-mesh sieve. Adjust the thickness of the glaze as needed.

3 Store the glaze covered in the refrigerator for up to 1 week.

Streusel

Streusel

Makes about 3½ cups
(547 grams)

½ cup (115 grams) unsalted
butter, at room temperature

⅔ cup (130 grams)
granulated sugar

1¼ cups (200 grams)
gluten-free flour blend
(see pages 1 to 3)

1 cup (100 grams)
almond flour

1 teaspoon (2 grams)
ground cinnamon (optional)

Streusel, an Alsatian pastry element, is a sweet, crunchy crumble that can be sprinkled raw over pastries before baking. Streusel can also be baked and sprinkled on the bottom of tarts to act as a moisture barrier.

Method

1 In a stand mixer fitted with the paddle attachment, combine the butter and sugar and beat on low speed just until combined.

2 Add the gluten-free flour, almond flour, and cinnamon, if using, and mix on low speed until crumbly, about 2 minutes, scraping the inside edges and bottom of the bowl with a silicone spatula to ensure even distribution of the ingredients.

3 The raw streusel can be stored in a covered plastic container in the refrigerator for up to 1 week.

4 To bake the streusel: Preheat the oven to 325°F (165°C).

5 Line a baking sheet with parchment paper. Sprinkle an even layer of streusel onto the parchment paper and bake, stirring occasionally, for 20 minutes, or until golden brown. Remove from the oven and set on a cooling rack to cool completely.

6 Store the baked streusel in an airtight container in the freezer until ready to use. Baked or raw streusel will keep in the freezer for up to 1 month.

Almond Cream

Crème d'amande

Makes about 4 cups
(650 grams)

¾ cup (170 grams) unsalted
butter, at room temperature

1⅔ cups (170 grams)
confectioners' sugar, sifted

1¾ cups (170 grams)
almond flour

1 tablespoon (8 grams)
gluten-free flour blend
(see pages 1 to 3), sifted

2 teaspoons (6 grams)
cornstarch, sifted

2 large eggs (110 grams)

1 tablespoon (16 grams)
dark rum or kirsch

You will find almond cream used as a base for the gorgeous rustic baked fruit tarts that adorn the shelves in French pâtisseries. It is a standard recipe in French baking and indispensable in its uses in various pastries. Mix it with pastry cream to make a lighter filling for baking or to use when making almond croissants. Spread a thin layer across the bottom of galettes or tarts to add protection from excess moisture and a touch of extra flavor and texture. Be careful to not overbeat the batter or it will rise too much when it is baked. This easy-to-make recipe scales readily to larger quantities and keeps well refrigerated or frozen in a plastic container.

Method

1 Place the butter, confectioners' sugar, and almond flour into the bowl of a stand mixer fitted with the paddle attachment. Beat at medium speed until the ingredients are well blended, about 1 minute.

2 Add the gluten-free flour and cornstarch and beat briefly at medium speed to incorporate.

3 With the mixer running on medium speed, beat in the eggs one at a time. Turn the mixer off and, using a silicone spatula, scrape the inside edges and bottom of the bowl. Return the mixer to medium speed and beat for 1 minute, or until the cream is homogenous. Reduce the mixer speed to low, add the rum, and beat briefly, until the almond cream has a smooth texture.

4 The almond cream is ready to be used immediately, or cover with plastic wrap, pressing it directly against its surface to ensure an airtight seal. Refrigerate the cream for up to 1 week or freeze for up to 1 month.

Frangipane

Frangipane

Makes about 3½ cups
(780 grams)

¾ cup (170 grams) unsalted
butter, at room temperature

2 tablespoons (28 grams)
granulated sugar

1½ cups (400 grams) almond
paste, broken into walnut-size
pieces

2 large eggs (110 grams)

1 tablespoon (16 grams)
dark rum or kirsch

¼ cup plus 2 tablespoons
(55 grams) gluten-free flour
blend (see pages 1 to 3), sifted

Frangipane is an almond paste–based filling that emits the
sweet scent of almonds. One story of its origin says it is
named after an Italian nobleman who, while living in Paris,
invented a lovely scent made from bitter almonds. In their
culinary cleverness, the French transformed this aroma into an
elevating pastry filling that's used to fill King's Cake, Pithivier,
or Jalousie, or as a base in cakes or petits fours. Swipe a thin
layer of frangipane on the base of a fruit tart or galette to
absorb moisture and to add its alluring aroma and flavor to
your pastries. Frangipane scales up readily and keeps well
refrigerated or frozen.

Method

1 Place the butter and sugar into the bowl of a stand mixer
fitted with the paddle attachment. Beat at medium speed
until the ingredients are well blended, about 1 minute.

2 Increase the mixer speed to medium-high and add the
almond paste one piece at a time. When all of the almond
paste has been added, beat for 1 minute, or until the mixture
is smooth. Use a silicone spatula to scrape the inside edges
and bottom of the bowl.

3 With the mixer running on medium speed, beat in the eggs
until well combined, then add the rum. Turn the mixer off,
use a silicone spatula to scrape the batter from the paddle
and the sides of the bowl, then return the mixer to medium-
high speed and beat for 1 minute, or until the cream is
homogenous.

4 Reduce the mixer speed to low, add the flour, and mix for 30 seconds, or until combined. Remove the bowl from the mixer and, using a silicone spatula, give the frangipane a final quick mix.

5 The frangipane is ready for immediate use, or it can be refrigerated to use later. Cover the filling with plastic wrap, pressing it directly against its surface to ensure an airtight seal, and refrigerate for up to 1 week or freeze for up to 2 months.

King's Cake

On Epiphany, it is traditional to serve King's Cake—*gâteau des Rois* or *galette des Rois*—a round cake made with flaky pastry or brioche, respectively. The cake is decorated with stars and a crown, filled with frangipane, and a charm, called a *fève* (a bean), is hidden inside. Usually a child, *le petit roi* or *la petite reine* (the little king or queen), cuts and distributes the festive cake. Discovering the *fève* in your piece of frangipane cake wins you the royal honor of being crowned king or queen for the following year.

Pastry Cream

Crème pâtissière

Makes 3 cups (815 grams)

___

For the milk infusion

2 cups (480 grams)
whole milk

¼ cup plus 1 teaspoon
(55 grams) granulated sugar

1 vanilla bean, split and
scraped

For the custard

¼ cup plus 1 teaspoon
(55 grams) granulated sugar

½ cup plus 1 tablespoon
(38 grams) cornstarch

2 large eggs (110 grams)

¼ cup (55 grams) unsalted
butter, at room temperature,
in walnut-size pieces

Smooth and luxurious, this pastry cream is quick to make and versatile in baking treatments. Choose real vanilla beans to add depth of flavor, or substitute 1 teaspoon pure vanilla extract. Nut pastes, such as pistachio, hazelnut, or peanut butter paste, can be added to pastry cream. The finished pastry cream may be lightened with whipped cream or combined with buttercream or meringue.

Method

Make the milk infusion

1 In a medium saucepan, combine the milk, sugar, and vanilla bean seeds and pod. Whisk the ingredients together, place over medium heat, and cook until the milk mixture is near boiling.

2 Turn the heat off and set the mixture aside for 30 minutes to 1 hour for the vanilla bean to infuse the milk.

Make the custard

1 In a small bowl, whisk together the sugar and cornstarch. Add the eggs and whisk them into the dry mixture. Using a hand or electric whisk, whip the egg mixture until it is homogenous and well blended. Strain the mixture through a medium-mesh sieve into a small bowl.

2 When the milk mixture has finished infusing, remove the vanilla bean. Wash the vanilla bean with warm water and place it in an appropriate place to dry; you can use the dried vanilla bean to make vanilla sugar to use at a later time (see page 287).

3 Bring the infused milk to a boil over medium-high heat. Slowly pour the strained egg mixture into the milk, whisking vigorously, making sure to whisk around the inside edges and bottom of the pan. Continue whisking until all of the egg mixture is incorporated and the surface of the mixture begins to break large bubbles, about 4 minutes. At this point, remove the pastry cream from the stovetop and pour it into a medium heatproof bowl. Cool the cream to 140°F (60°C), stirring frequently. Slowly whisk the softened butter into the pastry cream, mixing until it is creamy and homogenous.

4 Cover the pastry cream by pressing plastic wrap directly against its surface; this will prevent a skin from forming. Refrigerate the pastry cream until cooled. Once the pastry cream has cooled, it will become firm and have a gelatinous consistency. When you are ready to use the pastry cream, beat it well to return it to a smooth, creamy consistency. The pastry cream will keep covered in the refrigerator for up to 1 week.

Swiss Meringue

Meringue Suisse

Makes about 4 cups
(340 grams)

About 4 egg whites
(120 grams)

⅛ teaspoon (1 gram)
sea salt

1 cup plus 2 tablespoons
(230 grams) granulated sugar

Luxurious and satiny, Swiss meringue is excellent for piping on pastries and browning with a chef's torch. It is also used for making hard-shelled meringues and Swiss buttercream. Swiss meringue is made with two parts sugar and one part egg whites. The number one rule for meringue preparation is to keep it free of fat, including traces of egg yolk, as fat will deflate the whites and their volume will not properly increase.

Method

1 In the bowl of a stand mixer, combine the egg whites, salt, and sugar and whisk together.

2 Set the bowl over a bain-marie over medium-high heat and whisk continually (this will prevent the whites from cooking on the sides of the bowl) until the mixture reaches 149°F (65°C), at the point when the egg whites become more stable, about 4 minutes.

3 Remove from the heat, attach to the stand mixer, and whip on high speed until the meringue has increased in volume and the bottom of the bowl is barely warm to the touch, 4 to 5 minutes. The meringue is now ready to use.

Italian Meringue

Meringue Italienne

Makes about 5 cups
(500 grams)

---

5 egg whites (175 grams),
at room temperature

½ cup (120 grams) water

1¼ cups (255 grams)
granulated sugar

⅛ teaspoon (1 gram)
sea salt

¼ teaspoon (2 grams)
cream of tartar

Gorgeously white and soft in texture, Italian meringue is used to top tarts or coat pastries, as in the Dancing Brioche Buns (pages 265 and 266), and is a primary component in Italian Meringue Buttercream (pages 32 and 33). Italian meringue can be piped into teardrop or other shapes or used free-form and torched.

Method

1 Wash the stand mixer bowl, making certain no residual fat remains on the inside of the bowl, which could cause the egg whites to destabilize. Pour the egg whites into the mixer bowl and attach to a stand mixer fitted with the whisk attachment.

2 In a medium saucepan, combine the water and sugar. Using a silicone spatula, very carefully stir the mixture without splashing the inside of the pan. Insert a digital thermometer and cook the syrup over medium-high heat until it reaches 242°F (116°C). Check the saucepan to see if any sugar crystals have built up on the sides and carefully wash them down using a wet pastry brush.

3 When the sugar syrup reaches 235°F (113°C), add the salt to the egg whites and whip at medium speed until frothy, then add the cream of tartar, increase the speed to high, and whip until soft peaks form. Keep a close watch on the sugar syrup as the temperature rises and on the egg whites as they grow closer to their desired texture. When the sugar syrup reaches 242°F (116°C), immediately remove the pan from the stovetop. With the mixer speed on high, rest the lip of the pan with the sugar syrup against the edge of the mixing bowl, then slowly pour a steady stream of syrup down the inside edge of the mixing bowl. Continue to whip on high speed for 2 minutes, then reduce the speed to medium and whip for about 3 minutes, until the bottom of the bowl feels cool to the touch. The meringue is ready for immediate use.

Lemon Cream (Curd)

Crème au citron

Makes about 4 cups
(900 grams)

Special tools: food processor
or blender, microplane,
instant-read thermometer

1 cup plus 1 tablespoon
(215 grams) granulated sugar

1 tablespoon (6 grams)
lemon zest

4 large eggs (220 grams)

¾ cup (168 grams) lemon
juice (from about 5 lemons)

1½ cups (340 grams) unsalted
butter, at room temperature

Heavenly, velvety smooth, with bright, tart flavor, this lemon cream is directly inspired from French pastry chef Pierre Hermé. The cream is slightly cooled before adding the butter, then blended in a food processor or blender to ensure a sublime, silky finish.

Method

1 Set up a bain-marie (see page 9) and bring the water to a simmer over medium heat.

2 In a medium heatproof bowl, combine the sugar and lemon zest. Using your fingers, vigorously rub together the sugar and zest for about 1 minute. The friction created from this action causes the oils in the zest to release and makes the sugar become fragrant and turn light yellow.

3 Add the eggs and whisk for about 30 seconds. Pour in the lemon juice, then gently whisk until all of the ingredients are homogeneous.

4 Place the bowl over the bain-marie and cook, stirring every few minutes with a large whisk and occasionally scraping the sides and bottom of the bowl with a heatproof silicone spatula. Continue to cook until the cream thickens, is uniform in consistency, coats the spatula, and reaches 170°F (77°C). Be patient—the texture of the cream will gradually change from foamy and thin to thick and creamy, but it may take up to 20 minutes to reach the desired temperature.

5 Strain the hot lemon cream through a fine-mesh sieve directly into a food processor. Allow the cream to cool to 140°F (60°C), about 5 minutes. Attach the food processor lid, then begin to add the pieces of softened butter through the open feed tube. Keep the feed tube open, allowing steam to release from the hot cream. After all the butter has been added, continue to process for 2 minutes; the cream will lighten in color and increase in volume.

6 Pour the lemon cream into a container and place in the refrigerator to cool. Cover with plastic wrap, pressing it firmly against the surface, to make an airtight seal. The lemon cream will keep for up to 1 week refrigerated or frozen for up to 1 month.

Italian Meringue Buttercream

Crème au beurre à la meringue Italienne

Makes about 6 cups
(900 grams)

Special tool: instant-read
thermometer

2 cups (455 grams) unsalted
butter, at room temperature,
softened

5 egg whites (175 grams),
at room temperature

½ cup (100 grams) water

1¼ cups (255 grams)
granulated sugar

¼ teaspoon (1 gram)
cream of tartar

Italian meringue buttercream is prepared by first whisking hot sugar syrup into stiffly beaten egg whites, then whipping the mixture until cool, and incorporating softened butter. This pure white and fluffy buttercream makes a rich, gorgeous frosting for cakes and plays well to other flavors, such as citrus, chocolate, coffee, or nut pastes. Its flavor versatility makes it an excellent filling for meringues and macarons. Make sure your egg whites are at room temperature and that your butter is nicely softened.

Method

1 In the bowl of a stand mixer fitted with the paddle attachment, beat the butter on medium speed for 4 minutes, or until it becomes very soft, aerated, and lightened in color. Transfer the butter to a separate bowl and set aside.

2 Wash the stand mixer bowl, making certain no residual fat remains on the inside of the bowl, which could cause the egg whites to destabilize. Pour the egg whites into the mixer bowl and attach to the stand mixer fitted with the whisk attachment.

3 In a medium saucepan, combine the water and sugar. Using a silicone spatula, very carefully stir the mixture without splashing the inside of the pan. Insert an instant-read thermometer and cook the syrup over medium-high heat until it reaches 242°F (116°C). As the sugar syrup cooks, check the saucepan to see if any sugar crystals have built up on the sides and carefully wash them down using a wet pastry brush.

4 When the sugar syrup reaches 238°F (114°C), begin whipping the egg whites at medium speed until frothy, then add the cream of tartar, increase the speed to high, and whip until soft peaks form. Keep a close watch on the sugar syrup as the temperature rises, and on the egg whites as they grow closer to their desired texture. When the sugar syrup reaches 242°F (116°C), immediately remove the pan from the stovetop. Turn the mixer speed to high, rest the lip of the sugar syrup pan against the edge of the mixing bowl, then slowly pour a steady stream of syrup down the inside edge of the mixing bowl. Continue to whip on high speed for 2 minutes, then reduce the speed to medium and whip for about 3 minutes, until the bottom of the bowl feels cool to the touch.

5 Reduce the mixer speed to low, then add one quarter of the soft butter to the meringue. Increase the speed to medium, then begin adding the remaining butter, 1 tablespoon at a time, working quickly. Increase the mixer speed to high and whip for 1 to 2 minutes, until the buttercream comes together in a fluffy, smooth, emulsified mixture. Do not overwhip or the meringue will deflate and lose its light, fluffy consistency.

6 Italian meringue buttercream is best used freshly made, but it may be kept refrigerated for up to 1 week or frozen for up to 1 month.

French Buttercream

Crème au beurre Francaise

Makes about 3 cups
(650 grams)

Special tool: instant-read
thermometer

1¼ cups (280 grams) unsalted
butter, at room temperature

6 large egg yolks (150 grams),
at room temperature

¼ cup (55 grams) water

1 cup (200 grams)
granulated sugar

1 teaspoon (5 grams)
pure vanilla extract

French buttercream is prepared by first whipping hot sugar syrup into beaten egg yolks. It is transformed into buttercream by cooling it, and then whipping in softened butter. This rich, silky buttercream makes a gorgeous frosting for cakes and takes well to other flavors, such as citrus, chocolate, coffee, or nut pastes. Be certain to have your egg yolks and butter at room temperature.

Method

1 Tear the softened butter into tablespoon-size pieces and set aside.

2 In the bowl of a stand mixer fitted with the whisk attachment, whip the yolks on medium speed for about 5 minutes, until foamy and lightened in color. While the yolks are whipping, begin making the sugar syrup.

3 Put the water and sugar in a medium saucepan. Using a silicone spatula, very carefully stir the mixture without splashing the inside of the pan. Check the saucepan to see if any sugar crystals have built up on the sides, and carefully wash them down using a wet pastry brush. Insert an instant-read thermometer and cook the syrup over medium-high heat until the temperature reaches 240°F (115°C). When the sugar syrup reaches 240°F (115°C), immediately remove the pan from the stovetop. With the mixer running at low speed, rest the lip of the saucepan against the edge of the mixing bowl, then slowly pour a steady stream of syrup down the inside edge of the bowl into the yolks. Increase the mixer speed to medium-high and whip for 4 to 5 minutes, until the mixture has increased in volume and the bottom of the bowl feels cool to the touch.

4 Reduce the mixer speed to low, then slowly add the soft butter to the egg mixture, 1 tablespoon at a time, waiting for each addition to be incorporated before adding the next. Add the vanilla extract, increase the mixer speed to medium-high and whip for 3 to 5 minutes, until the buttercream becomes fluffy and smooth. Do not overwhip or the buttercream will deflate and lose its light consistency.

5 French buttercream is best used freshly made, but it may be kept covered and refrigerated for up to 1 week or frozen for up to 1 month.

Dark Chocolate Ganache

Ganache au chocolat noir

Makes about 2½ cups
(585 grams)

---

2 cups (300 grams)
dark chocolate

1 cup (230 grams)
heavy cream

¼ cup (55 grams)
unsalted butter, softened

Chocolate ganache can give pause to revelry, especially if you choose your chocolate and cream thoughtfully. My young friend Ella Scaggs, who is a serious chocolate connoisseur, prefers it straight off the spoon, and so do I. Use ganache as a glaze, frosting, or filling for meringues, tarts, and cakes, as well as to make truffles, fondue, and real hot chocolate.

Method

1 Chop the dark chocolate into ¼-inch pieces and place them in a medium heatproof bowl. You will want to leave plenty of room for when you stir the hot cream into the chocolate, so choose a generously sized bowl.

2 Pour the cream into a small saucepan and bring to a boil over medium heat. Immediately remove the cream from the heat and pour over the chopped dark chocolate. Allow the mixture to sit for 1 minute, then, using a hand whisk, gently stir the cream into the chopped chocolate in a slow circular motion. Stir for about 2 minutes, until they are well blended. Add the softened butter and stir slowly to allow the three ingredients to emulsify and become a shiny, smooth, thick ganache.

3 Cover with plastic wrap, placing it directly onto the ganache, and refrigerate for 2 hours, or until firm. The ganache will keep for up to 2 weeks.

4 When you are ready to use the ganache, allow it to sit at room temperature for 30 minutes, or until it has softened to a workable consistency. If necessary, gently stir or whisk the ganache to ensure a creamy, homogenous mixture. You may also re-melt the ganache to bring it to a liquid form. Do this by placing the ganache over a bain-marie (see page 9) and stirring gently with a silicone spatula.

Chocolate Chai Ganache

Ganache chocolat et aux épices chai

Makes about 2 cups
(500 grams)

1½ cups (250 grams)
dark chocolate

¼ cup (50 grams)
milk chocolate

1 cup (230 grams)
heavy cream

1 tablespoon (8 grams)
chai spice mix (see Sources,
pages 14 and 15)

1 cinnamon stick

Method

1 Chop the dark and milk chocolate into ¼-inch pieces, then place in a stainless steel bowl. Choose a generously sized bowl so you have plenty of room to later stir in the hot cream without it spilling over the sides.

2 Pour the cream into a small saucepan, stir in the chai spice mix, and add the cinnamon stick. Heat the cream just to a boil over medium heat. Immediately remove from the heat and set aside for 1 hour for the cream and spices to infuse.

3 Pour the cream mixture through a fine-mesh sieve into a clean bowl. Discard the infused spices to your compost. Put the strained cream into a clean saucepan and bring to a boil over medium heat. Remove the cream from the heat and immediately pour it over the chopped chocolate. Allow the mixture to sit for 1 minute, then, using a whisk, gently stir the cream into the chopped chocolate in a slow circular motion. Stir for about 2 minutes, taking your time to allow the chocolate and cream to emulsify and create a shiny, smooth, thick ganache.

4 Cover the bowl with plastic wrap, placing it directly onto the ganache, then refrigerate for 2 hours, or until firm. The ganache will keep in the refrigerator for up to 1 week.

5 When you are ready to use the ganache, allow it to sit at room temperature for 30 minutes, or until it has softened to a workable consistency. If necessary, gently stir or whisk the ganache to ensure a creamy, homogenous mixture. You may also melt the ganache to bring it to a liquid form or to reset.

Pistachio Ganache

Ganache à la pistache

Makes about 5 cups
(600 grams)

10¾ ounces (300 grams)
white chocolate

1 cup (230 grams)
heavy cream

3 tablespoons (45 grams)
pure pistachio paste

¼ teaspoon (2 grams)
pure almond extract

Method

1 Place the white chocolate into a small heatproof bowl set over a bain-marie (see page 9) over low heat. Stir the chocolate frequently using a heatproof silicone spatula until melted, then remove from the heat.

2 In a small saucepan, bring the heavy cream to a low boil over medium heat. Add the pistachio paste and almond extract and whisk until the cream mixture is homogenous.

3 Pour the cream over the melted white chocolate and gently stir with a hand whisk until the ingredients are smooth and homogenous. Pour the ganache into a bowl and cover the top by pressing plastic wrap directly onto its surface. Refrigerate the ganache for 4 hours, or until the texture sets up.

Working with Ganache

Adjusting the proportions of chocolate, cream, or butter can change the density and flavor of ganache. More chocolate makes a thicker ganache, while more cream gives it a thinner consistency. Another method of thinning ganache is to add water; this is a technique practiced by some "purist" types—myself included—to keep the original chocolate flavor more pronounced. For a richer, softer ganache, add more butter to the recipe. To repair a broken ganache, slowly pour a tablespoon of cold cream into melted ganache and whisk gently until the ganache has emulsified. Add a touch of crème fraîche or sour cream to ganache to give it a tangy edge. You can make dark, milk, or white chocolate ganache and create endless flavors through the infusion of teas and spices or the addition of oils, compounds, powders, creams, or liquors. Incorporating textured ingredients, such as finely minced ginger, nuts, or crushed caramel, will further add to the complexity of a ganache.

Honey Chocolate Mousse

Mousse au chocolat et au miel

Makes about 4 cups
(860 grams)

---

6 ounces (170 grams)
dark chocolate, melted

½ cup egg whites (115 grams),
at room temperature

¼ cup plus 1 tablespoon
(55 grams) granulated sugar

¼ cup plus 2 teaspoons
(100 grams) honey

2 cups (460 grams)
heavy cream

Thanks to Master Baker Jeffrey Hamelman for sharing this chocolate with honey mousse recipe, and a nod of appreciation to the honeybees and their invaluable contribution to our blossoming gardens and farms. In this recipe, the bees supply their sweet, uplifting honey notes to the tang of the dark chocolate, while the Swiss meringue adds its velvety soft texture. You can eagerly lick this mousse right off the spoon or use it with various pastries. Try pairing it with the Hazelnut Chocolate Dacquoise (pages 221 to 223) for a sublime textural contrast and flavor buzz.

Method

1 Place the chocolate into a small heatproof bowl set over a bain-marie (see page 9) and melt, stirring occasionally with a silicone spatula. Once melted, set the chocolate aside in a warm place.

2 Place the egg whites, sugar, and honey into the bowl of a stand mixer. Set the bowl over a bain-marie and, using a large whisk, whip the whites to 125°F (52°C). Remove from the heat, secure the bowl onto the mixer, and whip the whites on high speed until the meringue is cool and holds stiff peaks.

3 Using a silicone spatula, gently fold the warm melted chocolate into the meringue.

4 Whip the cream just until it holds soft peaks, then gently fold it into the chocolate-meringue mixture until it is evenly incorporated. Do not overmix or the mousse will become grainy. Cover with plastic wrap and refrigerate for 1 hour, then gently whisk the mousse until it is smooth before piping it.

French Macarons

Macaron française

Makes about 144 shells,
enough for 72 macarons

Special tools: pastry bag
fitted with a ½-inch plain tip,
candy thermometer, pastry
brush, template

For the almond flour mixture

2 cups plus 2 tablespoons
(300 grams) almond flour

3 cups (300 grams)
confectioners' sugar

3 large egg whites
(115 grams), preferably
aged (see page 207),
at room temperature

Food coloring and/or
flavoring (optional)

For the meringue

3 large egg whites
(115 grams), preferably
aged (see page 207),
at room temperature

¼ cup plus 1 tablespoon
(75 grams) water

1½ cups (300 grams)
granulated sugar

The *macaron*—a simple yet complex filled meringue cookie confection—has been sweeping its way through American popular food culture to become a much sought-after specialty cookie. I have been making macarons for nearly a decade, after an enlightening trip to Pâtisserie Pierre Hermé in Paris introduced me to these gems. True origins for macarons abound, from Venetian monasteries to a bakery in Montmorillon, France, which boasts a dedicated macaron museum. To whoever made the first macaron, thank you for creating this celestial sweet.

This macaron recipe is directly inspired by Hermé's Italian meringue method, which provides the strongest stability and structure for the macaron shells. Italian meringue is accomplished by cooking sugar syrup to the soft-ball stage and slowly pouring it into the egg whites, which essentially cooks the whites to create a stable protein structure.

Method

Make the almond flour mixture

1 Make a template: cut a 12-by-17-inch piece of parchment paper, then use a cookie cutter or the bottom of a glass to trace 1½-inch circles, leaving 1 inch of space between each circle.

2 Line three 12-by-17-inch baking sheets with parchment paper or silicone mats and set aside.

3 In a food processor, combine the almond flour and confectioners' sugar and pulse until ground to a consistent, fine powder. Pour half of the mixture through a medium-mesh sieve and into a large bowl. If there are remaining bits of almonds, regrind them with some of the nut-sugar mixture that has already passed through the sieve. Use your fingers to press the mixture through if needed. Continue in this manner until all the nut mixture passes through the sieve.

4 Add the 3 egg whites. If you are using food coloring or flavoring, add it now. Do not stir.

Make the meringue

1 Place the 3 egg whites into the bowl of a stand mixer fitted with the whisk attachment.

2 Pour the water into a small stainless steel saucepan. Add the granulated sugar and stir to dissolve the sugar. Clip a candy thermometer to the edge of the saucepan and cook over medium heat, using a small pastry brush dipped in water to brush clean any sugar syrup that clings to the upper inside edges of the pan. When the syrup reaches 230°F (110°C), about 5 minutes, begin whipping the egg whites at high speed until they just start to form soft peaks. Continue cooking the syrup until it reaches 239°F (115°C) (soft-ball stage), about 2 minutes, then immediately remove from the heat.

3 Lower the speed of the mixer to medium-high, then carefully rest the lip of the saucepan on the edge of the bowl and slowly pour the hot sugar syrup down the inside edge of the bowl into the egg whites. Continue whipping for about 2 minutes, until the egg whites are glossy and hold firm peaks but are still warm to the touch.

4 Using a rubber spatula, scrape the meringue into the bowl with the almond flour mixture and fold the two together, stirring from the center outward to the sides and turning the bowl as you go. Fold the batter until it is shiny and flows like lava, combining well without overmixing.

5 Using the rubber spatula, transfer your macaron batter into a pastry bag fitted with a ½-inch plain tip. Place your template underneath the parchment paper. Pipe rounds of batter onto the prepared baking sheets, using your template as a guide. Tap the macarons on the countertop and shake the baking sheet from side to side to help settle the little knob on top if it is still visible. Remove the template and continue this process with the remaining batter. Allow the macarons to sit for 30 minutes in order to dry and form a skin on the top. When you touch the top of the shell, it should feel dry with no stickiness.

6 While the macarons are drying, preheat the oven to 350°F (175°C).

7 Place the macarons in the oven and bake for 10 to 12 minutes, until they appear dry and firm to the touch but retain a little give under your finger. Remove the baking sheets from the oven and slide the parchment paper or silicone mat off the baking sheet and onto a cooling rack and cool completely on the parchment paper before removing. (If you are using a silicone mat, allow the shells to cool for 5 minutes, then remove them from the silicone mat and place directly onto the cooling rack.)

8 Carefully release the cooled shells, one by one, by peeling the parchment from the bottom of each shell. Match your macaron tops and bottoms according to size.

9 Spoon the filling into a pastry bag fitted with a ½-inch plain tip. Pipe a generous mound of filling onto the inside of half of the shells, then gently top with the remaining shells.

10 Place your finished macarons in a covered container and refrigerate overnight. (This is an essential step to allow the macaron flavors to merge and the texture of the shells to soften to the ideal consistency.) Remove the macarons from the refrigerator 1 hour before serving. The macarons will keep refrigerated for 48 to 72 hours and are best eaten during this time. They may also be frozen for up to 2 weeks.

Chocolate Macarons

Macarons au chocolat

Makes about 50 shells,
enough for 25 macarons

Special tool: pastry bag fitted
with a ½-inch plain pastry tip

For the almond flour mixture

1 cup (100 grams)
almond flour

1¾ cups (175 grams)
confectioners' sugar

¼ cup (25 grams)
cocoa powder

For the meringue

2 extra-large egg whites
(85 grams), preferably aged
(see page 207), at room
temperature

2 tablespoons (30 grams)
granulated sugar

Macarons, the little beauties that they are, can be fussy. However, this chocolate macaron recipe consistently yields the two classic signatures of a successful macaron: a smooth, round top and a ruffled foot. These macarons are made with a simple French meringue method, and the addition of cocoa powder provides strength to the shells. As for any macaron recipe, your chances of success will greatly increase if you weigh your ingredients.

Part of the appeal of this recipe is that it is not as sweet as the non-chocolate variations and pairs well to highlight distinctive types of chocolate. My favorite flavor is fresh raspberry with 64% Dark Chocolate Ganache (page 36). This particular flavor macaron helped determine the fate of this book when my dear friend and talented cookbook author, Leda Scheintaub, reported how she swooned in a private moment of bliss when she tasted her first. Try these with Chocolate Chai Ganache (page 37), Coffee Buttercream (page 213), or Chocolate Strawberry Ganache (page 227), or be adventurous and take off with your own inspiration.

Method

Make the almond flour mixture

1 Line two 12-by-17-inch baking sheets with silicone mats or parchment paper and set aside.

2 In a food processor, combine the almond flour, confectioners' sugar, and cocoa powder and pulse until ground to a consistent, fine powder. Pour the mixture through a medium-mesh sieve into a large bowl.

Make the meringue

1 Place the egg whites in the bowl of a stand mixer fitted with the whisk attachment and whip until they hold soft peaks.

Continue whipping and begin to sprinkle the granulated sugar into the whites until they hold firm, glossy peaks.

2 Using a rubber spatula, scrape the meringue into the bowl with the almond flour mixture. Stirring from the center outward to the sides, fold the two together, turning the bowl as you go. Fold the batter until it is shiny and flows like lava, combining well without overmixing.

3 Using the rubber spatula, transfer the macaron batter into a pastry bag fitted with a ½-inch plain tip. Pipe 1-inch rounds of batter onto the prepared baking sheets, allowing 1 inch of space between each round. If there is a little knob visible on the top of the shells, tap the baking sheet on the countertop and shake it from side to side to help settle them. Allow the macarons to sit for 20 minutes to 1 hour in order to dry and form a skin on the top. When you touch the top of the shell, it should feel dry with no stickiness.

4 While the macarons are drying, preheat the oven to 325°F (165°C).

5 Place the macarons in the oven and bake for 10 to 12 minutes, until they appear dry and firm to the touch but still retain a little give under your finger. Remove the baking sheets from the oven and slide the silicone mats or parchment paper off the baking sheet and onto your work surface. Allow the macarons to cool completely on the parchment paper or mats.

6 Carefully release the cooled shells, one by one, by peeling the parchment from the bottom of each shell. Match your macaron tops and bottoms according to size.

7 Spoon the filling into a pastry bag fitted with a ½-inch plain tip. Pipe a generous mound of filling onto the inside of half of the shells, then gently top with the remaining shells.

8 Place your finished macarons in a covered container and refrigerate overnight. (This is an essential step to allow the flavors to meld and the texture of the shells to soften to the ideal consistency.) Remove the macarons from the refrigerator 1 hour before serving. The macarons will keep refrigerated for 48 to 72 hours, or they can be frozen for up to 2 weeks.

French Sponge Cake

Génoise

Makes two 9-inch cakes

Special tool: two 9-inch round cake pans

1 cup (160 grams) Steve's Gluten Free Cake Flour (see pages 1 and 2)

¾ teaspoon (3 grams) baking powder

1 cup plus 1 tablespoon (215 grams) granulated sugar

6 large eggs (330 grams), at room temperature

¼ cup (55 grams) unsalted butter, melted and slightly warm

Génoise is a sponge cake that acts as a supporting element for layering with creams, including various flavors of mousse and varieties of buttercreams. It generally is brushed with flavored simple syrup to moisten its typically dry texture before applying additional pastry components.

Method

1 Grease and line the cake pans with circles of parchment paper and preheat the oven to 350°F (175°C).

2 Sift together the flour and baking powder and set aside.

3 Combine the sugar and eggs into the detached bowl of a stand mixer. Using a hand whisk, whip the ingredients until combined. Set the bowl over a bain-marie (see page 9) and whisk nonstop until the mixture reaches 140°F (60°C). Whisking continuously ensures that the eggs do not cook against the inside of the bowl. Remove the bowl from the heat and set on the stand mixer fitted with the whisk attachment.

4 Turn the mixer to high and whip until the mixture cools to room temperature, 4 to 6 minutes. The batter should appear fluffy, lightened in color, and approximately tripled in volume. Check for the correct texture by lifting the whisk and allowing a "ribbon" to fall on top of the batter; the ribbon should hold its shape for about 10 seconds.

5 With a small hand whisk, stir about 2 tablespoons of the batter into the melted butter and set it aside.

6 Working with a large silicone spatula or large balloon hand whisk, gently fold the flour mixture into the batter in two or three additions. Be sure to scrape down to the bottom and sides of the bowl, where the flour can accumulate. Treat the batter gently and efficiently; as you fold, the batter will lose volume.

7 Add the butter mixture by pouring it down the inside edge of the bowl, then fold it into the batter, working gently and quickly. Immediately pour the batter into the two pans, distributing it equally. If the batter needs to be spread level, use a small metal spatula (preferably an offset spatula) to quickly smooth the top.

8 Bake the cakes for 30 to 40 minutes, until they are light golden brown and the center is soft but firm when gently touched. A metal cake tester can be inserted into the center of the cake to test for doneness; the tester should reveal no visibly wet particles. Remove the cakes from the oven and set them on a cooling rack for 10 minutes. To unmold, run a small, flat metal spatula around the inside edge of the pan. Flip the cake pan over, releasing the cake onto your hand (or a cake circle), then carefully flip it upright and set it on the rack to cool. When the cakes have cooled completely, they are ready to assemble. Store the cakes, well wrapped, in the refrigerator for 1 week or frozen for up to 1 month.

Sweet Dough

Pâte sucrée

Makes 2 pounds (910 grams)

1⅓ cups (300 grams) unsalted butter, at room temperature

1½ cups (150 grams) confectioners' sugar, sifted

½ teaspoon (3 grams) sea salt

¾ cup (75 grams) almond flour

½ teaspoon (3 grams) pure vanilla extract

2 large eggs (110 grams)

2¾ cups (440 grams) gluten-free flour (see pages 1 to 3), sifted

Pâte sucrée is a sweet dough used to line tart pans. The dough is made sturdy by the inclusion of almond flour, yielding a crust that is resilient to moisture and takes well to tarts with moist fillings, such as pastry cream or lemon cream or baked fruit. The crumb of pâte sucrée is tighter than its cousin *pâte sablée*, which is a richer, more crumbly crust often used as a cookie base or an element in a complex dessert creation. Gluten-free pâte sucrée is firm yet pliable to handle. The dough is temperature sensitive and must be warm (and soft) enough to roll without cracking, but cool (and firm) enough to hold its shape. If the dough becomes difficult to handle, allow it to sit at room temperature covered with plastic wrap so it does not dry out until it is pliable or refrigerate it for 10 minutes to firm up, then resume working.

Method

1 In the bowl of a stand mixer fitted with the paddle attachment, combine the butter, confectioners' sugar, and salt and beat on medium speed for about 1 minute. You do not want to incorporate air into the dough, so beat just long enough to combine the ingredients.

2 Add the almond flour and vanilla and beat on medium speed for 30 seconds, or until combined.

3 Gradually add the eggs and beat on medium speed until they are well incorporated. Using a silicone spatula, scrape the inside edges and bottom of the bowl, then beat for an additional 20 seconds.

4 Add the flour, one-third at a time, beating on low speed until each addition is just incorporated. Scrape the sides and bottom of the bowl, then continue mixing on low speed until the dough comes together in a uniform texture.

5 Scrape the dough into a large freezer bag or onto a large sheet of plastic wrap. Form the dough into a ½-inch-thick rectangle, then refrigerate for at least 2 hours. The dough will keep refrigerated for up to 3 days or frozen for up to 1 month. If the dough is frozen, place it in the refrigerator to thaw overnight before using.

6 When you are ready to use the dough, remove it from the refrigerator and allow it to sit at room temperature for 5 minutes, or until it is pliable enough to work with, but not too soft. If at any point the dough becomes too soft, refrigerate it for 10 minutes, then resume working. When handling, you may need to press the dough back together where it develops small cracks. Use minimal amounts of flour when rolling the dough out, and always brush excess flour from the front and back of the dough before final application.

Pastry Dough

Pâte brisée

Makes about 1½ pounds
(680 grams), enough to make
two 9-inch crusts

1¾ cups (280 grams) Steve's
Gluten Free Cake Flour
(see pages 1 and 2)

4 teaspoons (20 grams)
granulated sugar

½ teaspoon (3 grams) sea salt

2 large egg yolks (45 grams)

6 tablespoons (85 grams) cold
milk, plus more if needed

1 cup (230 grams) cold
unsalted butter, cut into
½-inch pieces.

Pâte brisée is a buttery, flaky pastry dough made with a small amount of sugar that is suitable for rustic, free-form tarts, small or large fruit tarts, and quiches. The dough is made by cutting in broken pieces of fat to the flour. It is temperature sensitive and must be warm (and soft) enough to roll without cracking, but cool (and firm) enough to hold its shape. If the dough becomes difficult to handle, allow it to sit out, covered with plastic wrap, until it is pliable or refrigerate it for 10 minutes, then resume working. This recipe can be made in a food processor, with a stand mixer, or by hand.

Method

1 In a food processor fitted with the blade, combine the flour, sugar, and salt and pulse briefly to incorporate.

2 In a small bowl, whisk together the egg yolks and milk and set aside.

3 Add the butter to the flour mixture and pulse until the butter breaks down to ¼-inch pieces that remain visible in the flour.

4 Gradually pour in the milk and egg mixture, pulsing the machine until the mixture begins to clump but dry particles are still visible. Dump the mixture onto a work surface. Using the heel of your hand, begin to smear the dough across the work surface, incorporating the remaining loose flour and butter. Continue until the dough is cohesive with no loose particles, and bits and streaks of butter are visible in the finished dough. If necessary, add small amounts (1 teaspoon at a time) of cold milk to incorporate the final loose particles into the dough.

5 Form the dough into a disc and put it into a large freezer bag. Using a rolling pin, flatten the dough to ½ inch thick and refrigerate for at least 2 hours. The dough will keep refrigerated for up to 3 days or frozen for up to 1 month. If the dough is frozen, place it in the refrigerator to thaw overnight before using.

6 When you are ready to use the dough, remove it from the refrigerator and allow it to sit at room temperature for 5 minutes, or until it is pliable enough to work with but not too soft. If at any point the dough becomes too soft, refrigerate it for 10 minutes, then resume working. When handling, you may need to occasionally press the dough back together where it develops small cracks. Use minimal amounts of flour when rolling the dough out, and always brush excess flour from the front and back of the dough before the next steps.

Cream Puff Pastry Dough

Pâte à choux

Makes about 3½ cups
(700 grams)

½ cup (125 grams) whole milk

½ cup plus 2 tablespoons
(150 grams) water

7 tablespoons (100 grams)
unsalted butter, cut into
¼-inch pieces

1 tablespoon (15 grams)
granulated sugar

½ teaspoon (3 grams) sea salt

¾ cup (120 grams) Steve's
Gluten Free Cake Flour
(see pages 1 and 2), sifted

4 large eggs (200 to 225
grams), beaten, at room
temperature, plus more if
needed

Cream puff–type pastries are made with a loosely textured, egg-rich dough that is piped from a pastry bag into various shapes and sizes. When *pâte à choux* dough is baked, the pastry rises and releases steam, creating a hollow-like center for the filling. Learning the correct texture for the batter is important—there's a fine line between too loose and too stiff. It is always better to add a little less beaten egg than too much at once.

Method

1 In a medium saucepan, combine the milk, water, butter, sugar, and salt and bring to a boil over medium-high heat. Reduce the heat to low and add the flour all at once. Stir vigorously with a wooden spoon until the dough congeals to form a sticky, cohesive ball. Work quickly to prevent small lumps of flour from forming. Continue to stir vigorously for 1 to 2 minutes, until a light coating of dough forms on the bottom of the pan.

2 Immediately transfer the dough into the bowl of a stand mixer fitted with the paddle attachment. Turn the mixer to medium speed and beat for 30 seconds, allowing the dough to cool slightly.

3 Add the beaten eggs in four additions, one at a time, beating until each egg is incorporated before adding the next one. After the addition of the third egg, turn the mixer off and use a silicone spatula to thoroughly scrape the paddle and the sides and bottom of the bowl. When all the eggs have been added, scrape the inside of the bowl and paddle using the silicone spatula to release any buildup of dough.

4 Increase the mixer speed to high and beat briefly until the dough is uniformly smooth. The dough is the correct consistency when it is smooth, glossy, and slowly falls from a spatula, or you can remove the paddle from the bowl and the dough forms a softly hanging downward arrow shape. If the dough is too stiff, add additional beaten egg, 1 teaspoon at a time. The dough's final consistency should be able to hold a soft mound when piped. Pipe into shapes immediately.

Brioche Dough

Pâte à brioche

Makes about 1 pound
3 ounces (540 grams)

⅓ cup (80 grams) warm
(110°F/43°C) milk

1¾ teaspoons (5½ grams)
instant yeast

3 tablespoons (45 grams)
granulated sugar

1 cup (160 grams) Steve's
Gluten Free Cake Flour
(see pages 1 and 2)

3 large eggs (165 grams),
at room temperature

¼ teaspoon (2 grams) sea salt

6 tablespoons (85 grams)
unsalted butter, cut into
pieces, at room temperature

Brioche is a rich, tender, classic French yeast bread developed with milk, butter, and eggs that can be made lean, medium, or rich, the latter containing the highest ratio of butter. Wheat-based brioche relies on the strength of gluten strands to support its high butter content. Baking brioche gluten- and gum-free requires a different method that eliminates the usual need for long kneading to create the final product. The dough will be loose and sticky when you give it a first rise, then it is refrigerated overnight before proceeding. This method will develop the dough's flavor and firm its texture for hand shaping. Alternately, the dough can be used immediately through piping or smoothing with a spatula and the final product will have a flat top. To shape the brioche by hand, you will need to chill the dough for at least 2 hours before forming it into your desired shape.

Method

1 In the bowl of a stand mixer, combine the warm milk, yeast, and 1 tablespoon of the sugar. Whisk together by hand, then sprinkle the top with 1 tablespoon (8 grams) of the flour. Allow the mixture to sit for 5 minutes, or until cracks appear in the top of the flour, proving the yeast is active.

2 Fit the mixer with the paddle attachment, then add the eggs and beat at medium-low speed until the mixture is homogeneous. Add the remaining flour, the remaining sugar, and the salt and mix until the dough comes together in a cohesive blend, about 2 minutes.

3 Increase the mixer speed to high, then add the pieces of butter, one at a time, beating until they are incorporated into the dough, about 3 minutes. The dough should lighten in color and be smooth, loose, and sticky—the texture should be like a thick batter.

4 Scrape the dough into a greased bowl and cover with plastic wrap. Let the dough sit out at room temperature to rise for 1 to 2 hours, until it doubles in size. Gently deflate the dough by pressing your hands down over the plastic wrap, then refrigerate for at least 2 hours or overnight before proceeding with the recipe's next steps.

Puff Pastry Dough

Pâte feuilletée

Makes about 2 pounds (1 kg)

Special tools: pastry brush, bench brush

For the butter block
1 cup (225 grams) unsalted butter, at room temperature

For the dough
1⅓ cups (220 grams) Steve's Gluten Free Cake Flour (see pages 1 to 3)

2 teaspoons (8 grams) potato flour

1 teaspoon (4 grams) baking powder

1½ teaspoons (3 grams) chia powder

¾ teaspoon (6 grams) sea salt

2 cups (460 grams) heavy cream, plus more as needed

This highly versatile and buttery dough, called *pâte feuilletée* in French, translates to "leaf" or "sheets." Puff pastry is made by dough lamination, an elaborate folding and rolling technique that results in micro-thin pastry layers, or leaves, that bake to a golden buttery crispness. Here the laminating process is accomplished by making six three-fold turns that create alternating layers of dough and butter. Gluten-free puff pastry cannot rely on the strength of wheat gluten to help it rise, so this gluten-free recipe calls for the addition of leavening to help give a lift to the pastry. To prevent sticking, roll the dough between sheets of plastic wrap or silicone mats, liberally flour the dough while rolling, and always brush excess flour from the dough before making the next fold. Chill the dough between rolling, but make sure the butter stays soft enough inside the dough to easily accept its next rolling. If the butter hardens and breaks, it will be more difficult to work with. Depending on the condition of the dough, give it time to soften at room temperature or refrigerate it to chill before working on the next fold.

Although the process of making puff pastry is particular and labor intensive, the rewards are many: once you have the method down, you will have achieved one of the most important tools of gluten-free French pastry making, preparing you for classics including *Mille-Feuille* (pages 299 and 300), *Palmiers* (pages 285 to 287), Apple Slippers (pages 283 and 284), and *Sacristains* (pages 293 and 294).

Method

Make the butter block
1 Place the butter in the bowl of a stand mixer fitted with the paddle attachment. Beat the butter on medium-high speed until it lightens in color, about 1 minute.

2 Using a silicone spatula, scrape the butter out of the bowl and into a mound on a sheet of parchment paper, and shape the butter into an 8-by-6-inch rectangular block. Fold the parchment paper up over the sides and top of the butter block and place in the refrigerator to chill until firm. The butter block may be prepared a few hours or up to 1 week ahead of time and stored in the refrigerator until you are ready to use it.

Make the dough

1 Remove the butter block from the refrigerator and place it on your work surface, keeping it wrapped in the parchment paper. Allow the butter to sit out for 1 hour, or until it has softened to an optimal working consistency; when you press your fingertip on the top of the butter block, it should make a slight indentation but not squish down into the butter. For successful rolling and laminating, it is essential that the butter block and dough have the same temperature and feel.

2 To make the dough, combine the cake flour, potato flour, baking powder, chia powder, and salt in the bowl of a stand mixer fitted with the paddle attachment. Turn the mixer to low speed to briefly stir the dry mixture together, then steadily pour in the heavy cream and mix for 30 seconds. The dough will initially appear shaggy and a bit dry. Turn off the mixer and scrape the dough away from the center of the paddle and continue mixing until the dough takes a cohesive shape and holds together. If the dough is too dry, add additional cream, 1 tablespoon at a time, until the dough is soft and sticky, but holds a cohesive shape. Remove the dough from the bowl and shape it into a rough rectangle that's about 1 inch thick. Wrap the dough in plastic and refrigerate for 15 minutes before beginning the lamination process.

3 Remove the dough from the refrigerator and place it on a large piece of lightly floured parchment paper or plastic wrap. Sprinkle the dough with flour and cover with a large piece of plastic wrap to help prevent sticking. Using a rolling pin, firmly begin to roll the dough into a 17-by-7-inch rectangle, using your hands to help keep the rectangular shape when needed. Brush away any remaining flour from the top of the dough; this is an important step that will help make a flaky, tender puff pastry. Place the butter block in the center of the dough. Fold one side of the dough over the butter; it should reach to the center of the butter block. Then fold the remaining half of the dough to overlap slightly onto the other side, fully encasing the butter in the dough. If the edges of the dough crack, simply press them back together using your fingers.

4 Dust the work surface and the top and bottom of the dough with flour. Begin to firmly press the rolling pin down into the dough, making ridges across the length of the dough. The dough should begin to slightly lengthen. Then, beginning at the outside edge and working toward the center, roll the dough in even strokes. Repeat this rolling method with the other side of the dough, primarily rolling from the outside edge toward the center. Pay close attention to how much pressure you use with the rolling pin; the goal is to effectively distribute the butter in an even layer inside the dough without pushing the butter out the ends of the dough or tearing the dough. Roll the dough to a flat 18-by-8-inch rectangle with squared corners. Brush any remaining flour off the dough and use your hands to help shape the dough. Lightly score the rectangle into three equal portions to prepare to make a three-fold dough, just like you would fold a business letter: fold one end of the dough over the center third, then fold the remaining third across the top of the other two-thirds to complete the first turn. Transfer the dough onto a small baking sheet and cover with plastic wrap. Refrigerate the dough for 10 to 15 minutes for it to firm up enough to be ready for the next roll and fold. This resting period is crucial for the layers of dough to become established; the butter needs to chill to prepare for its next rolling but not become so cold that it cracks inside the dough.

5 Remove the dough from the refrigerator and place it on a large piece of floured plastic wrap. Cover the dough with a large piece of plastic wrap. The open ends should be facing vertically on the table in front of you. Repeat the same rolling and folding process to complete the second turn. Wrap and refrigerate the dough as before and allow a 15- to 20-minute rest. Continue this rolling, folding, and resting process until you have completed six turns. Keep track of how many turns you have given the dough by pressing a very light finger mark on top of the dough before you refrigerate it each time.

6 Once all six turns are complete, refrigerate the dough for 1 hour. Remove the dough from the refrigerator and roll it into a 16-by-24-inch rectangle that is ¼ inch thick. Brush off excess flour from the front and back of the dough. Cut the puff pastry dough in half and place one half on a baking sheet lined with parchment paper. Cover this sheet of dough with a piece of parchment paper, then place the remaining sheet of puff pastry on top and cover with another piece of parchment paper. Wrap the top of the dough securely in plastic or place in a large plastic bag. Allow the dough to rest in the refrigerator for 1 hour; at that point the dough is ready to use. The dough may be stored, wrapped well, in the refrigerator for up to 24 hours or frozen for up to 1 month. To defrost, remove the amount of dough you plan to use and defrost it, covered, in the refrigerator.

Croissant Dough

Pâte croissant

Makes about 2½ pounds
(1 kg 100 grams)

For the butter blocks

½ cup (113 grams) unsalted
butter, at room temperature

1 tablespoon (8 grams)
Steve's Gluten Free Cake
Flour (see pages 1 and 2)

For the dough

½ cup (112 grams)
full-fat ricotta cheese

½ cup (112 grams)
full-fat sour cream

1 large egg (55 grams)

1 tablespoon (8 grams)
instant yeast

1 cup (240 grams) water, plus
more as needed

¼ cup (50 grams)
granulated sugar

2¼ cups (360 grams) Steve's
Gluten Free Cake Flour
(see pages 1 and 2)

1 tablespoon (12 grams)
potato flour

2 teaspoons (8 grams)
baking powder

The flavor of this croissant dough is the real deal, boasting full-bodied buttery deliciousness—just what you would expect from a fresh croissant. Included in this dough are ricotta cheese and sour cream, which provide the yeast enough protein to feed on and endure the rolling and rising of this gluten-free croissant variation. The process for making this croissant dough remains the same as the traditional method, which requires rolling out the dough multiple times to make four turns with three folds. The lamination process is made easier by rolling the dough out between two large pieces of plastic wrap, which helps prevent sticking. Turn this dough into regular croissants or twice-baked almond croissants, or alter the rolling pattern to make *Kouign-amann* (pages 279 to 281).

Method

Make the butter blocks

1 Place the butter in the bowl of a stand mixer fitted with the paddle attachment. Add the flour and beat on low speed until the flour and butter begin to come together. Increase the speed to medium-high and beat until the mixture is fluffy and has lightened in color, about 1 minute.

2 Using a silicone spatula, scrape the butter out of the bowl and into a mound on a sheet of parchment paper. Divide the butter into two 2-ounce (60-gram) portions, then use a metal spatula to shape the butter into two 5-by-4-inch rectangles. Fold the parchment paper up over the sides and top of each butter block and place in the refrigerator to chill for 1 hour, or until firm. The butter blocks may be prepared a few hours or up to 1 week ahead of time and stored in the refrigerator until you are ready to use them.

1 tablespoon (4½ grams) chia powder

1 teaspoon (7 grams) sea salt

2 tablespoons (30 grams) cold unsalted butter, cut into ½-inch pieces

3 When you begin to prepare the dough, allow the butter block to sit out for 1 hour, or until it has softened to an optimal working consistency; when you press your fingertip on the top of the butter block, it should make a slight indentation but not squish down into the butter. For successful rolling and laminating, it is essential that the butter block and dough have the same temperature and feel.

Make the dough

1 In a medium bowl, combine the ricotta, sour cream, and egg. Whisk until the ingredients are homogeneous, then set aside.

2 Sprinkle the yeast into a small bowl and pour the water over it. Add 1 tablespoon (15 grams) of the sugar, whisk until well blended, sprinkle the top with 1 tablespoon of the cake flour, and set aside to proof the yeast. After 5 minutes, the flour on top should develop cracks, and the liquid should begin to foam and bubble.

3 In the bowl of a stand mixer fitted with the paddle attachment, combine the cake flour, potato flour, the remaining sugar, baking powder, chia powder, and salt. Add the cold butter, then beat on low speed until the butter breaks down to pea-size particles.

4 Next, whisk the yeast mixture into the ricotta mixture. With the mixer running on low speed, pour the wet mixture into the dry ingredients. Turn off the mixer and scrape the dough away from the center of the paddle, then continue mixing until the dough forms a loose but uniform texture. If the dough is too dry, add more water, 2 tablespoons at a time, until the dough is soft and sticky and just holds its shape.

5 Scrape the dough into another large bowl, cover with plastic wrap, and set aside at room temperature to rise for 1 hour or until doubled in size. Lightly flour your hands, and deflate the dough. Do this by folding the dough over onto itself, then repeat this folding step once more. Cover the bowl with plastic wrap and refrigerate the dough overnight.

6 When you are ready to make the croissants, remove the butter block from the refrigerator to come to the correct consistency, about ½ to 1 hour. When you press your fingertip on the top of the butter block, it should make a slight indentation but not squish down into the butter. For successful rolling and laminating, it is essential that the butter block and dough have the same temperature and feel.

7 Generously flour the top of your work surface, remove the dough from the refrigerator, and scrape it from the bowl and onto the work area. Divide the dough into two portions, about 20 ounces (580 grams) each. Liberally flour the bottom and top of the dough throughout the rolling process, but always brush excess flour from the dough before making the folds. Shape the dough into a rectangle and, using a rolling pin, gently and evenly begin to roll the dough into a 10-by-5-inch rectangle, using your hands to help keep the rectangular shape when needed. Use a dry pastry or bench brush to sweep away any remaining flour from the top of the dough. Place the butter block in the center of the dough. Fold one side of the dough over the butter; it should reach to the center of the butter block. Then fold the remaining half of the dough to slightly overlap onto the other side of the dough, fully encasing the butter in the dough. Repeat these steps with the other piece of dough and its butter block. Proceed through the remainder of the recipe, alternating the rolling of each separate piece of dough.

8 Liberally dust the work surface and the top and bottom of the dough with flour. Begin to press the rolling pin down across the dough, making slight indentations, beginning at the outside edge and working toward the center. Pay close attention to how much pressure you use with the rolling pin; the goal is to effectively distribute the butter in an even layer inside the dough without pushing the butter out the sides of the dough or tearing the dough. Roll the dough to a level 12-by-6-inch rectangle with squared corners, using your hands to help shape the dough when necessary. Brush any remaining flour off the dough. Lightly score the rectangle into three equal portions to prepare to make a three-fold turn, as you would fold a business letter. Fold one end of the dough over the center third, then fold the remaining third across the top of the other two-thirds to complete the first turn. Brush free any excess flour, wrap in plastic, and place the dough on a small baking sheet. Refrigerate the dough for 10 to 15 minutes for it to firm up enough to be ready for its next roll and fold. This resting period is crucial for the layers of dough to become established; the butter needs to chill to prepare for its next rolling, but not so much that it cracks inside the dough. This is a delicate step in dough lamination. If the dough cracks along the sides, simply press it back together using your fingers. Keep the dough well floured throughout the rolling process.

9 Remove the dough from the refrigerator and place it vertically on the work surface, with the open ends facing you. The folded sides should be to your right (like the spine of a book) and left. Repeat the same rolling and folding process to complete the second turn. Wrap and refrigerate the dough as before and allow it to rest for 10 to 15 minutes. Continue this rolling, folding, and resting process until you have completed four turns. Keep track of how many turns you have given the dough by pressing a very light finger mark on top of the dough before you refrigerate it each time.

10 Once all four turns are complete, wrap the dough in plastic wrap and refrigerate it for 15 to 20 minutes. Remove the dough from the refrigerator and proceed with your recipe instructions.

Tempered Chocolate

Tempérage du chocolat

Makes about 1 pound
(455 grams)

Special tool: chocolate
thermometer or instant-read
thermometer

1 pound (455 grams)
bittersweet couverture
chocolate, finely chopped,
or fèves, or pistoles

Tempering chocolate will result in a glossy finish, strength that has a nice snap, and a smooth, firm texture. Likewise, untempered chocolate will set slowly and "bloom," meaning it will exhibit dull gray streaks and splotches on the surface and lose its shine, strength, and smooth finish. For recipes that call for dipping in chocolate, tempering ensures that the chocolate sets up properly. Once tempered, you have the option of creating various decorative chocolate designs and forms that will hold their shape. The chocolate to use for tempering is couverture chocolate, which contains a high cocoa butter content. Do not attempt to temper chocolate chips or chunks. Do not allow the chocolate to overheat or it will scorch and separate into cocoa particles and liquid. Also do not allow the chocolate to come into contact with the tiniest bit of moisture, which will cause the chocolate to "seize" and become a solid grainy mass. You can salvage seized chocolate to add to an icing or filling by adding a tablespoon of warm water at a time and mixing until the chocolate becomes smooth and creamy, but it will no longer be suitable for tempering.

The following is a seeding method for tempering chocolate, essentially binding the chocolate crystals by adding a portion of already tempered chocolate.

Dark, milk, and white chocolate temper at different temperatures. Keep an eye out for specific tempering charts for different chocolate brands. I normally use dark chocolate pistoles (see Sources, pages 14 and 15) that are ready for melting and do not require chopping. The easiest method for chopping chocolate is to use a serrated knife on a chopping board.

Method

1 In a small bowl, set aside one-third (152 grams) of the chocolate. This is the seed chocolate.

2 Place the remaining two-thirds (303 grams) of the chocolate into a medium heatproof bowl and set over a bain-marie (see page 9). Keep the heat very low to prevent steam from rising up the sides of the bowl and ruining the chocolate for tempering. Using a silicone spatula, stir the chocolate often until fully melted. Keep close track of the temperature by inserting the thermometer into the chocolate (not touching the bottom of the bowl) to take regular readings. When the chocolate reaches 115°F (46°C) to 122°F (50°C), remove it from the bain-marie, and using a kitchen towel, wipe the moisture from the bottom of the bowl.

3 Add the reserved one-third of the chocolate (the seed) to the melted chocolate. Stir the chocolate continuously until the temperature lowers to between 90°F (32°C) and 86°F (30°C). Use the thermometer to check often for accurate readings.

4 The chocolate will remain in good temper as long as it stays close to its working temperature. If the chocolate begins to cool, return it to the bain-marie and carefully reheat briefly to bring it back to the correct temperature.

CHAPTER THREE

Cookies

Cookies

Les biscuits

No cookie is safe within sight at my house. Nor out of sight. Hiding the jar only means breaking out the ladder to climb up and reach into the dark corner of a tall cabinet to pull out an irresistible sweet. To me, cookies portray innocence: a small, individual serving-size pastry that a young hand can hold, tuck inside a pocket, or slip quietly out of a jar. And since few adults outgrow their secret visits to the cookie jar, we cookie lovers are young at heart.

Needless to say, the sight of an empty cookie jar is a sad state indeed. To help prevent this possibility, I've shared with you a pinch more than a baker's dozen of my favorites. We'll start with six variations on sablé cookies. *Sablé* translates to "sand," which refers to the original method for making these cookies, by hand: when you rub together the cold butter, flour, and sugar, the result is a sandy texture. Paradoxically, not all sablé cookies are sandy in texture— some are also flaky, more or less buttery, or more or less sweet. But, ultimately, sablés are buttery, shortbread-type cookies or tea biscuits (sablé biscuits usually contain less sugar). They can be flavored with nuts, zest, or chocolate, sandwiched, shaped into logs, rolled and cut, piped, or set as a base for other desserts.

A climb up the cookie ladder will also reveal hand-shaped Linzer Quenelles, with their crunchy texture, slightly acidic raspberry notes, and sensual shape. *Lunettes*, a roll and cut cookie resembling spectacles, are starkly gorgeous and simple to prepare. Bordeaux Biscuits are just a little sweet, loaded with generous flavor, and perfect alongside a cup of tea. The intriguing Coconut *Congolais* are a miniature French version of a coconut macaroon.

Moving along to wafer-style cookies, Hazelnut Wafers are a mouthful of *oh my*, and the intriguingly named Cat's Tongues are enchanting in their crisp, snappy texture and smooth dark chocolate contrast. *Tuiles* are also part of the wafer cookie category; the name means "tiles," and the cookies resemble the curved ceramic roof tiles found atop French country homes. These beautiful cookies gracefully adorn ice cream and other soft desserts, such as Honey Chocolate Mousse (page 39).

As you bake through this collection of recipes, you will amply fill the treasured cookie jar. Prepare to climb the ladder for a baker's game of hide and seek for cookies in hand . . . and mouth.

Chocolate Sea Salt Sablés

Sablés au chocolat et fleur de sel

Makes about 24

5 ounces (150 grams)
dark chocolate

Scant ¾ teaspoon (4–5 grams)

1 cup plus 2 tablespoons
(175 grams) Steve's Gluten
Free Cake Flour
(see pages 1 and 2)

⅓ cup (30 grams)
cocoa powder

½ teaspoon (3 grams)
baking soda

⅓ cup plus 1 tablespoon
(95 grams) unsalted butter, at
room temperature

¼ cup (50 grams)
granulated sugar

⅔ cup (120 grams)
light brown sugar

1 teaspoon (5 grams)
pure vanilla extract

These perfectly devilish dark chocolate sablés are crumbly, crunchy, and buttery, with their intense chocolate flavor accented by an ample toss of coarse sea salt. They have been known to cause serious hankerings and secret stashing behavior. Use any kind of good-quality chocolate you prefer, from a high-end favorite brand or plain and simple chocolate chips. You can also change the recipe by switching out half of the dark chocolate for milk chocolate and tossing in ½ cup of toasted nuts.

Method

1 Line two 12-by-17-inch baking sheets with parchment paper or silicone mats.

2 Working with a food processor fitted with a steel blade, or by hand, chop the chocolate into small to medium pieces. Add the salt and briefly process with the chocolate.

3 Sift the flour, cocoa powder, and baking soda into a medium bowl and set aside.

4 Place the butter into the bowl of a stand mixer fitted with the paddle attachment. On medium speed, beat the butter until it is creamy and lightens in color, about 1 minute.

5 Add the granulated sugar, brown sugar, and vanilla extract. Continue to beat on medium speed just until the sugars combine with the butter, about 1 minute. The objective is not to cream the sugars with the butter, but rather just to beat them to the point where they evenly combine and are still granular. Use a rubber spatula to thoroughly scrape the sides and bottom of the bowl, then reduce the speed to low and beat for 10 seconds.

6 Turn the mixer off and add the dry ingredients. Turn the mixer to low speed and beat just until the dry ingredients are nearly incorporated. Turn the mixer off, then add the chopped chocolate. Return the mixer to low speed and mix just until the chocolate and dough have incorporated. The dough will be somewhat loose and crumbly.

7 Turn the dough out onto a large sheet of parchment paper and separate it into two equal portions. With your hands, form each portion into a loose log shape that's approximately 1½ by 7 inches. Squeeze the dough together on one side, then roll the dough over and squeeze the other side, working to form a cylindrical cookie dough log. To assist with obtaining uniformity, wrap the edge of the parchment paper across the top of the dough log, then roll the dough log up in the parchment. Keep your hands on the paper and gently but firmly roll the log back and forth a few times. Unroll the parchment to observe the log and gently press in their outer ends to ensure they remain intact.

8 Wrap the cookie logs in plastic and allow them to rest and chill in the refrigerator for 1 hour. Alternately, the dough will keep refrigerated for up to 3 days or frozen for up to 2 months.

9 When you are ready to bake the sablés, preheat the oven to 325°F (165°C).

10 Remove the cookies from the refrigerator and allow them to sit out at room temperature for 15 minutes, or until they have softened slightly, making them easier to slice. Use a sharp serrated or thin-bladed knife to cut ½-inch-thick slices from the logs. If the cookies break apart, simply press them back together. Place the cookies on parchment paper–lined baking sheets 1½ inches apart and bake for 10 to 12 minutes. The cookies will spread, crack, and puff up a little. The ideal moment to remove them from the oven is when they are firm around the edges and the center is still slightly soft but has not yet fallen.

11 Remove the sablés from the oven and place them on a cooling rack. The cookies will firm up as they cool. They are delicious slightly warm, at room temperature, or chilled, or try crumbling them over ice cream. Store the sablés in an airtight container for up to 2 weeks or freeze for up to 2 months.

Almond Red Raspberry Sablés

Sablés aux framboises et amande

Makes 15

For the dough

1 cup plus 2 tablespoons (180 grams) Steve's Gluten Free Cake Flour (see pages 1 and 2), sifted

1 cup (100 grams) almond flour

Rounded ½ teaspoon (4 grams) sea salt

1 cup (225 grams) unsalted butter, at room temperature

½ cup (100 grams) granulated sugar

1 teaspoon (5 grams) pure vanilla extract

1 teaspoon (5 grams) pure almond extract

For rolling

½ cup (75 grams) finely chopped or crushed almonds

Egg Wash (page 19)

For sandwiching

½ cup (170 grams) raspberry jam

These sandwiched almond and raspberry shortbread-like cookies are a perfect marriage of taste and texture. Nutty, buttery almonds mingle with the fruity acidity of sweet red raspberry, with pure almond extract heightening the flavor profile. Rolling them in crushed almonds adds textural contrast to keep your senses fully engaged.

Method

1 Line two 12-by-17-inch baking sheets with parchment paper or silicone mats.

2 In a medium bowl, whisk together the cake flour, almond flour, and salt and set aside.

3 Place the butter into the bowl of a stand mixer fitted with the paddle attachment. On medium speed, beat the butter until it is creamy and lightens in color, about 1 minute. Add the granulated sugar, vanilla extract, and almond extract and continue to beat on medium speed just until the sugars combine with the butter, about 1 minute. The objective is not to cream the sugars with the butter, but rather to beat them just to the point where they combine evenly but are still granular. Use a rubber spatula to scrape the sides and bottom of the bowl, then lower the speed to low and mix for 10 seconds.

4 Turn the mixer off and add the dry ingredients, then turn the mixer to low speed and beat just until the dry ingredients are incorporated. The dough should be a loosely formed mass.

5 Turn the dough out onto a large sheet of parchment paper and separate it into two equal portions. With your hands, form each portion into a long rectangle, approximately

2 by 6 inches. Squeeze the dough together on one side, then roll the dough over and squeeze the other side, working to form a cylindrical cookie dough log. To assist with obtaining uniformity, wrap the edge of the parchment paper across the top of the dough log, then roll the dough log up in the parchment. Keep your hands on the paper and gently but firmly roll the log back and forth a few times. Unroll the parchment to observe the log and gently press in the outer ends to ensure they remain intact.

6 Wrap the cookie dough logs in plastic and allow them to rest and chill in the refrigerator for 1 hour. Alternately, the dough will keep refrigerated for up to 3 days or frozen for up to 2 months.

7 When you are ready to make the sablés, preheat the oven to 350°F (175°C).

8 Remove the cookie dough logs from the refrigerator and allow them to sit out at room temperature for 10 to 15 minutes, until they have softened slightly, making them easier to slice.

9 Lay out a large sheet of parchment paper and sprinkle with the chopped almonds. Brush the dough logs with the egg wash, then roll them in the almonds; press the logs firmly down into the almonds to help them adhere. Use a sharp serrated or thin knife to cut ½-inch-thick slices from the logs. If the cookies break apart, simply press them back together. Place the cookies on parchment paper–lined baking sheets 1½ inches apart and bake for 10 to 12 minutes. The cookies will spread and puff up a little. They are done when they are firm and light golden brown around the edges, and the center is still slightly soft.

10 Remove the sablés from the oven and place them on a cooling rack to cool completely, then sandwich them with the raspberry jam. Store the sablés in an airtight container for up to 2 weeks or freeze for up to 2 months.

Caen Sablés

Sablés de Caen

Makes about 24

Special tools: 3-inch fluted square cookie cutter or other cutter of your choice, pastry brush

For the dough

¾ cup (170 grams) unsalted butter, at room temperature

⅔ cup plus 2 teaspoons (85 grams) confectioners' sugar, sifted

2 large egg yolks, hard boiled and pressed through a medium-mesh sieve

2 tablespoons (28 grams) whole milk

1½ teaspoons (8 grams) pure vanilla extract

1¼ cups (200 grams) Steve's Gluten Free Cake Flour (see pages 1 and 2)

⅛ teaspoon (1 gram) sea salt

For glazing

Egg Wash (page 19)

Handsomely eye-catching, these fluted *sablés* contain hard-boiled eggs, which contribute to their extraordinarily rich, tender texture. With their subtle buttery, not very sweet flavor, these sablés sit in the category of biscuit, and their fluted square shape and pretty almond decoration will beckon an afternoon cup of tea. The recipe can be made with natural (skin-on) or blanched almonds, though blanched almonds give the cookies a more dramatic appearance. The work of pastry chefs Bruce Healy and Paul Bugat, whose baking books have inspired me to become a better baker, kindled this recipe.

Method

1 Line two 12-by-17-inch baking sheets with parchment paper or silicone mats.

2 Place the butter and confectioners' sugar into the bowl of a stand mixer fitted with the paddle attachment. Turn the mixer to medium speed and cream the butter and sugar until smooth, about 1 minute. Use a rubber spatula to scrape the sides and bottom of the bowl.

3 Add the egg yolks, then reduce the mixer speed to low and beat for a few seconds, until they're combined. Continue with the mixer running at low speed and slowly pour in the milk and vanilla extract. Mix for about 30 seconds, then turn the mixer off and scrape the bowl again.

4 Add the flour and salt, then mix on low speed for about 1 minute, stopping the mixer to scrape the bowl as necessary. The dough is ready when it is smooth and cohesive. Turn the dough out into a large plastic bag or onto a large sheet of parchment paper. Form the dough into a square pad about

For decorating
Approximately 100 blanched almonds (see page 76 for how to blanch almonds)

1 inch thick. Wrap the dough well and refrigerate for 1 hour before rolling out.

5 When you are ready to roll the dough, allow it to sit at room temperature for 5 to 10 minutes, until the dough is soft enough to roll but firm enough to handle. Lay down a large sheet of parchment paper topped with a large piece of plastic wrap. Turn the dough out onto the plastic wrap and cover it with a second piece of plastic wrap. If the dough is sticking to the plastic, lightly dust with flour. Roll the dough into a ⅛-inch-thick sheet. If the dough becomes too soft, slide it onto a baking sheet and refrigerate for 10 minutes, then resume rolling.

6 With the cookie cutter, cut as many squares as you can, saving the dough scraps for the next rolling. Use a wide metal spatula to transfer the cut sablés onto parchment paper–lined baking sheets, spacing them about ¾ inch apart. Place the first full sheet of sablés in the refrigerator, then proceed with rolling out the remaining dough.

7 Once both sheets are full, brush the tops of each sablé with the beaten egg, return them to the refrigerator, and allow them to sit while the egg wash dries, about 20 minutes.

8 Preheat the oven to 350°F (175°C).

9 Apply a second coating of egg wash to the sablés, then arrange 4 blanched almonds on the top of each with their points facing outward from the center of each square.

10 Bake the sablés until they are golden brown, about 15 minutes. Set the baking sheets on cooling racks to cool completely, then remove them with a wide metal spatula. Store the sablés in an airtight container for up to 1 week.

Blanching Almonds

Fill a medium saucepan with 4 cups of water, set it over high heat, and bring to a boil. Add 2 cups (280 grams) of natural, skin-on, whole almonds and boil for 2 minutes. Remove the pan from the heat and drain through a mesh strainer, shaking the almonds briefly to release residual water. Pour the almonds onto a baking sheet. Line another baking sheet with two layers of paper towels. Pick up one almond and squeeze the thicker end so the almond pops out of its skin. Set the blanched almond onto the paper towel to begin drying and toss the skin into the compost. Continue until all the almonds have been skinned, then set them aside to dry for 2 days. If you plan to grind your blanched almonds into flour, make certain they are completely dry before using.

Viennese Sablés

Sablés viennois

Makes about 36

Special tool: pastry bag fitted with a medium star tip (Ateco #825)

½ cup (60 grams) hazelnuts, natural or blanched, toasted

¼ cup (50 grams) granulated sugar

¼ cup (25 grams) confectioners' sugar

6 tablespoons (90 grams) unsalted butter, at room temperature

1 large egg (55 grams), at room temperature, lightly whisked

1 teaspoon (5 grams) pure vanilla extract

½ teaspoon (4 grams) sea salt

¾ cup (120 grams) gluten-free flour blend (see pages 1 to 3), sifted

For decorating
Tempered Chocolate (see pages 62 and 63)

½ cup (60 grams) toasted, finely chopped hazelnuts

This type of cookie, a piped *sablé*, gets its name, *Viennois*, from its popularity in Viennese pastry. Versatility and visual appeal are attributes of this delicious cookie. Play with shapes by piping the batter into fingers, shells, or hearts, or make rosettes and stud them with a joyful glacé cherry before baking. You can also sandwich the baked fingers, shells, or hearts with jam or dip them in chocolate. These quintessential cookies are traditionally stacked high onto a platter or packaged into tins for a sweet special occasion gift.

Method

1 Line two 12-by-17-inch baking sheets with parchment paper or silicone mats.

2 Combine the hazelnuts, granulated sugar, and confectioners' sugar in the bowl of a food processor fitted with a blade attachment. Grind the mixture until it is fine and flour-like. Sift the mixture through a medium-mesh sieve into a bowl. Grind any remaining nuts a second time with small amounts of the powdered nut mixture, then sift again until all the nut and sugar mixture has passed through the sieve.

3 In the bowl of a stand mixer fitted with the paddle attachment, combine the butter and nut and sugar mixture and beat on medium speed for 1 minute. Add the egg, vanilla extract, and salt and continue to beat on medium speed until the ingredients combine, about 1 minute. Turn the mixer off and, using a silicone spatula, scrape the sides and bottom of the bowl, and then beat again briefly.

4 Turn off the mixer and add the flour, then beat on low speed for 1 minute, or until blended. Remove the bowl from the mixer and give the batter a final hand mixing with a silicone spatula.

5 Preheat the oven to 375°F (190°C).

6 Fill the pastry bag with batter and pipe into shell shapes, approximately 1 inch wide and 1½ inches long, on the prepared baking sheets. Begin by piping a thicker mound while gradually pulling away to end with a pointed tip, spacing the cookies 1½ inches apart.

7 Bake the cookies for 8 to 10 minutes, until the scalloped edges of the cookies turn light golden brown. Remove the baking sheet from the oven and set it on a cooling rack to cool completely before finishing the cookies.

8 Finish the cookies by dipping them into tempered chocolate, then into the toasted hazelnuts. Alternately, sandwich the shells by spreading a thin layer of jam between them before dipping in chocolate. Store the cookies in an airtight container for up to 2 weeks.

Diamond Sablés

Sablés diamants

Makes 16

---

1 cup (225 grams) unsalted butter, at room temperature

⅔ cup (70 grams) confectioners' sugar, sifted

1 teaspoon (5 grams) pure vanilla extract

1 tablespoon (5 grams) lemon zest

1 large egg (55 grams)

1¾ cups (280 grams) Steve's Gluten Free Cake Flour (see pages 1 and 2), sifted

½ teaspoon (4 grams) sea salt

1 cup (200 grams) sparkling or demerara sugar

Egg Wash (page 19)

A roll in diamond sugar gives a pretty sparkle to these delicate lemon *sablés*. They have a delicate "short" crumb, which makes them remarkably tender, a characteristic typical of a fine shortbread-type cookie. The sablés are formed into small cylinder shapes, which helps hold their tender structure intact. The cylinders are then brushed with egg, embedded with crystal sugar, chilled, sliced, and baked. Although diminutive in size, their twinkling diamond edges and subtle flavor make this cookie a memorable one.

Method

1 Line two 12-by-17-inch baking sheets with parchment paper or silicone mats.

2 Place the butter into the bowl of a stand mixer fitted with the paddle attachment. On medium speed, beat the butter until it is creamy and lightens in color, about 1 minute. Add the confectioners' sugar, vanilla extract, and lemon zest. Increase the speed to medium-high and beat until the ingredients combine, about 1 minute. Add the egg and continue to beat on medium-high speed for 1 minute. Turn the mixer off and use a silicone spatula to scrape the paddle, sides, and bottom of the bowl. Turn the mixer to medium speed and beat for another 10 seconds, or until the mixture is homogeneous.

3 Turn the mixer off, then add the flour and salt. Turn the mixer to low speed and beat just until the dry ingredients are incorporated.

4 Turn the dough out onto a large sheet of parchment paper and separate it into two equal portions. With your hands, form each portion into a long rectangle. Squeeze the dough together on one side, then roll the dough over and squeeze the other side, working to form a cylindrical cookie dough log, about 1½ inches in diameter. To assist with obtaining uniformity, wrap the edge of the parchment paper across the top of the dough log, then roll the dough log up in the parchment. Keep your hands on the paper and gently but firmly roll the log back and forth a few times. Unroll the parchment to observe the log and gently press on and smooth the outer ends of the log to ensure that they remain intact.

5 Wrap the cookie dough logs in plastic, place on a baking sheet, and allow them to rest and chill in the refrigerator for 1 hour. Alternately, the dough will keep refrigerated for up to 3 days or frozen for up to 2 months.

6 When you are ready to make the sablés, preheat the oven to 350°F (175°C).

7 Sprinkle the sparkling sugar in a long rectangular pile onto a sheet of parchment paper. Brush the long sides of the cookie logs with egg wash, then set them onto the sparkling sugar and roll the logs back and forth, pressing down until the sides are covered with sugar. Use a sharp serrated or thin knife to cut ½-inch-thick slices from the logs. If the cookies break apart, simply press them back together. Place the cookies on parchment paper–lined baking sheets 1½ inches apart and bake for 10 to 12 minutes. The cookies will spread, crack, and puff up a little. The ideal moment to remove them from the oven is when they are firm and golden brown around the edges and the center is firm.

8 Remove the sablés from the oven, then place them on a cooling rack to cool completely before serving.

9 Store the sablés in an airtight container for up to 2 weeks or freeze for up to 2 months.

Breton Sablés

Sablés Breton

Makes 4 dozen

Special tools: pastry brush, mini muffin pans

For the dough
Nonstick cooking spray

1½ cups (240 grams) gluten-free flour blend (see pages 1 to 3)

2 teaspoons (8 grams) baking powder

½ teaspoon (4 grams) sea salt

¾ cup (170 grams) unsalted butter, at room temperature

½ cup plus 1 tablespoon (115 grams) granulated sugar

5 large egg yolks (110 grams)

For the glaze
¼ teaspoon (2 grams) coffee extract, such as Trablit

½ teaspoon (3 grams) hot water

1 large egg yolk (22 grams)

This classic cookie has its origins in Brittany, known for its salt marshes and production of fleur de sel, or "flower of salt." Breton *sablés* are buttery and rich and contain a slightly salty peck that makes them uncommonly good. Form the dough into small logs, slice, and bake the dough in mini muffin tins, which help form a perfectly lovely round of these shortbread-like treats. The glaze contains a bit of coffee, which adds a beautiful finish, but it is not a necessity for the recipe, so feel free to omit the espresso powder if you choose.

Method
Make the dough
1 Lightly grease two 1-inch mini muffin pans, or coat them with nonstick cooking spray.

2 Sift together the flour, baking powder, and salt and set aside.

3 Place the butter into the bowl of a stand mixer fitted with the paddle attachment. On medium speed, beat the butter until it is creamy and soft, about 1 minute. Add the sugar and beat briefly on medium-high speed until the ingredients combine. Add the egg yolks and continue to beat on medium-high speed for 1 minute, or until they are incorporated. Using a silicone spatula, thoroughly scrape the sides and bottom of the bowl, then reduce the speed to medium and beat for 10 seconds.

4 Turn the mixer off, then add the dry ingredients all at once. Turn the mixer on low speed and beat just until the dry ingredients have almost incorporated. Remove the bowl from the mixer and finish mixing by hand using a large silicone spatula. Be careful to not overwork the dough.

5 Turn the dough out onto a large sheet of parchment paper and separate it into two approximately equal portions. Using your hands, form each portion into a long rectangle. Squeeze the dough together by pulling the sides in toward the top and cupping your hand over the log, then roll the dough over and squeeze the other side, working to form a cylindrical cookie dough log about 1 inch in diameter. To assist with obtaining uniformity, wrap the edge of the parchment paper across the top of the dough log, then roll the dough log up in the parchment. Keep your hands on the paper and gently but firmly roll the log back and forth a few times. Unroll the parchment to observe the log and gently press on and smooth the outer ends of the log to ensure that they remain intact. The length of the log is not important; the diameter is what matters and must be just shy of the bottom of the muffin cup's diameter so the sablés will sit flat on the bottom.

6 Wrap the cookie dough logs in plastic, place on a baking sheet, and allow them to rest and chill in the refrigerator for 2 hours. From this point the dough will keep refrigerated for up to 3 days or can be frozen for up to 2 months.

7 When you are ready to make the sablés, preheat the oven to 350°F (175°C).

Make the glaze
1 Combine the coffee extract with the hot water and stir until combined. In a separate small bowl, whisk the egg yolk, then slowly pour the coffee mixture into the yolk, whisking the whole time.

2 Remove the sablés from the refrigerator and use a sharp serrated knife to cut ½-inch-thick slices from the logs. If the cookies break apart, simply press them back together. Press the top of each sliced cookie with the tines of a fork, making a crisscross design. Using the pastry brush, apply a light coat of egg glaze to the top of each cookie. Set a cookie snug into the bottom of each muffin cup.

3 Bake the sablés for 7 to 10 minutes, until puffed, golden, and firm to the touch. Remove the sablés from the oven, place the pans on a cooling rack, and cool for 10 minutes. Then release the sablés by flipping the pans over onto a cooling rack. You may need to use a small metal spatula or the tip of a paring knife to release some of the sablés.

4 Store the sablés in an airtight container for up to 2 weeks or freeze for up to 2 months.

Spectacles

Lunettes

Makes about 10

Special tools: 3-by-5-inch fluted oval cookie cutter, 1-inch round cutter

½ cup plus 1 tablespoon (60 grams) almond flour

1 cup (160 grams) gluten-free flour blend (see pages 1 to 3)

¼ teaspoon (2 grams) sea salt

½ cup (115 grams) unsalted butter, at room temperature

½ cup plus 1 tablespoon (115 grams) granulated sugar

1 large egg (55 grams)

1 teaspoon (5 grams) pure vanilla extract

½ cup (170 grams) raspberry jam or other jam of your choosing

¼ cup (25 grams) confectioners' sugar

Named after their shape (*lunettes* is French for eyeglasses), these large oval cookies feature two glistening jammy "eyes" dramatically peering out from their pure white sugared tops. Lunettes make a bold presentation and are easy to make. To vary the shapes, use a cookie cutter of another shape or size or fill them with a different flavor jam or jelly.

Method

1 Line two 12-by-17-inch baking sheets with parchment paper or silicone mats.

2 Sift together the almond flour, gluten-free flour, and salt into a medium bowl and set aside.

3 Place the butter and granulated sugar into the bowl of a stand mixer fitted with the paddle attachment. Turn the mixer to medium speed and cream the butter and sugar until smooth, about 1 minute.

4 Add the egg, then the vanilla extract and continue to beat at medium speed until combined. Use a rubber spatula to scrape the sides and bottom of the bowl and mix again briefly.

5 Turn the mixer off and add the dry ingredients all at once. Beat on low speed for about 1 minute, until the dough becomes uniform in consistency. Turn the dough out into a large plastic bag or onto a large sheet of plastic wrap and cover with another sheet of plastic wrap. Using your hands or a rolling pin, press the dough into a 1-inch-thick square. Wrap the dough well and refrigerate for at least 2 hours or overnight. At this point the dough may be frozen for up to 1 month.

6 When you are ready to roll the dough, allow it to sit at room temperature for 5 to 10 minutes, until the dough is soft enough to roll but firm enough to handle. Roll the dough between two pieces of parchment paper or plastic wrap. If the dough is sticking, lightly dust it with gluten-free flour, then brush off any residual flour before cutting the shapes. Roll the dough into a ⅛-inch-thick sheet. If the dough becomes too soft, slide it onto a baking pan and refrigerate for 10 minutes, then resume rolling.

7 With the oval cutter, cut as many cookies as you can. In half of the cookies, cut out two small circles to create the "eyes." Gather up the dough scraps, flatten into a disk, wrap, and chill for the next rolling. Use a wide metal spatula to transfer the cookie shapes onto parchment paper–lined baking sheets, allowing 1 inch between each cookie. Refrigerate the cookies, then proceed with rolling out the remaining dough.

8 Preheat the oven to 350°F (175°C).

9 Arrange the cookie bottoms and tops on separate baking sheets. The cookie tops with the cut-out eye shapes will take a little less time to bake. Bake the cookies until they are light golden brown around the edges, about 15 minutes. Set the baking sheets on cooling racks to cool completely before assembling.

10 Spread 1 teaspoon of raspberry jam across the surface of the solid oval cookie. Dust the cookie tops with the cut-outs with confectioners' sugar, then set them on top of the jam-coated bottom cookie. Use a small spoon or a pastry bag fitted with a small open tip to carefully fill each eye cavity with approximately ¼ teaspoon of jam. The cookies are best served with 24 hours of their assembly. You can store the unfinished cookies in an airtight container for up to 1 week.

Bordeaux Biscuits

Croquets Bordelais

Makes 39

2 cups (200 grams) almond flour

1 cup (100 grams) hazelnut flour

1⅓ cups plus 1 tablespoon (225 grams) gluten-free flour blend (see pages 1 to 3)

2 teaspoons (8 grams) baking powder

1 teaspoon (7 grams) sea salt

⅔ cup plus 1 teaspoon (155 grams) unsalted butter, at room temperature

1½ cups plus 2 tablespoons (335 grams) granulated sugar

1 tablespoon (6 grams) orange zest

1 teaspoon (5 grams) pure vanilla extract

2 extra-large eggs (125 grams)

1 cup (115 grams) hazelnuts, lightly toasted and coarsely chopped

Egg Wash (page 19)

These unusual biscuits are inspired from Pascal Rigo's pastry shop, American Boulangerie, in San Francisco. Slightly reminiscent of biscotti, *croquets* are more buttery in flavor and more tender in texture than their Italian cousins. *Croquer* means "to crunch," which is fitting for these crispy, crunchy biscuits. Croquets are ideal for dipping and perfect alongside a hot drink, or try them with a glass of wine from the Bordeaux region, where these biscuits originate. For a variation, you can substitute almonds for the hazelnuts and lemon zest for the orange zest. The dough is frozen overnight before slicing and baking, so a bit of preplanning is required.

Method

1 Line a 12-by-17-inch baking sheet with parchment paper or a silicone mat.

2 In a large bowl, whisk together the almond flour, hazelnut flour, gluten-free flour, baking powder, and salt and set aside.

3 In a stand mixer fitted with the paddle attachment, cream the butter and sugar on low speed just until smooth. Add the orange zest and vanilla extract, then add the eggs one at a time, scraping the sides and bottom of the bowl as necessary. Add the flour mixture and continue to beat on low speed until the dough begins to hold together. Add the hazelnuts and beat briefly. Remove the bowl from the mixer and finish incorporating the nuts with a flexible spatula. Empty the dough onto a piece of plastic wrap and use a metal spatula to shape it into a 9-by-6 ½-inch rectangle. Cover the top and sides with plastic wrap, then smooth the shape even by running your hands and spatula over the surface and sides. Place the dough on a baking sheet and freeze overnight.

4 Preheat the oven to 375°F (190°C). Remove the dough from the freezer and place it on a cutting surface. Use a ruler to score the 9-inch-long side into three 3-inch lengths. Slice the dough into three 3- by-6½-inch bars. Score each bar into ½-inch slices for a total of thirteen 3-inch-long biscuits, then slice them accordingly. Repeat with the remaining dough or store in the freezer until you would like to make more.

5 Arrange 10 biscuits on each baking sheet and lightly brush the tops with the egg wash. Bake for 15 to 20 minutes, until they are golden brown. Remove the biscuits from the oven and place on a cooling rack to cool completely. Store the biscuits well wrapped at room temperature for up to 1 week or frozen for up to 1 month.

Linzer Quenelles

Sablés de Linz

Makes 2 dozen

For the dough

¾ cup (75 grams)
almond flour

¾ cup (120 grams)
gluten-free flour blend
(see pages 1 to 3), sifted

7 tablespoons (100 grams)
cold unsalted butter, cut into
½-inch pieces

½ cup (100 grams)
granulated sugar

½ teaspoon (3 grams) sea salt

1½ teaspoons (3 grams)
ground cinnamon

1 teaspoon (2 grams)
lemon zest

For sandwiching

½ cup (170 grams)
raspberry jam

These linzer cookies are shapely in their rounded oval presence, with a bit of raspberry jam peeking through their coupled sides to invite you in. Almonds, cinnamon, lemon, and raspberry deliver crisp texture and full-bodied flavor. Many years ago, I lamented to a regular customer, Hillary, that no one ever brought *me* baked goods. One day she showed up at market with a little ribbon-tied package containing cookies of this shape. I was moved by her gesture and enamored with her irresistibly delicious cookies, and I set out to create a version of my own. Forming the cookies is labor intensive and a task I recommend for a rainy day's contemplative project or sharing with friends and family for a special treat.

Method

1 Preheat the oven to 350°F (175°C).

2 Line a 12-by-17-inch baking sheet with parchment paper. Sprinkle the almond flour onto the baking sheet and shake the sheet to evenly distribute it into an even layer. Bake for 10 minutes, or until the almond flour turns light brown and becomes aromatic. Remove from the oven and set it onto a cooling rack for 10 minutes, or until cooled completely. Turn the oven off while you prepare the cookies.

3 Line two 12-by-17-inch baking sheets with parchment paper or silicone mats.

4 Combine the toasted almond flour and gluten-free flour in the bowl of a stand mixer fitted with the paddle attachment. Mix on low speed for 30 seconds, or until blended.

5 Add the cold butter to the dry mixture and beat on low speed until the butter is broken down into pea-size clumps.

Add the sugar, salt, cinnamon, and lemon zest and continue to mix on low speed until the ingredients are well blended and begin to barely hold together, 2 to 3 minutes. The mixture will appear dry and will not form a mass.

6 Press the dough firmly into a small, oval-shaped kitchen teaspoon, smoothing the top and sides. Carefully slide the dough out of the spoon by pushing against the side closest to the handle. Set the dough flat side down, ½ inch apart onto the parchment paper. Continue until all of the dough has been formed, then chill the shaped cookies for 1 hour before baking.

7 Preheat the oven to 350°F (175°C).

8 Bake the cookies until they turn golden brown around the edges and subtle cracks have formed on the tops, 10 to 15 minutes. Remove the baking sheets from the oven and place them on cooling racks to cool completely.

9 To assemble the cookies, spread a thin layer of raspberry jam on the flat side of one cookie half, then sandwich with the other half, creating a quenelle, or egg shape. Store the linzer quenelles in an airtight container for up to 2 weeks or freeze for up to 2 months.

Hazelnut Wafers

Gaufrettes aux noisettes

Makes about 36

Special tool: pastry bag fitted with a ½-inch open tip

¾ cup (120 grams) Steve's Gluten Free Cake Flour (see pages 1 and 2)

¾ cup (105 grams) hazelnuts, toasted

¼ teaspoon (2 grams) sea salt

⅔ cup (150 grams) unsalted butter, at room temperature

⅓ cup plus 1 tablespoon (80 grams) granulated sugar

1 large egg white (33 grams), at room temperature, lightly whisked

1 teaspoon (5 grams) pure vanilla extract

Confectioners' sugar

Hazelnuts lend their sweet buttery nut flavor to these kindly wafers, perfect for munching on any time of day. Though humble in appearance, these nubby looking cookies deliver full-on hazelnut flavor with a light, crisp texture that keeps you going back for just one more. Hazelnuts, cobnuts, and filberts, all in the same family, are interchangeable in this recipe. You can use either natural (skin-on) or blanched nuts.

Method

1 Line two 12-by-17-inch baking sheets with parchment paper or silicone mats.

2 Combine the flour, hazelnuts, and salt in the bowl of a food processor fitted with a blade attachment. Grind the mixture until it is fine and flour-like, then set it aside. Small nut particles may remain; this is okay.

3 In the bowl of a stand mixer fitted with the paddle attachment, combine the butter and granulated sugar and beat on medium speed for 1 minute. Add the egg white and vanilla extract and beat on medium speed until the ingredients are combined. Scrape the sides and bottom of the bowl with a silicone spatula and beat again briefly.

4 Add the flour mixture, then beat on low speed for 1 minute, or until blended. Remove the bowl from the mixer and give the batter a final hand mixing with the silicone spatula. The dough is ready when the consistency appears uniform.

5 Preheat the oven to 375°F (190°C).

6 Fill the pastry bag with batter and pipe 4-inch-long finger-shaped sticks or circles on the parchment paper, spacing them

1½ inches apart. If you pipe different sizes and shapes of cookies, keep them on separate baking sheets so their baking time is the same.

7 Bake the cookies for 8 to 10 minutes, until the edges turn golden brown and the center retains a lighter color. Remove the baking sheet from the oven and set on a cooling rack to cool before removing the cookies. Let the baking sheets cool before you begin the next batch.

8 When you are ready to serve, lightly sift confectioners' sugar onto the cookies. The hazelnut wafers will keep well wrapped at room temperature for 1 week.

Cat's Tongues

Langues de chat

Makes about 24

Special tool: pastry bag fitted with a ½-inch open tip

7 tablespoons (100 grams) unsalted butter, at room temperature

1 cup (100 grams) confectioners' sugar, sifted

2 large eggs (110 grams), at room temperature

½ vanilla bean, split and scraped

½ teaspoon (3 grams) pure vanilla extract

½ cup plus 1 tablespoon (90 grams) Steve's Gluten Free Cake Flour (see pages 1 and 2), sifted

½ teaspoon (4 grams) sea salt

Tempered Chocolate (pages 62 and 63) or Sugar Icing Glaze (page 21)

These whimsically named crisp, light wafers with hues of vanilla bean are elegant and playful in appearance and pleasing to both children and adults. They are perfect as an accompaniment to ice cream or mousse. Dip the cookies in tempered dark chocolate (pages 62 and 63) for stark, eye-catching contrast. Another option is to dip the cat's tongues in lemon icing or drizzle them with chocolate. Or keep them plain, unadorned, and delightfully simple. The recipe will make multiple batches; remember to cool your baking sheets before beginning the next round.

Method

1 Prepare a bain-marie (see page 9) over low heat.

2 Put the butter into the bowl of a stand mixer. Place over the bain-marie and stir continually until the butter softens to a creamy white consistency. You want the butter to become very soft but not melted to liquid form. Remove from the heat and attach to a stand mixer fitted with the paddle attachment.

3 Add the confectioners' sugar and beat at medium speed until it is incorporated. Remove the paddle and replace it with the whisk attachment.

4 Turn the mixer speed to medium and whip in the eggs, one at a time, turning the mixer off to scrape the sides and bottom of the bowl with a silicone spatula as needed. Turn the mixer speed to medium, add the vanilla bean seeds and vanilla extract, and whip for 30 seconds. Turn off the mixer, add the flour and salt, and whip on medium speed for 1 minute, or until incorporated. Turn the mixer off, remove the bowl, and finish mixing the batter with a silicone spatula. The batter should be creamy, smooth, and slightly loose.

5 Preheat the oven to 375°F (190°C). Line two 12-by-17-inch baking sheets with parchment paper or silicone mats.

6 Fill the pastry bag with batter and pipe 5-inch-long, dog bone–shaped sticks on the prepared baking sheet, spacing them 1½ inches apart. Begin by piping a slightly bulbous oval shape, transitioning to a straight line, and ending with a slightly bulbous oval shape.

7 Bake the cookies for 8 to 10 minutes, until the edges turn golden brown and the center retains a lighter color. Remove the baking sheets from the oven and set them on cooling racks to cool completely before removing them. Be certain to let your baking sheets cool before you begin the next batch.

8 Dip one end of each cookie into tempered dark chocolate or sugar icing. The Cat's Tongues will keep well wrapped at room temperature for up to 1 week.

Coconut Congolais or Rocks

Rochers à la noix de coco

Makes about 45

Special tools: 1½-inch silicone pyramid mold, pastry bag fitted with a small star tip

For the batter

6 large egg whites (215 grams)

1 cup (200 grams) granulated sugar

3½ cups (215 grams) unsweetened dried shredded coconut

3 tablespoons (42 grams) coconut oil, melted

1 teaspoon (5 grams) natural coconut extract

1 teaspoon (5 grams) pure vanilla extract

¾ teaspoon (5 grams) sea salt

Nonstick cooking spray

For the topping
Dark Chocolate Ganache (page 36), softened to room temperature

Miniature pyramids, evoking the mysteries of faraway lands, this pretty cookie's name—*congolais*—translates to coconut petit fours. Shape them into freeform balls and they become *rochers*, the French word for rocks. Although they may seem exotic, in actuality they are simply a French-style coconut macaroon. Be sure to use unsweetened coconut, otherwise the cookies will be cloyingly sweet, and if you don't have pyramid-shaped molds, scoop the cookies into mounds with a small ice cream scoop and squeeze them into pyramids, or scoop them rustic style by the spoonful to make rock-shaped drop cookies.

Method

1 In a medium heatproof bowl, combine the egg whites and sugar and whisk briefly to combine. Add the coconut, melted coconut oil, coconut extract, vanilla extract, and salt. Mix the ingredients together with a silicone spatula. Set aside for 30 minutes for the coconut to absorb the liquid.

2 Place the bowl over a bain-marie (see page 9) and cook over medium heat, stirring every few minutes with the spatula and scraping the sides and bottom of the bowl to prevent burning. Continue to cook until the egg whites turn translucent and the mixture has thickened slightly, about 10 minutes. Remove the bowl from the heat and set aside for 15 minutes.

3 Preheat the oven to 350°F (175°C).

4 Place the silicone mold onto a baking sheet and coat the mold lightly with cooking spray. Spoon the coconut batter into the individual pyramid cavities and level the tops with a small metal spatula.

5 Bake the macaroons for 10 minutes, or until the tops turn deep golden brown. Remove the pan from the oven and place it on a cooling rack. Carefully grab the corners of the silicone mold and flip it upside down to release the cookies. If necessary, use a small metal spatula to gently pry the pyramids loose. Set the pyramids upright and allow them to cool completely.

6 Fit a pastry bag with a small star tip and fill it with softened dark chocolate ganache. Pipe a small rosette of ganache on top of each mini pyramid. The coconut congolais will keep for up to 1 week covered and refrigerated.

Spiral Tile Cookies

Tuiles spirales

Makes about 50

Special tools: plastic tuile template, silicone baking mat or parchment paper, rolling pin, pastry bag fitted with a ¼-inch open pastry tip

½ cup (80 grams) Steve's Gluten Free Cake Flour (see pages 1 and 2)

1½ cups (150 grams) confectioners' sugar

4 large egg whites (130 grams) at room temperature, lightly whisked

1 teaspoon (5 grams) pure vanilla extract

6 tablespoons (85 grams) unsalted butter, melted

1 teaspoon (2½ grams) cocoa powder

¼ teaspoon (1¾ grams) coffee extract, such as Trablit

Named after the shapely arched roof tiles found on French country homes, *tuiles* are a crisp, curvy wafer cookie that serves as a contrasting accompaniment to softer desserts such as ice cream or mousse. Their classic arched shape must be formed while they are hot. Alternatively, tuiles may be left flat after baking or shaped into attractive cornets to embrace creamy fillings. Decorative tuiles made into three-dimensional forms can embellish desserts and are pleasing to play around with. Here we are making eye-catching spiral tuiles with a contrasting chocolate spiral embedded in the golden cookie. To simplify, you can skip the chocolate spiral and sprinkle the cookies with sliced almonds before baking. The recipe will make multiple batches, so plan ahead to allow your baking sheets to cool completely before beginning the next round.

Method

1 Line two 12-by-17-inch baking sheets with parchment paper or silicone mats.

2 Sift the flour and confectioners' sugar into the bowl of a stand mixer fitted with the paddle attachment. Add the egg whites and beat on medium speed until the mixture is smooth, about 30 seconds, scraping down the sides and bottom of the bowl with a silicone spatula as needed. Add the vanilla extract and beat for 30 seconds. Reduce the mixer speed to low, then slowly pour the butter into the mixture. When all the butter has been added, increase the mixer speed to medium and beat for 30 seconds, or until the ingredients are homogeneous and the batter is creamy but loose. Remove ½ cup of the batter and place it in a small bowl. Add the cocoa powder and coffee extract to the small bowl of batter and stir to combine.

3 Cover both bowls with plastic wrap and refrigerate for at least 1 hour or up to 3 days before using. This will help the batter firm up for spreading the tuile shapes.

4 Preheat the oven to 350°F (175°C).

5 Set the silicone mat or parchment paper on a flat work surface and place the tuile template on top. Fill the pastry bag with the cocoa tuile batter. Begin at the center of each template round and make a chocolate spiral inside. When you have finished with one pan, place it in the freezer for 15 minutes, or until the spiral batter is frozen.

6 Working quickly, spoon a small amount of batter inside each template round, then use a flexible or offset metal spatula to spread tuile batter level with the top of the template. (You will want to work efficiently so the chocolate spiral does not begin to thaw and smear throughout the cookie). Then remove the plastic template and set the baking mat onto a baking sheet. If you are not using a tuile template, spread the batter onto a parchment paper–lined baking sheet. Use your finger or the back of a spoon to evenly smooth the batter into a circle or oval. The batter should be just shy of ⅛ inch thick. Allow 2 inches between each shaped cookie.

7 Bake the tuiles for 5 to 8 minutes, until the edges turn golden but the center retains a lighter color. Remove the baking sheet from the oven and place onto a cooling rack. Immediately lift the tuiles from the pan with a metal spatula and drape each tuile over a rolling pin. Allow the tuiles to cool and set their curved shape, then remove them and set them aside. Be certain to let the baking sheet cool before you begin the next batch.

8 Tuile batter can be frozen for up to 2 months and thawed overnight in the refrigerator. Store baked tuiles well wrapped at room temperature for 1 week or frozen for up to 1 month.

Orange Tuiles

Tuiles à l'orange

Makes about 50

Special tools: plastic tuile template, silicone baking mat, rolling pin

½ cup (100 grams) light brown sugar

½ cup (100 grams) granulated sugar

Zest of 1 medium orange

½ cup plus 2 tablespoons (100 grams) Steve's Gluten Free Cake Flour (see pages 1 and 2)

½ cup plus 1 tablespoon (100 grams) fresh-squeezed orange juice

7 tablespoons (105 grams) unsalted butter, melted

Delicate and lacy, these elegant orange tile cookies have caramel overtones followed by citrusy orange notes. Their ornate appearance will gracefully accompany various flavors of mousse or ice cream. After forming the *tuiles*, be sure to set them in the freezer for 10 minutes to completely firm up before baking. Take the cookies out of the oven when they are golden brown with a lacy appearance and be sure to form their arch shape while the cookies are still warm, otherwise they will crack and break. Note that you'll be most successful at tuile making by using a professional plastic template. The recipe makes multiple batches; allow the baking sheets to cool completely before beginning your next round of tuiles.

Method

1 Line two 12-by-17-inch baking sheets with silicone mats.

2 In a medium bowl, combine the brown sugar and granulated sugar with the orange zest and rub the mixture between your fingers until it becomes moist and aromatic. Add the flour and, using a hand whisk, beat the flour into the sugar mixture until just combined. Pour in the orange juice and whisk to incorporate, then slowly pour the melted butter into the mixture, whisking the whole time until the batter becomes homogeneous.

3 Cover with plastic wrap and refrigerate for at least 1 hour or up to 3 days before using. This will help the batter firm up for spreading into the tuile shapes.

4 Preheat the oven to 350°F (175°C).

5 Set the silicone baking mat on a flat work surface and place the tuile template on top. Spoon a small amount of batter inside each round and use a flexible or offset metal spatula to spread the tuile batter level with the top of the template. Leave 2 inches between each shaped cookie. When you have finished spreading all of the template rounds, remove the plastic template and set the baking mat onto a baking sheet. Set the baking sheet into the freezer for 15 minutes to harden the tuiles.

6 Bake the tuiles for 5 to 8 minutes, until the cookies turn a dark golden brown. Remove the baking sheet from the oven and set it on a cooling rack. Allow the tuiles to rest for 2 to 3 minutes, until they firm up just enough to handle. Use a thin metal spatula to gently lift up one edge of the tuile and remove it from the silicone mat. Quickly drape the tuile over a rolling pin to create a curved shape. Allow the tuiles to cool and set their shape, then remove them and set aside. Be certain to let the baking sheet cool before you begin the next batch.

7 The tuile batter can be frozen for up to 2 months (thaw overnight in the refrigerator). Store baked tuiles well wrapped at room temperature for up to 1 week or frozen for up to 1 month.

The Charm of French Cookies

In the world of French pastry, cookies are quite straightforward, as they generally don't require advance preparation or have multiple components and can be turned out in a pinch. Cookies enamor with their unique charm, pretty appeal, ease of eating, and endless flavors. Styles range from roll-and-cut to hand-shaped to piped, and each of us has our personal favorites. Here are some helpful reminders for these three types of cookies.

Roll-and-cut cookies: Remember to brush excess flour from the dough. Use a ruler to check for dough thickness, and, if needed, dip your cutter into a container of flour to help reduce sticking. A wide metal spatula is helpful for transferring cut cookies onto the baking sheet. Experiment with different cutter shapes to change things up.

Hand-shaped cookies: Shaping cookie logs is best done on a large sheet of parchment paper. Using your hands, press the dough into a cylindrical shape and pull the paper up over the log to cover it. Squeeze your hands over the paper and roll the dough back and forth a few times to firm the shape up. Once the log is chilled and ready for slicing, use a serrated knife to slice round cookies; slice on the diagonal for an oval shape. When shaping individual cookies by hand, it can be helpful to wear disposable gloves or slightly moisten your hands with water to prevent sticking.

Piped cookies: These may take a bit of practice, but they're fun to make, and children enjoy experimenting with a pastry bag. Cookie dough needs to be at the correct temperature to easily pipe into and hold its shape. Fill the pastry bag halfway to make for easier piping.

Most cookie doughs and batters can be frozen and baked at a later date so you can bake the cookies on short notice for guests or impromptu teatime. And, remember to weigh your ingredients. Even the most modest of cookies will benefit from this practice!

CHAPTER FOUR

Tarts

Tarts

Les tarts

Growing up I baked delightful, good ole traditional American pies—apple pie, pumpkin pie, berry pie, and lemon meringue pie. But I had no idea about French tarts, and *ooh la la*, they are in a class of their own. Many French tarts are based on fruit: the zingy Lemon Tart with its creamy meringue topping insists on your full attention, and the Crème Brûlée Tart will leave you wistfully quiet, while the Pear Frangipane Tart is like a dear friend, longing for a return visit. Blueberries, lime, and molasses meet up in the Wild Blueberry Tart, and the Apple Normandy Tart features Calvados, an apple brandy made in the Normandy region. Fresh apricots baked into the Apricot Tart are passionate and intense with flavor, and the tart base takes well to any number of fruit variations. The Rustic Berry Galette, with the berries tucked into a free-form crust, is the recipe most similar to traditional American pie. The Raspberry Frangipane Tart is adorned with fresh berries, piped buttercream, and chocolate ganache. If there were a French version of a cupcake, perhaps this would be a contender. Completing this section are elegant Chocolate Coffee Tarts that deliver a teensy pick-me-up, like a café mocha you can sink your teeth into. Don your apron and grab the rolling pin, it's time for tarts!

Lemon Tarts

Tartes au citron

Makes twelve 3-inch tarts

Special tools: pastry brush, twelve 3-by-½-inch tart rings, culinary or chef's torch, pastry bag fitted with a large star tip, instant-read thermometer

For the crust
½ Recipe Sweet Dough (pages 47 and 48)

¼ cup (75 grams) Apricot Glaze (page 20), melted

For the filling
3 cups (675 grams) Lemon Cream (pages 30 and 31)

For the topping
1 recipe Swiss Meringue (page 28)

A sweet pastry crust, silky lemon cream filling, superbly light Swiss meringue, and torched marshmallow rosettes makes these tarts visually exciting. The lemon cream delivers a full tartness that is tempered by the sweet ethereal meringue. If you prefer, you could finish the tarts with a buttercream rosette and adorn them with a beautiful organic, edible flower, such as a garden rose, pansy, or even a snapdragon. Snip and gather cut flower heads, then check for friendly spiders that may be hiding from you. Gently rinse and lightly pat the flowers dry in paper towels. Settle the flowers in place and tap a little confectioners' sugar over the top of the tarts. The flowers will drink in the sugar, leaving a lovely white ring along the edge of the crust.

Method

1 Flour both sides of the pastry dough, then place the dough between two pieces of plastic wrap and set it onto your work surface. Roll the dough out to ⅛ inch thick, brush any excess flour from both sides of the dough, and cut out twelve 4-inch circles of pastry. Line the tart rings with the dough, gently pressing the dough into them and smoothing the dough flat along the inside edges. Using a rolling pin, press across the top of the tart to shear off excess dough. Place the tart rings on a baking sheet, cover them with plastic wrap, and refrigerate for at least 2 hours or overnight. At this point, the tarts may be put in an airtight container and frozen for up to 1 month.

2 When you are ready to bake the tart shells, preheat the oven to 350°F (175°C).

3 Blind bake the shells: Fill each one with a paper muffin cup filled with pie weights or raw beans, or prick them with a fork, and bake for 7 to 10 minutes, until golden brown. Leave the oven on.

4 Place the baking sheet with the baked shells onto a cooling rack for 5 minutes, then remove the paper cups, being careful to not tear the bottom crust. Brush the bottom crust lightly with melted apricot glaze—this will seal the bottom crust to prevent it from becoming soggy or leaking.

5 When the shells have completely cooled, use a medium spoon to fill each one with lemon cream, mounding it into the tart shell. Using a flat metal spatula, spread the cream smooth and level it off with the top of the tart and return the excess cream to the lemon cream container. Continue until all the tarts are filled and leveled smooth. Place the tarts on a baking sheet and put it in the oven for 5 minutes. This will give the tarts a shiny glaze and perfectly smooth surface without further cooking the lemon cream. Refrigerate the tarts for 1 hour to cool completely before finishing with the Swiss meringue.

6 Fill the pastry bag with the Swiss meringue, then pipe large rosettes on top of each lemon tart. Ignite the culinary torch and toast the meringues until they are nicely browned. Serve immediately, or refrigerate and serve within 24 hours.

Crème Brûlée Tarts

Tartes crème brûlée

Makes eight 3½-inch tarts

Special tools: eight 3½-inch tart pans with removable bottoms, small pastry brush, medium-mesh sieve, culinary torch

For the crusts
½ recipe Sweet Dough (pages 47 and 48)

¼ cup (75 grams) Apricot Glaze (page 20), melted

For the custard
4 cups (920 grams) heavy cream

¾ cup (150 grams) granulated sugar

½ vanilla bean, split and seeds scraped

9 large egg yolks (200 grams)

For the topping
¼ cup plus 2 tablespoons (80 grams) granulated sugar

Crème brûlée, a silky smooth custard capped with a thin crust of caramelized sugar, dates back to the seventeenth century. Although the country of origin remains debated, one amusing story recounts early versions of crème brûlée being served with a small chisel and hammer to crack a thick top layer of burnt sugar. Over time, crème brûlée has become the more refined dessert classic we know and love, highlighting a delicate caramelized top requiring only the faint tip of a spoon to break through.

For exceptional results, seek out local, organic cream and eggs. The ingredients are few, and choosing the best quality will reward you with dreamy results. Don't be surprised if things suddenly get pretty quiet around the dinner table after the first taste: this is a telltale sign of a spellbound guest.

Method

Make the crusts
1 Flour both sides of the dough, then place the dough between two pieces of plastic wrap and set it onto your work surface. Roll out the sweet dough to ⅛ inch thick and brush any excess flour from both sides. Cut eight 4-inch circles of pastry, then line the tart ring molds with the dough. Gently press the dough into the tart rings and smooth it flat along the inside edges. Using a rolling pin, press across the top of the tart to shear off any excess dough. Place the tarts on a baking sheet, cover them with plastic wrap, and refrigerate for at least 2 hours or overnight. At this point, the tarts may be put in an airtight container and frozen for up to 1 month.

2 When you are ready to bake the tarts, preheat the oven to 350°F (175°C).

3 Pierce the bottoms of the tart shells using the tines of a fork. Bake the shells for 7 to 10 minutes, until golden brown. Remove the shells from the oven and allow them to cool. To seal the bottom of the tarts, brush them with the melted apricot glaze.

Make the custard

1 In a large, heavy saucepan, combine the heavy cream and sugar and stir to combine. Split the vanilla bean in half lengthwise and use a small, sharp knife to scrape out the seeds. Add the vanilla bean and seeds to the cream mixture. Heat the cream over medium heat just to a boil, about 8 minutes. Set a timer and pay close attention to keep the cream from boiling over. Cover the pan and allow the cream to sit for 30 minutes to infuse with the vanilla bean.

2 Once the cream is finished infusing, remove the vanilla bean, rinse it, and set it aside to dry; you can use it later to make vanilla sugar (page 287).

3 Preheat the oven to 300°F (150°C).

4 Put the egg yolks into the bowl of a stand mixer fitted with the whisk attachment. Whip the yolks on low speed for 10 seconds, or until they are homogeneous.

5 Increase the mixer speed to medium and slowly pour the cream mixture into the egg yolks. Turn the mixer off, then scrape down the sides and bottom of the bowl with a silicone spatula. Mix again briefly until the mixture is homogeneous.

6 Place a medium-mesh sieve atop a clean bowl, then pour the mixture through the sieve. Straining removes any egg solids and ensures a smooth custard.

7 Pour the custard into the tart shells and cover with a second inverted baking sheet. This will help prevent the custard from overbrowning. Bake for 10 to 15 minutes, until the custard has set in the center. Remove the baking sheet from the oven and place on a cooling rack for 30 minutes, then refrigerate the tarts for at least 1 hour, or up to 4 days, allowing them to cool completely before the next step.

8 When you are ready to caramelize the custards to crème brûlée, remove them from the refrigerator. Sprinkle 2 teaspoons of sugar over the top of each custard, distributing it in an even layer. Use a kitchen torch to caramelize the top until it is crisp and golden brown.

Pear Frangipane Tart

Tarte frangipane aux poires

Makes one 8-inch tart

Special tool: 8-inch tart pan
with a removable bottom

½ recipe Pastry Dough
(pages 49 and 50)

½ recipe Frangipane
(pages 24 and 25), at room
temperature

3 Bosc or other pears

¼ cup (75 grams) Apricot
Glaze (page 20), melted

1 tablespoon (11 grams)
confectioners' sugar
(optional)

A lovely baked fruit tart, designed with thinly sliced pears fanned open across its top. The subtle sweetness of the pears meets the ready boldness of the almond frangipane filling. This inviting and sensual tart provides a comely dessert that is suitable for snack time as well as an elegant dinner party. For a change, the tart can be topped with thinly sliced apples or nectarines. Serve the tart warm or at room temperature, plated with a scoop of ice cream.

Method

1 Flour both sides of the pastry dough, then place the dough between two large pieces of plastic wrap and set it onto your work surface. Roll the dough into an 11-inch-diameter circle that's ⅛ inch thick. Brush any excess flour from both sides of the pastry. Gently lift the pastry and set it into the tart pan. Using your fingers, secure the pastry straight and firm against the inside edges of the pan. Gently press the dough into place, then trim off any excess pastry by applying a rolling pin across the top of the pan. Place the lined tart pan onto a parchment paper–lined baking sheet, wrap it in plastic, and refrigerate for at least 2 hours or overnight. At this point, the tart shell may be frozen for up to 1 month.

2 When you are ready to make the tart, preheat the oven to 350°F (175°C).

3 Spoon about 2 cups of frangipane into the tart shell. Using a long metal spatula, smooth the cream level across the top to the edge of the pan's rim. If needed, add additional frangipane to fill the tart pan. Refrigerate the tart for 1 hour to allow the frangipane to firm up.

4 Peel the pears, cut them in half, and core them. Depending on the size of the pears, you will need 5 or 6 halves. Cut each pear half into 10 thin slices, running vertically from top to bottom. Set the pear halves on top of the chilled frangipane cream, then gently press your hand down, fanning the pears while keeping them overlapping.

5 Bake for 30 to 45 minutes, until the tart is a deep golden brown and set in the center. Place the tart on a cooling rack to cool until it's barely warm. Release the tart from the ring by running a paring knife along the inside edge, being careful to not cut into the crust. Use the tip of the knife to cut through any adhered juices. Set the tart onto a plate, then brush with the apricot glaze. Dust lightly with confectioners' sugar and serve. Store the tart wrapped in plastic in the refrigerator for up to 1 week or freeze for up to 1 month.

Apricot Tart

Tarte aux abricots

Makes one 13-inch
rectangular tart

Special tools: 4-by-13-inch
tart pan with a removable
bottom, small pastry brush

½ recipe Pastry Dough
(pages 49 and 50)

½ cup (170 grams)
apricot jam

½ recipe Almond Cream
(page 23), at room
temperature

10 fresh apricots,
halved and pitted

2 tablespoons (30 grams)
granulated sugar

¼ cup (75 grams) Apricot
Glaze (page 20), melted

2 tablespoons (20 grams)
confectioners' sugar
(optional)

Fresh apricots provide outstanding flavor in this classic French take on a baked fruit tart. If you cannot find fresh apricots, canned ones will suffice. Fresh plums, peaches, pears, or apples are equally at home atop this fabulous tart. Serve the tart warm or at room temperature with whipped cream or ice cream. The tart can also be made in a 10-inch round pastry ring or tart pan with a removable bottom.

To release the tart from its long rectangular pan, I like to use an adequately padded kitchen towel draped down the length of my arm for protection rather than bulky oven mitts. This gives more control for handling the hot metal pan and lessens the risk of breaking the tart's lovely shape.

Method

1 Flour both sides of the pastry dough, then place the dough between two large pieces of plastic wrap and set it onto your work surface. Roll the dough into a 15-by-6-inch rectangle that's ⅛ inch thick. Brush any excess flour from both sides of the pastry, then gently lift the pastry and set it into the tart pan. Pull the sides of the pastry inward, toward the center of the pan. This will help the dough settle into the pan. Using your fingers, secure the pastry straight and firm against the inside edges and corners of the pan. Gently press the dough into place, then trim off any excess pastry by applying a rolling pin across the top of the pan. Place the tart pan onto a parchment paper–lined baking sheet, wrap in plastic, and refrigerate for at least 2 hours or overnight. At this point, the tart shell may be frozen for up to 1 month.

2 Spoon the apricot jam into the bottom of the tart shell, then use a small metal spatula to spread the jam into a smooth, even layer. Spread a thick layer of almond cream on top of the jam, then smooth the cream level to the edge of the pan's rim. Using a metal spatula, scrape three long indentations across the top of the tart, removing about ¼ cup of the cream and creating a shallow hollow area along the length of the tart.

3 Refrigerate the tart for 1 hour to help set up the almond cream.

4 Preheat the oven to 375°F (190°C).

5 With a sharp paring knife, cut the apricots in half and discard the stone pit. Place the apricots on top of the almond cream, setting them in two lines down the length of the tart. Sprinkle the tart with the granulated sugar, then bake for 45 to 60 minutes, until the crust is a deep golden brown and the filling is firm to the touch. Some juices might ooze out from the bottom of the tart pan; this is okay.

6 Set the baking sheet with the tart onto a cooling rack and allow it to cool for 20 minutes. Using a kitchen towel or oven mitts, remove the tart from the pan before it has completely cooled. Use a small, sharp paring knife to release any edges that may be sticking. If you wait too long, the baked juices from the tart may adhere to the pan, making the removal of the tart more difficult. Return the released tart to the cooling rack to cool completely. Using the pastry brush, lightly coat the apricots with the apricot glaze. Serve the tart at room temperature with a light sifting of confectioners' sugar, if using. Store the tart wrapped in plastic in the refrigerator for up to 1 week or freeze for up to 1 month.

Wild Blueberry Tart

Tarte aux myrtilles sauvagess

Makes one 9-inch tart

Special tools: 9-inch tart pan or ring, pastry brush

½ recipe Pastry Dough (pages 49 and 50)

2 tablespoons Frangipane (pages 24 and 25) or Almond Cream (page 23), at room temperature

2¼ cups (340 grams) frozen or fresh wild blueberries

¼ cup (50 grams) granulated sugar

1 tablespoon (20 grams) molasses

½ vanilla bean, split and seeds scraped

1 tablespoon (15 grams) water

1 tablespoon (18 grams) lime juice

1 teaspoon (3 grams) cornstarch

2 tablespoons (20 grams) confectioners' sugar, sifted

The purple violet hues of wild blueberries contrasting with the stark white rim make this a very pretty tart indeed. Wild blueberries are smaller and juicier than cultivated blueberries; a little cornstarch helps to bind the juices. Spreading the bottom of the tart with frangipane adds a hint of almond and helps absorb extra juices, which prevents the crust from becoming soggy. Blueberries, molasses, and lime add an unusual flavor depth to this lovely tart. For an elevated presentation, serve it alongside a scoop of vanilla bean ice cream.

Method

1 Remove the dough from the refrigerator and allow it to sit at room temperature for 5 minutes, or until it is pliable enough to work with but not too soft. If at any point the dough becomes too soft, refrigerate it for 10 minutes, then resume working. When handling, you may need to press the dough back together, as it may develop small cracks. Use minimal amounts of flour when rolling the dough out, and always brush excess flour clear from the front and back of the dough before lining the tart pan.

2 Flour both sides of the pastry dough, then place the dough between two large pieces of plastic wrap and set it onto your work surface. Roll the dough into a ⅛-inch-thick circle, then line a 9-inch tart pan or ring. Cover the tart in plastic wrap and refrigerate it for at least 1 hour or overnight.

3 Use a metal spatula to spread the softened frangipane evenly across the bottom of the tart, making sure to reach to the edges.

4 In a medium bowl, combine the blueberries, sugar, molasses, and vanilla bean seeds. In a small bowl, make a slurry by whisking together the water, lime juice, and cornstarch. Add the slurry to the berries and stir thoroughly with a large spoon or spatula. Set the berry mixture aside to macerate for 10 minutes.

5 Preheat the oven to 375°F (190°C).

6 Pour the blueberry filling into the tart shell. Take time to evenly distribute the filling and press the berries down into the small crevices along the edge of the pastry shell.

7 Bake for 30 to 40 minutes, until the berries are bubbling, set around the edges, and barely jiggling in the center, and the pastry is golden brown. Remove the tart from the oven and place it on a cooling rack to cool for 30 minutes, then carefully remove the tart from the ring. Sprinkle the rim of the tart with the confectioners' sugar before serving. Store the tart, well wrapped in plastic, in the refrigerator for up to 3 days.

Apple Normandy Tart

Tarte normande

Makes one 9-inch tart

Special tools: 9-inch tart pan with removable bottom or 9-inch ring, pastry brush

½ recipe Pastry Dough (pages 49 and 50)

3 medium Granny Smith or other baking apples, peeled, cored, and thinly sliced

1 tablespoon (15 grams) unsalted butter, melted

1 tablespoon (15 grams) plus 4 tablespoons (60 grams) granulated sugar

2 large egg yolks (45 grams)

¾ cup (172 grams) heavy cream

1 tablespoon (16 grams) Calvados or cognac

2 tablespoons (20 grams) confectioners' sugar

The region of Normandy is known for its prolific apple orchards, and this tart has many variations throughout the region. The tart is made with thinly sliced apples lined into a tart shell, sometimes paired with an almond mixture, other times with a custard cream. This version is made with custard cream scented with Calvados, an apple brandy that originates from Normandy. Ultimately simple, this tart is made wonderful by the earthly delights of the apple, a fruit that has thousands of varieties to its acclaim. Apples have different purposes; some are best enjoyed fresh out of hand, others for cooking, and some for distilling into spirits, such as cider and Calvados brandy. Try enjoying this simple apple tart paired with a local hard cheese.

Method

1 Remove the dough from the refrigerator and allow it to sit at room temperature for 5 minutes, or until it is pliable enough to work with but not too soft. If at any point the dough becomes too soft, refrigerate it for 10 minutes, then resume working. When handling, you may need to press the dough back together, as it may develop small cracks. Use minimal amounts of flour when rolling the dough out, and always brush excess flour clear from the front and back of the dough before lining the tart pan.

2 Flour both sides of the pastry dough, then place the dough between two pieces of plastic wrap and set it onto your work surface. Roll the dough into a circle that's ⅛ inch thick, then line a 9-inch tart pan with the dough. Cover the tart with plastic wrap and refrigerate it for at least 1 hour or overnight.

3 Preheat the oven to 375°F (190°C).

4 Arrange the sliced apples in an overlapping concentric circle, beginning at the outside of the tart pan. Brush with the melted butter, sprinkle with 1 tablespoon (15 grams) of the granulated sugar, then bake for 15 minutes, or until the apples begin to color.

5 In a medium bowl, whisk together the egg yolks, cream, the remaining 4 tablespoons (60 grams) of granulated sugar, and the Calvados. Remove the tart from the oven and slowly pour the custard mixture over the apples; allow the cream to gradually fill the tart. Bake for 10 minutes, then sprinkle the top with the confectioners' sugar. Continue to bake for 5 to 10 minutes, until the tart is golden brown.

6 Set on a cooling rack for 20 minutes, then serve warm. Store the tart wrapped in plastic in the refrigerator for up to 3 days.

Rustic Berry Galette

Galette rustique aux fruits rouges

Makes 12 galettes

Special tools: pastry brush, 6-inch metal cutter

1 recipe Pastry Dough (pages 49 and 50)

4 cups (650 grams) mixed berries, such as raspberries, blackberries, and blueberries

⅓ cup (65 grams) granulated sugar

1 teaspoon (6 grams) lemon juice

1 teaspoon (3 grams) cornstarch

¼ cup Almond Cream (page 23), at room temperature

Egg Wash (page 19)

¼ cup (55 grams) demerara or crystal sugar

Galettes are a flat, round, or free-form pastry. These galettes are open faced and bursting with a bright berry flavor that's complemented by the tender, buttery pastry. They emulate small volcanoes that are full of juicy joyfulness. You can also make this recipe with other fruits, such as peaches, pears, apricots, or cherries. These fruity galettes will likely bubble out some sticky juices, so the best choice for baking would be on a silicone mat for easiest removal after baking. *Pâte brisée*, the French version of pastry dough, handles much like pie dough and is tender yet stable to handle. If the dough becomes too soft to work with, refrigerate it for about 10 minutes, then resume working.

Method

1 When you are ready to use the dough, remove it from the refrigerator and allow it to sit at room temperature for 5 minutes, or until it is pliable enough to work with but not too soft. If at any point the dough becomes too soft, refrigerate it for 10 minutes and resume working. When handling, you may need to press the dough back together, as it may develop small cracks. Use minimal amounts of flour when rolling the dough out, and always brush excess flour clear from the front and back of the dough before final application.

2 Flour both sides of the pastry dough, then place the dough between two pieces of plastic wrap and set it onto your work surface. Roll the dough ⅜ inch thick, then cut out twelve 6-inch rounds. You will need to reroll the scrap pieces to complete all of the rounds. Place the cut-out rounds onto a parchment paper–lined baking sheet. Cover with parchment paper, then layer the next rounds on top. When all twelve

rounds are cut out, cover the baking sheet with plastic wrap and refrigerate for 20 minutes. Prepare the berries while the dough is resting.

3 In a medium bowl, combine the berries, granulated sugar, lemon juice, and cornstarch. Lightly toss the ingredients together, then set aside to macerate for 10 minutes.

4 When you are ready to assemble the galettes, bring the pastry dough rounds to the temperature that enables you to easily fold the dough without it breaking or tearing.

5 Using a small metal spatula, spread the center of each pastry round with 1 heaping teaspoon of almond cream. Pile ⅓ cup of berries into the center of the pastry on top of the almond cream. Cup the pastry upward and press a fold into the dough at the top, bottom, right, and left. Then rotate the pastry and press an additional fold between each previous fold for a total of eight overlapping folds, or pleats. Using your hand, gently but firmly press inward and upward on the dough so that it resembles a little volcano, where you can see the berries peering out from the center. There should be a spiral of pleated dough holding firm against the inner berry filling. Refrigerate the pastries for 15 minutes.

6 While the pastries are chilling, preheat the oven to 375°F (190°C).

7 Brush the pastries with egg wash, then sprinkle them with the demerara sugar.

8 Bake the pastries for 30 minutes, or until the crust is golden brown and the juices are bubbling. Place the baking sheet on a cooling rack to cool completely before removing. Store them wrapped in plastic at room temperature for up to 1 day or refrigerate for up to 1 week.

Raspberry Frangipane Tarts

Tartes frangipane aux framboises

Makes twelve 3-inch tarts

Special tools: twelve 3-inch fluted tart pans or 3-by-½-inch ring molds, pastry brush, pastry bag fitted with a medium star tip, pastry bag fitted with a small star tip

½ recipe Pastry Dough (pages 49 and 50)

½ cup (170 grams) raspberry jam

½ recipe Frangipane (pages 24 and 25), at room temperature

¼ cup (75 grams) Apricot Glaze (page 20), melted

48 fresh raspberries

2 cups (250 grams) Dark Chocolate Ganache, softened (page 36)

1 cup (150 grams) French Buttercream (pages 34 and 35) or Italian Meringue Buttercream (pages 32 and 33), softened

Chocolate decorations (optional)

Raspberries, with their pink and red juicy mounds waiting to explode their flavor into your mouth, hold my favor year-round. This raspberry frangipane tart exudes simplicity, elegance, and lusciousness. My inspiration for this recipe comes from an enchanting tiny Swiss walnut tart I learned to make at Hamelman's Bakery when I was twenty-three years old. Finished with little swirls of buttercream and a secret hidden filling, it was my favorite pastry to make. Although grander in scale, this raspberry tart can be made in smaller pans and finished as a petit four; I encourage you to play and discover your own creations.

Method

1 Flour both sides of the pastry dough, then place the dough between two pieces of plastic wrap and set it onto your work surface. Roll out the dough to ⅛ inch thick, then brush any excess flour from both sides. Cut twelve 3¾-inch circles of pastry, then line the tart pans or ring molds with the pastry dough; gently press the dough into the pans and firmly smooth it flat along the inside edges, while maintaining the same thickness. Use a rolling pin to press across the top of the tarts to shear off any excess dough. Use your hands to pull away extra dough from the pans. Place the tarts on a parchment paper–lined baking sheet, cover with plastic wrap, and refrigerate for at least 2 hours or overnight. At this point, the tarts may be put in an airtight container and frozen for up to 1 month.

2 Spoon about 1½ teaspoons of raspberry jam into the bottom of each tart shell. With a metal spatula, apply about ¼ cup of frangipane on top of the jam, then smooth the cream level across the top of the tart pan. As you initially smooth the frangipane into the tart, pull the cream outward, away from the center, deliberately working to secure the jam beneath the frangipane. When you are finished, each tart should be filled and the top level. If needed, add or remove frangipane cream to fill the tart pan. The tarts are ready to bake, or they can be covered with plastic wrap and refrigerated for up to 1 day before baking. Well-wrapped unbaked tarts can be frozen for up to 1 week.

3 Preheat the oven to 350°F (175°C).

4 Place the baking sheet with the tarts into the oven and bake for 15 to 20 minutes, until they are golden brown and lightly spring back in the center. Place the tarts on a cooling rack to cool completely before finishing.

5 Release the tarts from the pans by flipping them upside down, then place them upright. Lightly brush each tart with apricot glaze, then place four fresh raspberries in the center of each tart, nestled closely. The apricot jam will help the raspberries adhere to the top and also seal the top of the tart from drying out.

6 Fill the pastry bag fitted with the medium star tip two-thirds full with chocolate ganache. Pipe a total of four rosettes, spaced equally on top of the tart, placing one rosette between each raspberry. Fill the pastry bag fitted with the small star tip with buttercream. Pipe a small scroll design at the outer edge of each tart; there should be space for three scrolls. Return to the pastry bag filled with chocolate ganache and pipe a large rosette onto the center of the raspberries. If using a chocolate decoration, set it on top of the rosette. The tarts are now ready to eat, or cover and refrigerate for up to 1 day. If you refrigerate them, allow the tarts to sit out for a few hours to come to room temperature before eating.

Fresh Fruit Tart

Tarte aux fruits

Makes one 8-inch tart

Special tools: 8-inch tart pan, small pastry brush, pastry bag fitted with a ½-inch open tip

For the crust
½ recipe Sweet Dough (pages 47 and 48)

¼ cup (75 grams) Apricot Glaze (page 20), melted

For the filling
1 recipe Pastry Cream (pages 26 and 27)

1 cup (200 grams) fresh blueberries

1 cup (125 grams) fresh raspberries

1 cup (150 grams) fresh strawberries

Confectioners' sugar (optional)

In the world of French pastries, these fresh fruit tarts are fairly simple but present an uplifting visual effect for any occasion. The mix of vanilla bean-infused pastry cream, fresh fruit, and the buttery crispness of the tart shell embrace a span of pastry elements that deliver high on the pleasure scale. The star of this pastry is the fruit, so take advantage of seasonal, local, and organic produce for optimal flavor and freshness. Once cut, fresh fruit dries out quickly; a light brushing with apricot glaze seals the moisture in. Take your time assembling the tarts to create eye-catching designs and further enhance your eating enjoyment.

Method
Make the crust
1 Flour both sides of the sweet dough, then place the dough between two pieces of plastic wrap and set it onto your work surface. Roll the sweet dough out into a circle that's ⅛ inch thick and brush any excess flour from both sides. Line the tart mold with the sweet dough; gently press the dough into the pan and firmly smooth the dough flat along the inside edges. Use a rolling pin to press across the top of the tarts to shear off the excess dough. Place the tart pan on a baking sheet, cover with plastic wrap, and refrigerate for at least 2 hours or overnight. At this point, the tart can be put in an airtight container and frozen for up to 1 month.

2 When you are ready to bake the tart, preheat the oven to 350°F (175°C).

3 Pierce the bottoms of the shell using the tines of a fork. Bake the shell for 10 to 12 minutes, until medium golden brown. Remove the shell from the oven and place it on a cooling rack to cool. To seal the bottom of the tart, brush it with apricot glaze.

Make the filling

1 In a medium bowl, whisk the pastry cream until it is smooth and homogeneous. Fill the pastry bag two-thirds full with pastry cream, then pipe a spiral of pastry cream into the tart shell. Add additional pastry cream as necessary to reach within $\frac{1}{8}$ inch of the rim. Use a small metal spatula to smooth the top even. You want enough pastry cream to fill the shell with room for the berries to sit steadily on the top.

2 Place the berries on top of the tart in a circle or another design of your choice. If you slice your strawberries, brush the exposed cut side of the fruit with apricot glaze so it does not dry out or discolor.

3 Sprinkle the tart with confectioners' sugar, if using, and serve immediately.

Chocolate Coffee Tarts

Tartes chocolat café

Makes twelve 3-inch tarts

Special tools: twelve 3-inch tart rings, pastry bag fitted with ½-inch open tip, 2-inch-diameter plastic tuile template, silicone baking mat

For the tart

½ recipe Sweet Dough (pages 47 and 48)

2 tablespoons (35 grams) Apricot Glaze (page 20)

1 recipe Dark Chocolate Ganache (page 36)

1 tablespoon plus 1 teaspoon (28 grams) coffee extract, such as Trablit

¼ cup (56 grams) heavy cream

For the tuiles

½ cup (100 grams) light brown sugar

½ cup (100 grams) granulated sugar

¾ cup (120 grams) Steve's Gluten Free Cake Flour (see pages 1 and 2)

(continued on page 144)

An elegant confection in a pastry shell, the creamy chocolate coffee ganache lends itself to the contrast of the crisp buttery pastry shell, the light coffee whipped cream, and ultra-lacy coffee tuile with its fragile shattering texture. My preference for coffee extract is a deeply flavored Italian brand called Trablit, but you can use another type of coffee extract. If you'd like some extra coffee cream to spoon on the side, double up on the coffee extract and cream mixture. The tuiles can also be made as a separate recipe to enjoy on their own or adorn an ice cream or mousse parfait.

Method

Make the tarts

1 Flour both sides of the pastry dough, then place between two pieces of plastic wrap and set it onto your work surface. Roll the dough out to ⅛ inch thick, then cut out twelve 4-inch circles of pastry. Line the tart rings with the dough, gently pressing the dough into the tart rings and smoothing it flat along the inside edges. Using a rolling pin, press across the top of the tart pans to shear off the excess dough. Place the tarts on a parchment paper–lined baking sheet, cover with plastic wrap, and refrigerate for at least 2 hours or overnight. At this point, the tarts may be put in an airtight container and frozen for up to 1 month.

2 When you are ready to bake the tart shells, preheat the oven to 350°F (175°C).

3 Blind bake the shells; fill each one with a paper cup filled with pie weights or raw beans or prick them with a fork and bake for 7 to 10 minutes, until golden brown.

4 Place the baking sheet with the tart shells on a cooling rack for 5 minutes, then remove the paper cups, being careful not

⅔ cup (100 grams)
brewed espresso

7 tablespoons (100 grams)
unsalted butter, melted

¼ cup (25 grams) sliced
almonds, finely chopped

to tear the bottom crust. Brush the bottom crust lightly with the melted apricot glaze; this will seal the bottom crust and keep it from becoming soggy or leaking.

5 As you make the ganache and it has fully emulsified, add 1 tablespoon of the coffee extract and gently whisk by hand to combine. Use a hand ladle to spoon the chocolate coffee ganache into each baked tart shell and fill to the top. Refrigerate the tarts for 1 hour, or until firm.

Make the coffee tuiles

1 Line two 12-by-17-inch baking sheets with silicone mats.

2 In a medium bowl, combine the brown sugar and granulated sugar. Add the remaining ingredients, one at a time, and use a silicone spatula to mix the batter together. The mixture should appear homogeneous and thin but not runny.

3 Cover with plastic wrap and refrigerate for at least 1 hour or up to 3 days before using. Resting the batter will help it firm up for spreading into the tuile shapes.

4 Set the silicone baking mat on a flat work surface and place the tuile template on top. Spoon a small amount of batter inside each round, then use a flexible or offset metal spatula to spread the tuile batter level with the top of the template. When you have finished spreading all of the template rounds, remove the plastic template and set the baking mat onto a baking sheet. Set the baking sheet in the freezer for 15 minutes to harden the tuiles.

5 Preheat the oven to 375°F (190°C).

6 Bake the tuiles for 5 to 8 minutes, until the cookies turn dark golden brown. Remove the baking sheet from the oven and set it on a cooling rack to cool before applying them to the coffee tarts.

To assemble

1 Whip the cream until soft peaks begin to form, then add the remaining 1 teaspoon coffee extract and whisk briefly to combine. You want the cream to be at soft, firm peaks for piping but not stiff.

2 Fill a pastry bag fitted with the open tip with the coffee cream and pipe a ¾-inch mound on top of each tart. Set a coffee tuile at an angle resting against the cream. Serve immediately.

CHAPTER FIVE

Cakes

Cakes

Les gâteaux

Infinite sizes, shapes, flavors, fillings, components, constructions, and creative consideration fold their way through the realm of French cake making. Grab your apron, roll up your sleeves, and waltz your way through the wondrous world of enchanting French cakes made gluten-free.

We begin with a selection of tea cakes: miniature Pistachio Baby Cakes, traditional shell-shaped Madeleines and their brown-buttered cousins, *Financiers*, along with tangy Little Lemon Cakes. Individual-size cakes include Tiger Cakes, heavenly scented *Canelés*, and the deep chocolate cork-shaped cakes known as *Bouchons*. Sumptuous Apple Cakes and *Petits Savarin Chantilly* round out the selection of single-serving treats. Almond-encrusted Lemon Cake and Honey Spice Cake are homey, comforting loaf cakes. Slicing cakes for any occasion include the fetching *Gâteau Basque* with its pastry cream filling and tart-like structure, the revisited melt-in-your-mouth Soft Chocolate Cake, and Chocolate Almond Cake. Layered cakes offer enticing cross-sections and creamy fillings: Mocha Buttercream Cake is a classic, Lemon Mousse Cake is a visual feast, and we finish with Chocolate Strawberry Mousse Cake, featuring a beloved flavor combination. Let's bake!

Pistachio Baby Cakes

Petits gâteaux à la pistache

Makes 24

Special tools: mini cupcake pans, mini cupcake liners, pastry bag fitted with a ½-inch open pastry tip, pastry bag fitted with a medium star tip

For the cakes
2 tablespoons (55 grams) pistachio paste

¾ cup (200 grams) almond paste, broken into walnut-size pieces

2 large eggs, beaten (110 grams)

5 tablespoons (70 grams) unsalted butter, melted and cooled

For decorating
Pistachio Buttercream (see pages 237 to 240) or Dark Chocolate Ganache (page 36)

½ pound chunk of dark chocolate, at room temperature, to make chocolate curls (optional)

Dainty and bite-size, these cakes are simple, elegant, and notably bold in flavor. Reminiscent of petits fours, the cakes can be finished in a variety of styles—scattered with nuts, studded with rum-soaked fruit, or served plain. The cakes are finished with a luscious swirl of pistachio buttercream and sprinkled with chocolate curls. Alternately, you could fold mini chocolate chips into the batter and top the finished cakes with orange buttercream or dark chocolate ganache.

Method

1 Put the pistachio paste and almond paste into the bowl of a stand mixer fitted with the paddle attachment. Beat on medium speed until the two pastes combine, about 2 minutes. Some small particles may remain; this is okay.

2 With the mixer still on medium speed, slowly pour a thin, steady stream of the beaten eggs down the inside edge of the mixing bowl. Take your time, allowing the eggs to incorporate into the paste. After the eggs are well blended, scrape the bowl using a silicone spatula.

3 Reduce the mixer speed to low, then slowly pour in the melted butter. Once all of the butter is incorporated, increase the mixer speed to medium and beat until the batter is thick and smooth. Cover the batter with plastic wrap and refrigerate overnight.

4 When you are ready to make the cakes, remove the batter from the refrigerator and preheat the oven to 350°F (175°C).

5 Line the muffin pans with the mini cupcake liners.

6 Fill the pastry bag with the ½-inch open tip two-thirds full of batter. Fill each cupcake liner three-quarters full with batter.

7 Place the pans in the oven and bake the cakes for 10 to 12 minutes, until the tops spring back when gently touched in the center. Remove the pans from the oven and place them on a cooling rack. Allow the cakes to sit for 5 minutes, then flip the pans upside down to release the cakes and place them directly on the rack to cool completely. Fill the pastry bag fitted with the star tip with pistachio buttercream, then finish the cakes by piping a swirled rosette on top.

8 If you're making chocolate curls, hold the chunk of dark chocolate in one hand and use a vegetable peeler to scrape off curls of chocolate. As the chocolate warms up, the curls will become larger. Finish each cake with a sprinkling of chocolate curls atop the rosette.

9 Store the cakes in a plastic container in the refrigerator for up to 1 week.

Madeleines

Madeleines

Makes 24

Special tools: madeleine molds, zest grater, pastry bag fitted with a ½-inch open tip

1 cup minus 1 tablespoon (150 grams) Steve's Gluten Free Cake Flour (see pages 1 and 2)

1 teaspoon (4 grams) baking powder

⅛ teaspoon (1 gram) sea salt

Grated zest of 1 medium orange

¾ cup (150 grams) granulated sugar

¾ ounce (20 grams) honey

3 large eggs (165 grams)

1 teaspoon (5 grams) pure vanilla extract

1 tablespoon (16 grams) orange blossom water

10 tablespoons (140 grams) unsalted butter, melted

Nonstick cooking spray

Confectioners' sugar

A favorite among pastry chefs, madeleines are known for their delightful scalloped shell shape, light cake texture, and delicate crisp crust. Famous for their history and debated origin, legend has it that in the eighteenth century King Stanislaw Leszczynski of Poland tasted these cookies while in France. He was so enamored that he named the cookie after the local woman who baked them, Madeleine.

These lovely, diminutive treats have endless flavor options, but to be a true madeleine, they must rise and form a hump during their time in the oven. Ideally madeleines are eaten the same day that they're baked; they are at their peak of enjoyment fresh out of the oven and slightly cooled. However, day-old madeleines are excellent for dunking in or alongside a cup of hot chocolate, coffee, or tea. Note that the batter is prepared a day ahead of baking.

Method

1 Sift the flour, baking powder, and salt into a small bowl and set aside.

2 In a small bowl, combine the orange zest with the granulated sugar, rubbing them together using your fingers.

3 In the bowl of a stand mixer fitted with the whisk attachment, combine the sugar–zest mixture, the honey, and eggs. Whip on medium-high speed until the egg mixture thickens and lightens in color, about 4 minutes. Add the vanilla and orange blossom water and whip just until combined.

4 Reduce the mixer speed to low, gradually add the flour mixture, and whip until it is fully incorporated.

5 Keeping the mixer speed on low, slowly pour a thin, steady stream of the butter down the inside edge of the bowl, taking breaks if necessary to allow the butter to incorporate before adding more. Remove the bowl from the mixer and use a silicone spatula to scrape the sides and bottom of the bowl, then stir until the batter is homogeneous.

6 Firmly cover the madeleine batter by pressing plastic wrap against its surface, creating an airtight seal, and refrigerate overnight. Allowing the batter to rest will help ensure adequate development of the traditional madeleine hump.

7 When you are ready to make the madeleines, preheat the oven to 350°F (175°C).

8 Prepare the pans: spray each scalloped section of the pan with cooking spray or grease with melted butter and dust with flour.

9 Remove the madeleine batter from the refrigerator. Using a large silicone spatula, fill the pastry bag two-thirds full with the batter. Pipe the batter into each cavity until it's three-quarters full. Do not overfill the molds or the madeleines will have difficulty developing a prominent hump.

10 Bake the madeleines for 10 to 15 minutes, until they are light golden brown and the tops are soft but spring back after you touch them. Remove the madeleines from the oven and unmold them immediately by rapping the pan against a cooling rack. Serve the madeleines slightly warm or at room temperature, sprinkled with confectioners' sugar.

Financiers

Financiers

Makes 36

Special tool: mini muffin pans or other shaped pans

¾ cup plus 2 tablespoons (200 grams) unsalted butter

1 cup plus 1 tablespoon (110 grams) confectioners' sugar, sifted

⅔ cup (130 grams) granulated sugar

1 cup (100 grams) almond flour

½ cup (80 grams) gluten-free flour blend (see pages 1 to 3)

1 teaspoon (4 grams) baking powder

6 to 7 large egg whites (210 grams), at room temperature, lightly whisked

1 vanilla bean, seeds scraped and reserved, pod set aside to dry

Nonstick cooking spray

As the story goes, these cakes originated in the financial district of Paris near the stock exchange; they were baked in traditional rectangular molds, each representing a bar of gold. A combination of browned butter and vanilla bean gives these teacakes a delicate yet distinctive flavor. For an extra flourish, you can adorn the cakes with berries or nuts.

Financiers are a versatile, uplifting accompaniment to afternoon tea, an impromptu picnic, or dessert served with fresh fruit and cream. You can make them in batches (after each batch, cool the pans completely, wipe them clean with a soft cloth or paper towel, coat again with cooking spray, place on a baking sheet, and proceed from step 5) or bake them in tart molds or cake pans of various sizes; adjust the baking time up or down as needed. You could also keep half of the batter in the refrigerator or freezer so it's available when you're looking for a reliable treat on short notice.

Method

1 Brown the butter: place the butter in a medium saucepan and melt over medium heat, then cook until it turns a dark golden color and brown bits begin to form on the bottom of the pan, about 8 minutes. Pay close attention to the butter because it can quickly go from browned to burnt. Remove the butter from the heat and allow it to cool slightly.

2 Sift the confectioners' sugar, granulated sugar, almond flour, gluten-free flour, and baking powder into a medium bowl. Pour the dry mixture into the bowl of a stand mixer fitted with the whisk attachment. Add the egg whites and vanilla bean seeds and mix on medium speed just until combined.

3 Steadily begin to pour the browned butter down the inside edge of the mixing bowl while running the mixer at low speed. Scrape up all the toasty browned bits from the bottom of the pan to include in the batter. Once all the butter has been added, turn off the mixer and scrape the sides and bottom of the bowl with a silicone spatula. Turn the mixer to medium speed and beat for 1 minute, or until the texture of the batter is medium-thick and pourable. Cover the batter and allow it to sit in the refrigerator overnight. (At this point, you may store the financier batter in a covered container in the refrigerator for up to 1 week or freeze it for up to 1 month. When you are ready to use the batter, let it come to room temperature and stir it well.)

4 Preheat the oven to 375°F (190°C). Coat the pans lightly with cooking spray and place them on baking sheets.

5 Pour the batter into the prepared pans, leaving $\frac{1}{16}$ inch of room at the top.

6 Bake for 5 minutes, then reduce the oven temperature to 350°F (175°C) and bake for 7 more minutes, or until the edges are nicely browned and the center is still light in color but firm to the touch. Remove from the oven and place the baking sheet on a cooling rack to cool for 20 minutes.

7 To release the cakes from the pans, flip the pans upside down and gently rap them against the cooling rack. You may need to run the tip of a small, sharp knife around the edges of the cakes to help nudge them out. Store the teacakes well wrapped at room temperature for up to 2 days, or store them in the freezer for up to 2 weeks.

Little Lemon Cakes

Petits gâteaux au citron

Makes 36

Special tools: round or square mini savarin molds, pastry bag fitted with a ½-inch open tip

For the cakes

1 cup (255 grams) almond paste, broken into walnut-size pieces

2 large eggs (110 grams) at room temperature, well beaten

5 tablespoons (70 grams) unsalted butter, melted and cooled

Nonstick cooking spray

For finishing

½ cup Lemon Cream (pages 30 and 31)

½ cup (150 grams) Apricot Glaze (page 20), melted

¼ cup (42 grams) candied lemon or orange peel, sliced ⅟₁₆ inch thick, or small, fresh, edible flowers, such as lemon gem or tangerine marigolds

A Pierre Hermé adaptation, these miniature lemon bites burst with almond and lemon flavor and entice with their shiny finish. Add them to a platter of petits fours and they will be gleefully gobbled up. If you prefer, you can eliminate the lemon cream and finish the cakes with Italian Meringue Buttercream (pages 32 and 33), French Buttercream (pages 34 and 35), or Pistachio Ganache (page 38) rosettes. Decorate the cakes with thin slices of candied lemon or orange peel or small, fresh, edible flowers.

Method

1 Put the almond paste into the bowl of a stand mixer fitted with the paddle attachment.

2 Turn the mixer to medium speed and slowly pour the beaten eggs in a thin, steady stream down the inside edge of the mixing bowl. Take your time, allowing the eggs to incorporate into the paste. After the eggs are well blended, scrape the sides and bottom of the bowl using a silicone spatula.

3 Turn the mixer to low speed and slowly pour the melted butter into the batter. Once all of the butter is incorporated, increase the mixer speed to medium and beat until the batter is thick and smooth. Cover the batter with plastic wrap and refrigerate overnight.

4 When you are ready to make the cakes, remove the batter from the refrigerator and preheat the oven to 350°F (175°C).

5 Prepare the mini savarin molds by spraying them lightly with cooking spray.

6 Fill the pastry bag two-thirds full of batter. Fill each mold cavity three-quarters full with batter.

7 Place the pans into the oven and bake the cakes for 8 to 10 minutes, until the tops spring back after being gently touched on the edge. Remove the pans from the oven and flip the pans upside down to release the tiny cakes onto a cooling rack. This will prevent the cakes from continuing to bake. Allow the cakes to cool completely before the next steps.

8 Stir the lemon cream until it is smooth and homogeneous. Fill the pastry bag with the lemon cream, then pipe a dollop in the center cavity of each cake. Place the cakes onto a parchment paper–lined baking sheet and freeze for 30 minutes.

9 Dip the frozen cakes into the warm apricot glaze, then set them onto a cooling rack to set up. Garnish with a thin slice of candied lemon or orange peel or fresh, edible flowers. These cakes are best eaten the same day they are made.

Tiger Cakes

Gâteaux tigré

Makes 16

Special tools: two sheets of 2½-by-2½-by-1-inch square or round savarin silicone molds or other molds, pastry bag without a tip, pastry bag fitted with a ½-inch star tip

For the cakes

2⅓ cups (235 grams) almond flour

¾ cup (150 grams) granulated sugar

⅓ cup (55 grams) gluten-free flour blend (see pages 1 to 3)

⅛ teaspoon (1 gram) sea salt

7 large egg whites (240 grams), at room temperature

1 tablespoon (21 grams) honey

1 teaspoon (5 grams) pure vanilla extract

Nonstick cooking spray

1 cup minus 1 tablespoon (210 grams) unsalted butter

(continued on page 163)

Tigers are a bold type of teacake with a luscious texture similar to a pound cake. The cake is made with almond flour and stippled with chocolate bits and bears a tight, buttery crumb that contrasts its slightly crisp exterior. They are finished with a creamy rosette of dark chocolate ganache. Inspired by a recipe of Dorie Greenspan's, I have adapted the recipe by browning the butter, switching out corn syrup for honey, adding vanilla, and making it gluten-free. Tigers are quite appealing unadorned, though the intensity of the creamy ganache swirl meeting the notes of honey and dense texture of the cake is irresistible. These tigers can be finished with various flavors of ganache or buttercream and made in many shapes and sizes, ranging from petits fours to cupcakes.

Method

1 In a medium bowl, whisk together the almond flour, sugar, gluten-free flour, and salt.

2 Place the egg whites into the bowl of a stand mixer fitted with the whisk attachment. Whip the egg whites on low speed for about 30 seconds, until they are uniformly liquefied but not frothy.

3 Add the dry mixture and whip for 1 minute, or until the batter is homogenous. Add the honey and vanilla and whip for 30 seconds, or until the batter is smooth.

4 Remove the bowl from the stand mixer and use a silicone spatula to give the batter a final mix. Cover the batter with plastic wrap and refrigerate overnight.

5 When you are ready to make the cakes, remove the batter from the refrigerator and attach the bowl to the stand mixer fitted with the whisk attachment.

¾ cup (145 grams) bittersweet mini chocolate chips or finely chopped dark chocolate

For decorating
Dark Chocolate Ganache (page 36), at room temperature

6 Lightly coat the savarin molds with cooking spray and place them on a baking sheet.

7 Preheat the oven to 350°F (175°C).

8 Heat the butter in a small saucepan over medium heat until it melts and turns a dark golden color, about 8 minutes. Browned bits will begin accumulating at the bottom of the pan; this is a sign that the butter is nearly finished. Brown butter can quickly burn, so watch it closely. Remove the browned butter from the heat and scrape the bottom of the pan with a metal spatula to remove all the browned butter bits. With the mixer running on low speed, slowly pour the hot browned butter into the batter. Once all of the butter is incorporated, increase the mixer speed to medium and whip until the batter has cooled and the bottom of the bowl is cool.

9 Reduce the mixer speed to low and add the chocolate chips. Whip the batter for 30 seconds, or until the chips are evenly distributed.

10 To pipe the cake batter, use a medium pastry bag without a pastry tip inserted. The larger bag opening will provide an easier flow of batter into the molds. Fill the pastry bag two-thirds full with batter, then squeeze the batter into the savarin molds until they are three-quarters full.

11 Place the baking sheet with the molds into the oven and bake the cakes for 12 to 15 minutes, until the tops are light golden brown. The cakes will not rise very high but will crack slightly in the middle when they are done. Remove the baking sheet from the oven and place it on a cooling rack. Using a kitchen towel, gently but firmly grab the sides of the silicone mold and flip it upside down to release the cakes onto the rack. This will prevent the cakes from continuing to bake. Cool completely.

12 Fill the pastry bag with the ½-inch tip with the softened chocolate ganache. Pipe a rosette into the center of each cake. The cakes will keep in a plastic container for up to 1 week in the refrigerator, or in the freezer for up to 1 month.

Canelés

Canelés

Makes 16

Special tools: 16 copper canelé molds, pastry brush, medium-mesh sieve, instant-read thermometer

For the molds

½ cup pure beeswax, melted

For the batter

4 cups (960 grams) whole milk

1 vanilla bean, split and scraped

¼ cup (50 grams) cold unsalted butter, cut into ½-inch cubes

1 cup plus 2 tablespoons (180 grams) Steve's Gluten Free Cake Flour (see pages 1 and 2)

1¾ cups (355 grams) granulated sugar

8 large egg yolks (180 grams)

2 tablespoons (32 grams) dark rum

There is a ritualistic nature to the baking of canelés. They require the unusual ingredient of beeswax (available from a natural food store or your local beekeeper), and the equipment needed to make them—baking sheet, pastry brush, molds, and kitchen towel—will become coated with beeswax, rendering them solely for canelé making. Canelés receive a long bake, with their visible bottoms nearly black and their fluted sides a deep caramel color. Give them their due time in the oven and your home will be scented with the heavenly gift of the honeybees.

Method

1 Melt the beeswax in a small saucepan over low heat. Using a small pastry brush, apply a thorough coating of beeswax to the bottom and inside channels of the seasoned canelé molds. Space the canelé molds 1½ inches apart on a parchment paper–lined baking sheet.

2 In a medium saucepan, combine the milk and vanilla bean. Place over medium-high heat and bring to a boil. Add the butter, remove from the heat, and set aside to cool slightly.

3 Combine the flour and sugar in the bowl of a stand mixer fitted with the whisk attachment. Turn the mixer to medium-low speed, add the egg yolks, and whip until blended, about 1 minute. The mixture will be somewhat stiff.

4 Remove the vanilla bean from the hot milk, rinse it, and set it aside to dry. Reduce the mixer speed to low, then slowly pour the warm milk in a thin, steady stream into the bowl. Remove the bowl from the mixer and use a silicone spatula to scrape down the sides and bottom of the bowl, incorporating any residual egg yolk.

5 Set the sieve over a medium bowl, then pour the custard batter into the sieve. Using the silicone spatula, press the batter through the sieve. There may be small lumps of batter remaining; if so, lower the sieve into the custard batter, allowing the warm mixture to soften the little bits of batter, then push them through the sieve until there are no remaining particles of batter in the sieve.

6 Add the rum to the custard batter and gently stir with the silicone spatula until thoroughly combined. Cover with plastic wrap and refrigerate for a minimum of 48 hours and up to 72 hours.

7 When you are ready to bake the canelés, preheat the oven to 450°F (230°C).

8 Remove the canelé batter from the refrigerator and stir it with a silicone spatula to reincorporate the ingredients (there will be naturally occurring separation). Pour the batter into a heatproof bowl and cook over a bain-marie (see page 9) until it reaches 110 to 113°F (43 to 45°C) on an instant-read thermometer. Use a silicone spatula to stir the batter continuously. As the batter heats, it will begin to partially cook and thicken slightly. In order to prevent sticking, be sure to scrape the bottom of the bowl repeatedly. When the desired temperature is reached, immediately remove the batter from the heat and pour through a medium-mesh sieve into a large measuring cup or pouring device, pressing any lumps through in the same manner as step 5. The batter should be smooth, creamy, and homogenous. Pour the batter within ⅛ inch of the top of each canelé mold. Stir the batter between each pouring to distribute the vanilla beans and maintain a homogeneous mixture.

9 Bake the canelés for 25 minutes, then reduce the oven temperature to 425°F (220°C) and bake for an additional 20 minutes. Lower the oven temperature once more to 400°F (205°C) and bake for 20 to 30 minutes more, until the canelés are dark brown–blackish on top.

10 Test one canelé by unmolding it before removing the whole batch from the oven. Using a well-padded kitchen towel, carefully and firmly grasp the copper mold (an oven mitt will be too clumsy to handle the small, hot metal mold) and remove it from the baking sheet, leaving the remaining canelés still in the oven. Turn the mold upside down and rap it against a cooling rack, releasing the canelé with its rounded crown up. The canelé should appear to be very dark brown, with no obvious yellow hues on the crown. When they are ready, release all of them onto a cooling rack to cool until slightly warm or at room temperature before enjoying.

Canelés ⌒⌐ Heavenly Fluted Crowns

Originating in Bordeaux, these dark and slightly burnished custardy pastries have a historical archive that includes their registration with the Parliament of Bordeaux in the mid-1600s, limiting their production to specialty bakers, or *canauliers.* Further distinctions include the spelling. The name may include one or two *n*'s; the removal of one *n* took place during the late 1900s by a confederation of bakers in the Bordeaux region, thereby ensuring *canelé* as the true name for France's national records. Such concern over a pastry seems warranted; these divine little pillars are unusual in their preparation and mysterious in their flavor and texture profile.

Canelé means "fluted," which speaks to the shape of the traditional copper molds they are baked in. The molds are brushed with beeswax, which caramelizes into the canelé's crusty, chewy exterior, imparting an integral yet mysterious flavor, while the interior surrenders to a contrast of soft, vanilla bean–speckled custard scented with dark rum. Silicone molds are a less costly alternative and make acceptable quality canelés. However, the copper canelé molds brushed with pure beeswax are far superior and will yield greater development of the essential crust, not to mention the visual and tactile pleasures of working with these artful molds. Over time the copper molds will age with character and sit beautifully in your treasure chest of baking tools, lasting a lifetime.

Chocolate Corks

Bouchons au chocolat

Makes 12

Special tools: 12 timbale or baba au rhum nonstick mold pans, large pastry bag

⅔ cup (100 grams) gluten-free flour blend (see pages 1 to 3)

1 cup (100 grams) Valrhona cocoa powder

½ teaspoon (3 grams) sea salt

1¼ cups (280 grams) unsalted butter

3 large eggs (165 grams)

1½ cups plus 2 tablespoons (325 grams) granulated sugar (or reduce sugar by 2 tablespoons for a less sweet final product)

½ vanilla bean, split, seeds scraped, and pod set aside

1⅓ cups (225 grams) chocolate chunks or chips

Nonstick cooking spray

Named after its resemblance to a champagne cork, the *bouchon* is the French version of a stand-up brownie and is studded with dark chocolate chunks. Bouchons are easy to make yet intensely delicious with their moist, dark, cakey texture and melty chocolate chunks. My preference is to use Valrhona cocoa powder and the highest cocoa percentage, largest chocolate chunks or chips I can find. Or make your own chunks with your favorite brand of chocolate. Keep the bouchons on hand in the freezer for a quick dinner party dessert; simply thaw, heat, and serve. Embellish them with ice cream and red raspberries and your guests will remember the evening with big smiles.

Method

1 Sift the flour, cocoa powder, and salt into a small bowl and set aside.

2 Allow the butter to sit out at room temperature to soften. If necessary, place the butter into a medium saucepan over low heat and heat briefly, stirring until the butter is softened but not melted.

3 Combine the eggs, sugar, and scraped vanilla bean into the bowl of a stand mixer fitted with the whisk attachment. Whip on high speed until the mixture thickens and lightens in color, about 3 minutes.

4 Reduce the mixer speed to low and alternately add the cocoa–flour mixture and the butter, whipping well between each addition until the batter is homogenous, about 2 minutes. Using a silicone spatula, scrape down the sides and bottom of the bowl a few times between mixing. The batter should be thick and well combined.

5 Add the chocolate chunks and mix on medium–high speed until evenly distributed and the batter lightens a bit in color, about 1 minute.

6 Scrape the batter into a large stainless steel bowl and use a silicone spatula to do a final mixing by hand, evenly distributing the chocolate chips. Cover with plastic wrap, pressing the wrap directly onto the batter. Refrigerate overnight or up to 2 days before using.

7 Remove the batter from the refrigerator, place in a warm place, and allow it to come to room temperature. The batter should be soft enough to easily stir with a silicone spatula.

8 Preheat the oven to 350°F (175°C).

9 Spray the molds with cooking spray, then set them on a baking sheet.

10 Using a silicone spatula, stir the batter until the consistency is uniform. Fill a large pastry bag that does not have a tip inserted. Squeeze the batter into the molds, filling to within ¼ inch of the top.

11 Bake for 20 to 25 minutes, or until the sides feel firm and the center is firm yet tender when you touch it. The top of the bouchons may crack as they bake, and this is okay.

12 Remove the baking sheet from the oven and place it on a cooling rack to cool for 15 minutes. Then grasp the mold, turn it upside down, and gently swivel the bouchons back and forth to encourage them to release. The bouchons can be eaten at room temperature or warmed and served with ice cream. Store at room temperature, well wrapped in plastic, for up to 5 days, or freeze for up to 2 months.

Lemon Pound Cake

Quatre-quarts au citron

Makes three 6-by-2½-inch loaves or one 9-inch loaf

Special tools: 6-by-2½-inch loaf pans or one 9-inch loaf pan, pastry brush

For the pans

¼ cup (55 grams) unsalted butter, at room temperature

½ cup (40 grams) sliced almonds

¼ cup (50 grams) granulated sugar

For the cakes

1¼ cups plus 1 tablespoon (210 grams) Steve's Gluten Free Cake Flour (see pages 1 and 2)

¾ teaspoon (3 grams) baking powder

½ teaspoon (4 grams) sea salt

4 large eggs (220 grams), at room temperature

1¼ cups (250 grams) granulated sugar

½ cup plus 3 tablespoons (155 grams) unsalted butter, softened

(continued on page 173)

In France, this type of loaf cake is referred to as a Weekend, or Traveling Cake, meant to last the weekend and ideal for transporting to a picnic or neighbor's home. These quick to put together lemon citrus cakes are almond encrusted, adding a delightful crunchy contrast to the buttery soft crumb of the cake. To make an orange citrus cake, simply substitute orange for the lemon throughout the recipe. The recipe can be made in tiny loaf shapes as well.

Method

Prepare the pans

1 Preheat the oven to 350°F (175°C).

2 Generously coat the loaf pans with butter, then sprinkle them with almonds, turning the pan from side to side and helping them adhere by pressing them against the pan with your fingers. Place the pans in the freezer for 5 minutes. Remove the pans from the freezer and divide the sugar among the pans, swirling it around to coat the bottoms and sides of the pans. Return the pans to the refrigerator while you make the cake batter.

Make the cakes

1 Sift the flour, baking powder, and salt into a medium bowl and set aside.

2 Place the eggs and sugar into the bowl of a stand mixer fitted with the whisk attachment. Whip on medium speed for 4 to 5 minutes, until the texture becomes fluffy and the mixture lightens in color. Remove the bowl from the mixer.

3 In a separate bowl, using a medium hand whisk, whip together the butter and lemon juice. Pour the cream into the

2 tablespoons (36 grams) lemon juice

¼ cup (60 grams) heavy cream, at room temperature

3 tablespoons (15 grams) lemon zest

For the syrup
¼ cup (58 grams) water

¼ cup (50 grams) granulated sugar

1 tablespoon (16 grams) lemon juice

mixture, whipping to incorporate, then add the lemon zest and mix to blend. The mixture should be creamy and smooth.

4 Using a silicone spatula, gradually fold the flour mixture into the egg and sugar mixture. Pour the lemon, butter, and cream mixture down the inside edge of the bowl, then fold it in, turning the batter just until it is homogeneous.

5 Bake the cakes for 25 to 35 minutes, until the edges turn golden and the center is firm to the touch. As the cake bakes, a crack may appear down the center; this is to be expected.

Make the syrup and finish the cakes
1 While the cakes are baking, prepare the soaking syrup. Combine the water and sugar in a small saucepan and cook over medium heat until it comes to a boil. Remove the syrup from the heat and allow it to cool for 10 minutes. Add the lemon juice and whisk to combine, then pour into a bowl and refrigerate.

2 When the cakes are done, place the pans on a cooling rack to sit for 5 minutes. Then remove the still-hot cakes from the pans, handling them carefully so as to not break the almonds. Using a cake tester or similar implement, gently pierce the top the cake (fifty times for the smaller cakes, one hundred times for the larger). Using a pastry brush, coat the tops of the cakes with the soaking syrup, distributing it evenly. Allow the cakes to cool completely on the cooling rack. Store the cakes, wrapped well, at room temperature for up to 3 days, or freeze for up to 1 month.

Honey Spice Bread

Pain d'épices au miel

Makes three 5-by-3-inch
loaves

Special tools: three 5-by-3-
inch loaf pans, pastry brush

For the cakes
½ cup (72 grams) white
buckwheat flour

1 cup (160 grams) Steve's
Gluten Free Cake Flour
(see pages 1 and 2)

1½ teaspoons (6 grams)
baking powder

1 tablespoon (3 grams)
ground ginger

2 teaspoons (4 grams)
ground cinnamon

¼ teaspoon ground nutmeg

¼ teaspoon ground allspice

¼ teaspoon ground cloves

½ teaspoon (4 grams) sea salt

¾ cup (170 grams) unsalted
butter, at room temperature

2 tablespoons (30 grams)
dark brown sugar

1 cup (300 grams) honey

⅔ cup (225 grams)
orange marmalade

(continued on page 176)

Traditionally made with rye flour, here I have substituted
a combination of white buckwheat flour and a gluten-free
flour blend. With its origins in Reims, *pain d'épices* is now
a specialty cake of the city of Dijon. Early versions of pain
d'épices were made by setting a thick paste of rye flour
and honey into a trough to ferment for months, and then
later adding spices, yolks, and milk before baking the stiff,
unleavened dough in loaf pans. The modern-day version
relies on baking soda or baking powder for leavening.
Pain d'épices au miel is sweetened with honey; the type
of honey you use will impart a large presence in the cake's
taste. I prefer a dark or buckwheat honey to marry with the
buckwheat flour used in the recipe.

Method
Make the cakes
1 Grease three nonstick loaf pans, then line the bottoms with
parchment paper.

2 Preheat the oven to 350°F (175°C).

3 Sift together the buckwheat flour, gluten-free flour, baking
powder, ginger, cinnamon, nutmeg, allspice, cloves, and salt
into a medium bowl.

4 Combine the butter and brown sugar in the bowl of a stand
mixer fitted with the paddle attachment. Beat on medium
speed for 1 minute, then turn off the mixer and add the honey
and orange marmalade. Resume beating on medium speed
until the ingredients are combined, about 2 minutes. Add the
eggs, one at a time, and mix until the eggs are incorporated.
Turn the mixer off, then scrape the sides and bottom of the
bowl with a silicone spatula. Beat the mixture on medium
speed for approximately 30 seconds more to combine.

2 extra-large eggs
(130 grams)

For the glaze
1 cup (100 grams)
confectioners' sugar, sifted

1 tablespoon (16 grams)
orange juice

2 teaspoons (12 grams) water,
plus more as needed

5 Turn the mixer off, then add the dry ingredients to the bowl. Beat on low speed until the batter is homogenous. Remove the bowl from the mixer and give the batter a final mixing by hand with a silicone spatula.

6 Scrape the batter into the loaf pans, filling them three-quarters full. Using a small offset spatula, level the surface of the batter. Place the loaf pans in the oven and bake for 20 to 30 minutes, until the tops have cracked open and are firm to the touch. Remove the cakes from the oven and set on a cooling rack to cool for 10 minutes. Leave the oven on. While the cakes are cooling, make the glaze.

Make the glaze and finish the cakes
1 In a small bowl, combine the confectioners' sugar, orange juice, and water, and whisk to combine. Slowly add additional water as needed to make it smooth and thick enough to be spread with a pastry brush but not so thin as to be runny.

2 To release the cakes from the loaf pans, run a small metal spatula along the inside edges of the pan. Flip the pan over, releasing the loaf into your hand, then set the loaf back onto a parchment paper–lined baking sheet. Brush the top of each loaf with the orange glaze. To avoid excess dripping down the sides, go slowly and paint the tops from the center outward to the edges. Put the cakes into the oven and bake for 5 minutes, or until the sugar crackles and sets. Watch the cakes carefully so the sugar does not burn. Remove the cakes from the oven and place on a cooling rack to cool completely. Store the cake wrapped in plastic at room temperature for up to 1 week or in the freezer for up to 1 month.

Spoon Gingerbread

Pain d'épices is a spice bread reminiscent of American-style gingerbread. Warm, homey, and down to earth, this spiced loaf cake can be enjoyed alongside the hearth year-round. Gingerbread was a staple in my home growing up, where I became smitten with this spicy, softly yielding cake. As children, we often ate gingerbread on Sunday evening after a long day romping in the fields of our grandparents' farm in rural Vermont. Sometimes we had gingerbread for lunch or as a grand snack, sliced and spread with peanut butter. For the most memorable gingerbread, split it while still warm, nestle it into your favorite bowl, top with a large dollop of softly whipped cream, and eat with a spoon.

French Apple Cake

Gâteau aux pommes Francaise

Makes 12 individual-size cakes or one 10-inch cake

Special tools: twelve 2-by-3½-inch entremet rings or one 10-inch springform pan

For the cake

Nonstick cooking spray

½ cup (85 grams) dark raisins

6 tablespoons (85 grams) dark rum

1 cup plus 1 tablespoon (170 grams) gluten-free flour blend (see pages 1 to 3)

1¼ teaspoons (6 grams) baking powder

¼ teaspoon (2 grams) sea salt

½ vanilla bean, split and scraped

¾ cup (170 grams) unsalted butter, melted and cooled

3 large eggs (165 grams)

1 cup plus 2 tablespoons (225 grams) granulated sugar

½ teaspoon (1 gram) lemon zest

6 Empire, Cortland, or other baking apples, peeled, cored and cut into ½-inch cubes

This exceptionally moist dessert exemplifies the simplicity of a French-style homemade cake. The contrast between the abundance of apples and minimal coating of batter is precisely what allows this cake to feature the apples of your choice or a mix of apple varieties. Macerating the raisins in rum will plump them, so they'll be ready to burst with their tangy juices as a complement to the softer notes of the apples. The mingling of dark rum, vanilla bean, and lemon add to this cake's full-bodied flavor profile. Dress this cake up by serving it with vanilla ice cream.

Method

Make the cake

1 Preheat the oven to 350°F (175°C).

2 Line a 12-by-17-inch baking sheet with a silicone mat or parchment paper and set aside. Spray the rings or pan with cooking spray. If using a springform pan, line it with a circle of parchment paper.

3 In a small bowl, combine the raisins with the rum and set aside to macerate.

4 Sift together the flour, baking powder, and salt into a medium bowl.

5 In a small saucepan, combine the vanilla bean seeds and pod with the butter and melt over medium-low heat. Set the butter mixture aside to cool, then remove the vanilla bean pod.

6 In the bowl of a stand mixer fitted with the whisk attachment, combine the eggs and sugar, then whip on medium-high speed for 2 minutes, or until the mixture thickens slightly and lightens in color. Add the lemon zest and whip for 30 seconds.

For the topping

1 egg (55 grams)

¼ cup (55 grams) plus 2 tablespoons (28 grams) granulated sugar, plus more as needed

3 tablespoons (40 grams) unsalted butter, melted and cooled

7 With the mixer running at low speed, slowly pour the melted butter mixture into the batter and whip for 1 minute, or until the butter is fully incorporated.

8 Add the rum and raisins, then continue to whip on low speed for 1 minute.

9 Add the flour mixture all at once and mix on low speed until it is well blended.

10 Add the chopped apples and mix on low speed for 1 minute. Using a silicone spatula, scrape down the sides and bottom of the bowl, then mix until the apples are coated with the batter. Remove the bowl from the mixer and use the silicone spatula to finish combining the batter by hand.

11 Using a large spoon, evenly distribute the batter into the pans. Using a small, flat metal spatula, smooth the tops even.

12 Place the cakes into the oven and bake for 15 minutes, or until the tops are light golden brown and just firm to the touch. While they are baking, prepare the topping.

Make the topping and finish the cakes

1 In a small bowl, whisk together the egg and ¼ cup (55 grams) of the sugar. Slowly pour in the melted butter and whisk briefly, about 15 seconds, until incorporated.

2 Remove the cakes from the oven and place them on a cooling rack. Using a large spoon, gently pour the topping evenly over each cake. It may run down the sides of the entremet rings; that is okay. Be sure to use all of the topping, then sprinkle the cakes with the remaining 2 tablespoons (28 grams) of sugar. Return the cakes to the oven and bake for an additional 5 to 10 minutes, until the topping has turned a deep golden brown and the sugar has formed a crackly crust.

3 Remove the baking sheet from the oven and place it on a cooling rack to cool for 20 minutes. To release the cakes, run a flat metal spatula or small paring knife around the inside edge of the rings or pan. Well wrapped, the apple cakes can be stored in the refrigerator for up to 3 days. Rewarm the cakes at 350°F (175°C) for 5 minutes to restore their crispy topping.

Basque Cake

Gâteau Basque

Makes one 9-inch cake

Special tool: one 9-by-1-inch round, straight-edged tart pan with a removable bottom

For the dough
1¾ cups (280 grams) Steve's Gluten Free Cake Flour (see pages 1 and 2), sifted

3 tablespoons (45 grams) granulated sugar

2 tablespoons (30 grams) light brown sugar

½ teaspoon (2 grams) baking powder

1 teaspoon (6 grams) sea salt

2 large egg yolks (45 grams)

6 tablespoons (90 grams) cold milk

1 cup plus 2 tablespoons (255 grams) cold unsalted butter, cut into small pieces

For the filling
3 cups (755 grams) Pastry Cream (pages 26 and 27)

1 teaspoon (5 grams) dark rum

(continued on page 183)

Similar in construction to a pie or tart, *Gâteau Basque* is a traditional dessert from the Basque region of France. The cake consists of a thick layer of pastry cream encased by a sweet pastry crust. The pastry cream is made aromatic with vanilla bean, rum, and almond extract, and then it's studded with cherries. Typically, the top of the dough is scored with a crosshatch pattern before baking and given an egg wash that results in a shiny top design. The cake can also be made with other types of fresh berries or a thin layer of jam across the bottom before adding the pastry cream.

Method

Make the dough

1 In a food processor fitted with a blade, combine the flour, granulated sugar, brown sugar, baking powder and salt and pulse briefly to incorporate.

2 In a small bowl, whisk together the egg yolks and milk and set aside.

3 Add the butter to the flour mixture and pulse until the butter breaks down to ¼-inch particles that remain visible in the dough.

4 Gradually pour in the milk and egg mixture and pulse just until the mixture begins to clump but with dry particles still remaining. Remove the bowl from the processor and dump the mixture onto a work surface. Using the heel of your hand, begin to spread the dough across the work surface, incorporating the remaining loose flour and butter. Continue until the dough is cohesive—there should be no loose particles, and you should be able to see bits and streaks of butter in the finished dough. If necessary, add small amounts

¼ teaspoon (2 grams)
pure almond extract

24 wild or black cherries
(see Sources, pages 14 and 15),
pitted

For glazing
1 drop of coffee extract
(optional)

Egg Wash (page 19)

(1 teaspoon at a time) of cold water to incorporate the final
loose particles into the dough.

5 Divide the dough into two equal portions and form
them into flat, round discs. Wrap them in plastic wrap and
refrigerate for 1 hour. The dough will keep refrigerated for up
to 3 days or frozen for up to 1 month.

6 When you are ready to use the dough, remove it from
the refrigerator and allow it to sit at room temperature for
5 minutes, or until it is pliable enough to work with but not too
soft. If at any point the dough becomes too soft, refrigerate it
for 10 minutes, then resume working. When handling, you may
need to press the dough back together, as it may develop
small cracks. Use minimal amounts of flour when rolling the
dough out, and always brush excess flour clear from the front
and back of the dough before final application.

Assemble the cake
1 Between two pieces of plastic wrap, roll the first pastry
round into a 12-inch circle that's ⅛ inch thick. Brush any excess
flour from both sides of the pastry. Gently lift the pastry and
set it into the round pan. Pull the sides of the pastry inward,
toward the inside edge of the pan, to help settle it snugly
into the bottom edge. Using your fingers, secure the pastry
straight and firm against the inside edges of the pan. Gently
press the dough into place, then trim off any excess pastry
by running a rolling pin across the top of the pan. Place the
lined tart pan onto a parchment paper–lined baking sheet,
cover it with plastic wrap, and refrigerate for 1 hour. Roll the
top crust between two pieces of plastic wrap into an 11-inch
circle that's ⅛ inch thick. Using the tines of a fork, lightly score
a crosshatch pattern into the top of the crust. Slide the crust
onto a baking sheet and refrigerate for 30 minutes.

2 Preheat the oven to 350°F (175°C).

3 Remove both the tart shell and the separate top from the refrigerator. In the bowl of a stand mixer fitted with the whisk attachment, whip together the pastry cream, rum, and almond extract. Spoon the pastry cream into the lined tart shell, then use a metal spatula to smooth the surface to ⅛ inch below the top of the pan. Stud the pastry cream with the cherries by pushing them down into the top of the pastry cream. Use the metal spatula to spread a bit more pastry cream over the top of the cherries so they are barely visible. Wet your finger with a little water, then dab it along the top edge of the pastry dough. Carefully slide the top scored layer of dough over the tart pan, then gently press the edge to secure it to the rim. Use a sharp paring knife to cut away the excess dough from the rim. Then, with the tip of the knife, create a small ⅛-inch hole in the center of the cake to allow steam to escape.

4 If using the coffee extract, add it to the egg wash. With a pastry brush, lightly coat the top crust with the egg wash.

5 Place in the oven and bake for 45 to 55 minutes, until the cake is golden brown. Remove from the oven and set the cake on a cooling rack to cool completely. To unmold, push the removable bottom upward and slide the cake onto a serving plate. Store the cake wrapped in plastic in the refrigerator for up to 3 days.

Petit Savarin Chantilly

Petit savarin Chantilly

Makes 16

Special tools: two 2½-by-2½-by-1-inch round or square silicone savarin molds or other molds, pastry bag fitted with a ½-inch open tip, pastry bag fitted with a large star tip, pastry brush

For the cakes

Nonstick cooking spray

1¾ teaspoons (5.5 grams) instant yeast

⅓ cup (80 grams) warm milk (110°F/43°C)

3 tablespoons (45 grams) granulated sugar

4 large eggs (220 grams)

1 cup plus 2 tablespoons (180 grams) Steve's Gluten Free Cake Flour (see pages 1 and 2)

¼ teaspoon (2 grams) sea salt

6 tablespoons (90 grams) unsalted butter, at room temperature, cut into pieces

(continued on page 187)

This yeasted, ring-shaped cake is named in honor of Brillat Savarin, a politician and gourmand who is said to have developed the secret of the soaking syrup. Savarin is cousin to a similar pastry, baba au rhum, traditionally made with raisins and baked in a tall mold. Beginning as a not-so-sweet cake, Savarin is engorged by a soak in rum syrup, then topped high with Chantilly cream and garnished with fresh fruit. You'll find this Savarin recipe swollen with a gingered lemon and rum syrup, then swirled with vanilla bean cream and elevated with fresh juicy peaches. As an eating experience, Savarin is undeniably moist, even wet, as that is the essence of this easy yet elaborate pastry.

Method

Make the cakes

1 Lightly coat the savarin molds with cooking spray and place them on a baking sheet.

2 Whisk together the yeast, milk, and 1 tablespoon (15 grams) of the sugar in the bowl of a stand mixer fitted with the paddle attachment. Once the yeast dissolves, turn the mixer to medium-low speed and beat in the eggs, one at a time, until well blended, about 1 minute. Add the remaining 2 tablespoons (30 grams) sugar, the flour, and salt and beat at medium speed until the mixtures come together to form a soft mass, about 2 minutes. Scrape the sides and bottom of the bowl with a silicone spatula as necessary.

3 Increase the mixer speed to medium-high and beat for 1 minute.

4 Begin adding the small pieces of soft butter, one at a time, allowing each piece to incorporate before adding the next one. The dough's texture will be like a creamy batter. If the

For the syrup

1½ cups (345 grams) water

1 cup (200 grams) granulated sugar

1 tablespoon (10 grams) grated fresh ginger

¼ cup (64 grams) dark rum

1 tablespoon (18 grams) lemon juice

For finishing

½ cup (150 grams) Apricot Glaze (page 20), melted

1½ cups (337 grams) heavy cream

½ teaspoon (1 gram) granulated sugar

½ vanilla bean, split and scraped

3 fresh peaches, skinned and thinly sliced (optional)

½ cup (120 grams) finely chopped candied ginger

batter breaks, replace the paddle with the whisk attachment and whip at medium-high speed until the batter comes together.

5 Fit a pastry bag with the ½-inch open tip and fill it two-thirds full of batter, then squeeze the batter into the savarin molds until they are half full. Set the molds aside to rise for 45 to 60 minutes, until they double in volume and reach the top of the mold but are not above the top.

6 Preheat the oven to 350°F (175°C).

7 Place the baking sheet with the molds into the oven and bake the cakes for 12 to 15 minutes, until the tops (which will become the bottoms) are golden brown. Remove the sheet from the oven and place the molds on a cooling rack. Using a kitchen towel, gently but firmly grab the sides of the silicone mold and flip it upside down to release the cakes onto the rack. Allow the cakes to cool completely before finishing. The cakes can sit, well wrapped, overnight before finishing.

Make the syrup

1 Combine the water, sugar, and fresh ginger in a small saucepan and bring to a boil over medium-high heat. Remove from the heat and allow the mixture to infuse for 20 minutes. Bring the liquid to a boil again, then immediately strain the liquid through a fine-mesh sieve into a shallow bowl. Add the rum and lemon juice and stir to combine.

2 Dip each savarin cake into the hot syrup: submerge the cake briefly, then remove with a flat slotted spatula or spoon. You want each cake to be well soaked. Set the cakes on a cooling rack set over a baking sheet to drip and allow the cakes to cool.

To finish

1 Use a small pastry brush to gently apply a light coating of the melted apricot glaze to the sides and top of each savarin.

2 Fit a medium pastry bag with a large star tip. Place the heavy cream into the bowl of a stand mixer fitted with the whisk attachment. Whip the cream at high speed until it barely begins to form soft peaks. Add the sugar and vanilla bean seeds, then whip until the cream begins to hold medium peaks. Do not overwhip, otherwise it will become grainy. Fill the pastry bag with the whipped cream and pipe a tall rosette into the center of each cake. Top with fresh peach slices, if using, then sprinkle the cakes with the candied ginger. Drizzle extra syrup around each plate and serve immediately.

Soft Chocolate Cake

Moelleux au chocolat

Makes one 9-inch cake

Special tool: one 9-inch round cake pan

Nonstick cooking spray

½ cup plus 2½ tablespoons (155 grams) unsalted butter, at room temperature

5 ounces (150 grams) dark chocolate, chopped

¼ cup (32 grams) gluten-free flour blend (see pages 1 to 3)

1 tablespoon (7 grams) cocoa powder

⅛ teaspoon (1 gram) sea salt

5 large egg yolks (110 grams), at room temperature

¾ cup (150 grams) granulated sugar

8 large egg whites (265 grams) at room temperature

¾ cup (195 grams) Dark Chocolate Ganache (page 36), melted

Deep, mellow, and tender, this revisit of a classic is finished with a thick swirl of dark chocolate ganache. The cake's sheer chocolate notes and yielding consistency indulge the shyest of palates and is a triumph for chocolate purists. When baked, the cake puffs high, and as it cools it will fall and settle in the center. Ultimately, the top reveals a striking, shiny, thatch-like appearance amid the swirl design. Warm up this cake before serving and the ganache will soften and intensify the experience. The cake can be dressed up with a big dollop of Chantilly cream and fresh berries.

Method

1 Spray the cake pan with cooking spray, then line it with a circle of parchment paper.

2 In a heatproof bowl, combine the butter and dark chocolate and place over a bain-marie (see page 9). Use a silicone spatula to stir occasionally, until the mixture is melted and homogenous, then set it aside in a place where it will remain warm.

3 While the butter and chocolate are melting, sift the flour, cocoa powder, and salt into a small bowl and set aside.

4 Preheat the oven to 350°F (175°C).

5 In a large heatproof bowl, whip together the egg yolks and half of the sugar. Place the bowl over the bain-marie and whip until the mixture thickens. Remove the bowl from the heat and use a silicone spatula to scrape the sides and bottom of the bowl, then set it aside.

6 Pour the egg whites into the bowl of a stand mixer fitted with the whisk attachment. Turn the mixer to medium speed

and whip until the whites become frothy and begin to foam. Increase the mixer speed to high, then add the remaining sugar in a slow, steady stream, whipping until the whites hold firm peaks. Set the bowl aside.

7 Using a silicone spatula, fold one-third of the yolk mixture into the warm (not hot) melted chocolate and butter mixture. Add the remaining yolk mixture and gently combine the ingredients until incorporated.

8 Add one-third of the whipped egg whites to the chocolate mixture and gently fold them in. Sift the dry ingredients into the chocolate mixture, then fold until the flour is just incorporated. Add the remaining egg whites and fold them in gently until the batter is smooth and homogenous.

9 Pour the batter into the cake pan and use a small offset spatula to gently smooth the top level. Pour the melted ganache in a spiral on top of the cake batter. With a table knife, cut 1 inch deep into the cake and quickly marble a design into the batter, being careful not to touch the bottom of the pan.

10 Bake 25 to 30 minutes, until the edges are set and the center puffs up and is set but still soft. Remove the cake from the oven and cool on a cooling rack for 30 minutes before removing the cake from the pan. Store the cake, wrapped in plastic, in the refrigerator for up to 3 days. Allow the cake to sit out at room temperature for 2 hours or warm it slightly before eating.

Chocolate Almond Cake

Gâteau chocolat amandes

Makes one 9-inch cake

Special tool: 9-inch springform pan

Nonstick cooking spray

1 cup plus 2 tablespoons (255 grams) unsalted butter, at room temperature

12 ounces (340 grams) pure almond paste

1⅓ cups (265 grams) granulated sugar

¾ cup (85 grams) unsweetened Dutch-processed cocoa

¼ teaspoon (2 grams) sea salt

6 large eggs (330 grams)

1 teaspoon (5 grams) pure vanilla extract

Confectioners' sugar

Pure almond paste takes center stage in this rustic yet elegant cake that has a boldly intense almond flavor with a seductively moist consistency. The recipe is near foolproof—it's easy to prepare and needs only a simple, stunning visual finish to whet your appetite and please the palates of anyone you serve it to. Be certain to use pure almond paste rather than macaroon paste or marzipan (see sidebar). Consider adding another flavor element to the cake by tossing a cup of fresh raspberries into the batter. You can also experiment by making the cake in individual molds or as a sheet cake, cut into shapes and layered—the recipe can successfully scale up times two. Serve the cake plain or with berries and cream.

Method

1 Preheat the oven to 350°F (175°C).

2 Lightly coat the springform pan with cooking spray, then place a circle of parchment paper in the bottom.

3 Combine the butter and almond paste in the bowl of a stand mixer fitted with the paddle attachment. Beat at medium-low speed until the ingredients begin to soften and combine, about 3 minutes. Increase the mixer speed to high, then beat until the mixture lightens in color and increases slightly in volume. There may be a few small bits of almond paste visible; this is okay.

4 While the butter and almond paste are mixing, sift the sugar, cocoa powder, and salt into a medium bowl. Once the butter and almond paste have reached the desired consistency, reduce the mixer speed to low, then add the cocoa mixture in three additions. Beat on low speed until the batter is uniform in color and texture. Increase the mixer speed to medium and beat for 30 seconds, then scrape the sides and bottom of the bowl with a silicone spatula.

5 Turn the mixer to medium speed again and add the eggs, one at a time, beating for about 30 seconds after each addition, allowing each egg to incorporate before adding the next one. Once all the eggs are incorporated, add the vanilla and mix for 30 seconds. Turn the mixer off and use a silicone spatula to scrape the sides and bottom of the bowl. Return the mixer to medium-high speed and beat for 1 minute to ensure a homogeneous batter.

6 Scrape the batter into the springform pan and use a small offset metal spatula to distribute and smooth the batter evenly in the pan.

7 Place the springform pan in the oven and bake for 45 minutes, or until the cake jiggles slightly and reveals small cracks in the center. Remove the cake from the oven and place on a cooling rack to cool for 1 hour, then remove it from the springform pan and allow to sit until completely cooled. Serve at room temperature, or cover in plastic wrap and refrigerate for up to 2 weeks. The cake may also be wrapped well and frozen for up to 1 month.

8 To serve the cake, bring the cake to room temperature if necessary and sprinkle with a light dusting of confectioners' sugar. For a fancier finish, use a template of your choosing: lay a design template or a piece of lace on top of the cake and dust with confectioners' sugar. Remove the template, and voilà!

Almond Paste and Its Cousins

Almond paste, marzipan, macaroon paste, and almond extract are related, yet each is unique in its flavor, texture, and usage. Almond paste holds the highest percentage of almonds to sugar, making it a high-quality baking ingredient known for its intense almond flavor. Marzipan is a sweeter, drier version of almond paste and is used as modeling dough to create unbaked, edible sculptural pieces. Macaroon paste is a less flavorful product, made with a smaller percentage of almonds, but it can still be substituted for almond paste. Almond extract in its pure form can be added to dough and batter to emulate the flavor of pure almond paste, but with less depth of flavor and a candy-like scent. Look for these almond products in the baking section of supermarkets or online (see Sources, pages 14 and 15).

Mocha Buttercream Cake

Gâteau moka

Makes one 9-inch cake

Special tools: two 9-inch round cake pans, pastry brush, pastry bag fitted with a medium star tip

1 recipe Italian Meringue Buttercream (pages 32 and 33) or French Buttercream (pages 34 and 35), softened

1 tablespoon plus 2 teaspoons (35 grams) coffee extract such as Trablit, plus more if you like

¼ cup Dark Chocolate Ganache (page 36) or plain dark chocolate, melted

½ cup (145 grams) Simple Syrup (page 20)

1 tablespoon (16 grams) dark rum (optional)

1 recipe Génoise (pages 45 and 46)

⅔ cup Dark Chocolate Ganache (page 36), softened to room temperature

1 cup (140 grams) toasted almonds, finely chopped

Chocolate-covered coffee beans

Génoise is a wonderfully versatile cake, and here it is a welcome foundation for the deep flavors of coffee, set off with chocolate, and tinged with rum. Slice the tender génoise cake layers carefully by sawing back and forth rather than trying to force the knife. Making a crumb coat is a helpful step to ensure the finished cake appears creamy and smooth against the striking cross section of chocolate and coffee layers.

Method

1 In a large bowl, combine the buttercream, 1 tablespoon (21 grams) of the coffee extract, and the melted chocolate ganache. Whisk together briefly, until smooth and well blended. Taste for flavor and add more coffee extract if you like.

2 Combine the simple syrup, the remaining 2 teaspoons (14 grams) of coffee extract, and rum in a small bowl.

3 Using a long serrated knife, slice the baked génoise into three layers. Save the flat bottom layer for the top. First you will make a crumb coat on the cake, which will allow for a final thin application of buttercream that results in a visually clean cake. Set the first (the top from the cake you just sliced) cake layer onto a board, then brush one-third of the simple syrup mixture evenly over the top of the cake. Spoon approximately 1 cup (180 grams) of buttercream onto the center of the cake and use a metal spatula to spread the buttercream level across the top, reaching to the edges. Then spread a thin, even layer of the softened chocolate ganache over the buttercream.

4 Add the second layer of cake and repeat the above steps.

5 Top with the third cake layer, brush with the remaining simple syrup mixture, and spread ½ cup (90 grams) of buttercream over the top, pushing outward from the center to cover the top completely. Smooth the sides with buttercream, using extra from the bowl if needed and scraping off any excess. When the cake is smooth and uniform in shape, place it into the refrigerator to chill for 1 hour.

6 Remove the cake from the refrigerator and spoon about 1 cup (180 grams) buttercream onto the top of the cake. Using a metal spatula, spread the buttercream over the top and onto the sides of the cake, smoothing it flat and consistent. If the buttercream chills on the cake, it may become difficult to handle. You can warm your spatula by running it under hot water, wiping it clean, and quickly applying it to the areas that need attention.

7 To finish the cake, coat the sides with the toasted almonds, then fill the pastry bag with ½ cup (90 grams) buttercream and pipe a decorative shell border around the top edge. Stud the juncture of each shell with a chocolate-covered coffee bean.

8 When you are ready to serve the cake, allow it to sit out at room temperature for 2 to 3 hours. This provides adequate time for the buttercream to soften and become creamy again before eating. The cake may be stored in a plastic container in the refrigerator for up to 1 week.

Lemon Mousse Cake

Gâteau mousse au citron

Makes one 8-inch dome

Special tools: 12-by-17-inch baking pan, dome mold(s), pastry brush, pastry bag fitted with a large serrated swag tip, pastry bag fitted with a medium open tip, culinary torch

For the cake

1 recipe Génoise (pages 45 and 46), baked in a 12-by-17-inch baking pan and cooled

6 tablespoons (110 grams) Simple Syrup (page 20)

1 teaspoon (5 grams) pure vanilla extract

1 tablespoon (16 grams) dark rum

1 tablespoon (18 grams) lemon juice

3 cups (690 grams) heavy cream

2 cups (400 grams) Lemon Cream (pages 30 and 31)

½ cup (90 grams) fresh blueberries

(continued on page 200)

Luscious and enchanting, the dramatic appearance and creamy layers of this fruity dome hold court for your guests. The meringue swag draws you in, and the multiple components create a dreamy explosion of melding flavors—citrusy, soft, and sensual. Visually inspired by a Pierre Hermé photo, this recipe can also be made as individual cakes by using smaller round molds. The cake is versatile: choose a different type of fresh fruit for inside the cake or swap out the lemon mousse and syrup for Honey Chocolate Mousse (page 39) and straight rum syrup for a chocolate sensation.

2 tablespoons (35 grams) Apricot Glaze (page 20), melted

Method

Assemble the cake

1 Choose a mold to work with: it can be a large metal bowl that has a flat bottom section or is fully rounded. Later, when you release the cake, you will be flipping the bowl upside down, so the rounded bottom will be inverted to become the top. If the bowl top will be flat, cut a thin, round piece of cardstock to set in the bottom before adding the mousse.

2 Cut out one 8-inch circle and one 3-inch circle from the génoise; cover both with plastic wrap and set aside.

3 In a small bowl, whisk together the simple syrup, vanilla extract, rum, and lemon juice and set aside.

4 In a stand mixer fitted with the whisk attachment, whip the heavy cream until soft peaks just begin to form. Add 1¼ cups (250 grams) of the lemon cream and finish whipping by hand. Be careful to not overwhip, as it will make the mousse grainy.

5 Spoon about 1½ cups (325 grams) of the mousse into the mold and smooth it with an offset metal spatula. Set the

To finish

1 recipe Italian Meringue
(pages 32 and 33)

½ cup (90 grams)
fresh blueberries

1 fresh peach, thinly sliced

3-inch circle of génoise on top. Use a pastry brush and lightly soak the top of the cake with the lemon-rum sugar syrup. Spread ¾ cup (150 grams) of lemon cream on top of the cake, then add enough mousse to reach within 2 inches of the open end of the bowl. Smooth the surface level with an offset metal spatula, then press the fresh blueberries into the mousse until you can barely see them. Smooth the top over with extra mousse. Set the 8-inch circle of génoise on top of the mousse and settle it firmly in place by pressing down gently with your hand. Brush the cake with the remaining lemon-rum sugar syrup. Cover the cake with plastic wrap and freeze it for at least 3 hours or overnight before finishing.

6 Release the frozen cake by wrapping the sides of the bowl in a moist, hot towel or blasting with a blow-dryer on high heat. As the sides warm up, the cake will begin to loosen and slide around. When ready, set a cake plate on top of the open end of the bowl and turn it over so the cake releases onto the plate. Place the cake in the freezer while you make the Italian meringue.

Finish the cake

1 Fit a pastry bag with a large serrated swag tip and fill it two-thirds full with the meringue. Pipe long, curved swags from the bottom of the cake upward to the top. Continue in a circle until you have completely decorated the sides of the cake. Using the pastry bag fitted with the open tip, pipe beads of meringue in a circle at the top of the swag, making an enclosure to hold the blueberries and peach slices.

2 Use a culinary torch to brown the meringue, then decorate the top with the fresh blueberries and peach slices. Brush the fruit with the apricot glaze and serve immediately.

Chocolate Strawberry Mousse Cake

Gâteau mousse aux fraises et chocolat

Makes one 8-inch cake

Special tools: 9-inch cake pan, 8-by-2¼ inch metal ring mold

1 recipe Soft Chocolate Cake (pages 189 to 191), minus the ganache swirl, baked in a 9-inch cake pan and cooled

2 tablespoons (32 grams) Simple Syrup (page 20)

1 teaspoon (5 grams) pure vanilla extract

1 tablespoon (16 grams) Amaretto (optional)

2 cups (340 grams) fresh strawberries, plus more for topping if you like

1 recipe Honey Chocolate Mousse (page 39)

½- to 1-pound (225- to 445-gram) chunk of chocolate for curls or fans for decorating (optional; see pages 62 and 63 for tempering)

In France, rich creams and mousses are a welcome component in pastries, including this layered mousse cake. This sumptuous cake requires a few steps, but is surprisingly easy to turn out. The base is a soft chocolate cake brushed with an optional Amaretto syrup, which sets the stage to build upon. Next, the Honey Chocolate Mousse shares the scene with fresh sweet strawberries, and the cake is finished with chocolate shavings, curls, or fans. Another option is to increase the fruity pleasure by topping the cake with plain or chocolate-dipped whole fresh strawberries.

Method

1 After you release the Soft Chocolate Cake from the pan, slice it in half horizontally, then wrap one half in freezer wrap and freeze for a later use. Set the remaining half aside.

2 Set the ring mold onto a cardboard circle or other finishing surface that will fit into the freezer. Set the chocolate cake into the bottom of the ring mold. If the cake is a little big, use the ring mold as a cutter; set the ring mold on top of the cake and bear down, effectively cutting the precise size to fit snug into the bottom of the ring.

3 In a small bowl, mix together the simple syrup, vanilla extract, and Amaretto. Using a pastry brush, lightly soak the top of the cake with the syrup.

4 Rinse, and gently pat dry the strawberries with paper towels. Hull the strawberries and slice them approximately ¼ inch thick. Line the inside edge of the ring mold with uniformly shaped and sized strawberries with the pointed ends up; these will be showcased when the mold is removed. You may need to gently press the strawberries against the side of the mold to help them adhere.

5 Spoon the mousse into the ring mold, then use a metal spatula to smooth the mousse level to about ¼ inch from the top. Pay attention to spreading the mousse adequately to the edges—this will help secure the strawberries against the inner wall of the ring mold. Add the remaining strawberry slices by pressing them down into the chocolate mousse. Add a bit more chocolate mousse on top, then use a metal spatula to gently but firmly set the mousse into place. Scrape the mousse level across the mold, removing any excess. The result should be a smooth, flat surface. Chill the cake in the refrigerator for 2 to 3 hours or overnight.

6 Allow the chunk of dark chocolate to sit out at room temperature. Set a piece of parchment paper onto a baking sheet. Using a vegetable peeler, scrape against the chocolate chunk to create curls, letting them drop onto the parchment as you are peeling. The chocolate will begin to warm in your hand; when this happens, flip the chunk over and continue to run the blade over the chocolate, adding to a growing pile of shavings, which will vary from dry to smooth, changing as the temperature of the chocolate yields differently beneath the blade. Alternately, temper the chocolate and set your hand to making large curls or fans.

7 To unmold the cake, wrap a moist, hot towel around the edge of the metal ring or use a blow-dryer to heat the sides of the metal ring. After a few minutes, the ring will loosen. Pull the ring up off the cake in one continuous motion.

8 Decorate the cake with chocolate decorations and strawberries if you like. Serve the cake immediately, or store in a plastic container in the refrigerator for up to 1 day.

CHAPTER SIX

Meringues

Meringues

Les meringues

Meringues play an immeasurable function in pastry making. Among their many roles, they are used to lighten mousse and leaven cakes, and they make their way into various toppings for desserts where they are torched, revealing their three-dimensional characteristics. After developing their structure, meringues can be flavored with nuts, chocolate, or spices, but no fats, because fats will deflate the meringue. Always make sure your mixing bowl and whisk are perfectly free of any fat deposits before beginning your meringue production, and work quickly so the meringue doesn't lose its necessary volume and strength to perform its purpose.

This chapter highlights flourless pastries that use meringue as the primary ingredient. We begin with macarons, the darling confections that have become hugely popular in recent years. A master macaron recipe acts as a backdrop for a selection of fillings, from pistachio to classic chocolate.

From the charming macaron we move to the Giant Meringue, a truly mountainous sculpture with a sharply contrasting crunchy exterior and soft marshmallow interior. Another type of meringue is the sublime Dacquoise: nut meringues piped in spirals, baked, filled, and cured for a sensational eating experience. The Concorde, a historical pastry feat performed by a famous French pastry chef, is a wonder that you can create in your home kitchen, and the Chocolate Strawberry Meringues conclude the chapter on a delightfully playful note.

Macaron Minutiae

Eating a good macaron is a memorable experience: upon biting into the cookie there is first the luscious collapse of the shell, followed by the sensual expansion of the filling as it melts in your mouth. Possible flavor combinations are endless: think of your macaron as a canvas onto which you can mix and match your choice of colors and flavors, or create your own palette with any number of natural food colorings, nuts, flavorings, compounds, herbs, spices, teas, and powders for a truly personalized macaron experience.

Making macarons is a perfect reason to acquire a baking scale, joining the growing number of Americans who are practicing precision and enjoying the positive results of baking by weight. I cannot emphasize this enough! Weighing your ingredients can be the determining factor in whether or not you turn out successful macarons.

Ovens vary in temperature. Macarons with added food coloring are vulnerable to discoloration if the oven temperature is too high. If the macarons are starting to brown, adjust the oven temperature down to reach your desired outcome.

Use aged egg whites if possible. As egg whites age, they become more fluid, which enables you to whip them to the correct consistency without becoming grainy. To age egg whites, separate the whites from the yolks and save the yolks for another recipe. Place the egg whites in a bowl and cover the bowl with plastic wrap. Pierce the wrap with a sharp knife and refrigerate for 2 to 4 days. Allow the whites to come to room temperature before beginning your recipe.

Use silicone baking mats if you have them; the macarons will release easier from silicone mats than from parchment paper.

Be generous with the filling—this is where your macarons deliver the biggest hit of flavor.

To make the macarons more decorative and flavorful or to add texture, try sprinkling the top shells with cacao nibs, a light dusting of cocoa powder, finely chopped almonds, colored sugars, or another garnish of your choice. Add the garnish after you have piped the shells, before setting them aside to dry.

Pistachio Macarons

Macarons à la pistache

Makes 70 macarons

Special tools: pastry bag fitted with a ½-inch plain pastry tip, candy thermometer, pastry brush, template

For the shells

1 recipe French Macarons (pages 40 to 42)

¼ teaspoon (1 gram) liquid green food coloring

¼ teaspoon (1 gram) liquid yellow food coloring

1 cup (120 grams) finely chopped pistachios

For the filling

1¼ cups (225 grams) Italian Meringue Buttercream (pages 32 and 33), softened

¼ cup (60 grams) pure pistachio paste, softened

¾ cup (90 grams) Pistachio Ganache (page 38)

These pastel colored macarons feature notable pistachio flavor heightened by the small addition of almond extract in the creamy filling. Sprinkle the tops of the shells with chopped pistachio nuts, and their distinctly green and rose hues will add visual appeal. Keep a close watch and adjust your oven temperature down if the macarons begin to brown.

Method

1 Prepare the French Macaron recipe, adding the food colorings during step 4. After the macarons have been piped, sprinkle them lightly with the chopped pistachios before they are set aside to dry. Continue as directed until the macarons are ready for assembly.

2 To assemble, sort the macaron shells, arranging them into compatible sizes. Turn half of the shells over, revealing the flat side, where you will pipe the filling.

3 In a medium bowl, combine the buttercream, pistachio paste, and pistachio ganache and whisk until the ingredients are smooth and creamy.

4 Fit a pastry bag with a ½-inch tip and fill the bag two-thirds full with pistachio filling. Pipe a generous amount of filling onto each turned-up shell, then top with the remaining shells and lightly press down to sandwich the two shells together, forming a macaron.

5 Place the macarons in an airtight container and refrigerate for 24 hours to "cure," then allow the macarons to sit out at room temperature for 1 hour before eating.

Lemon Macarons

Macarons au citron

Makes 70 macarons

Special tools: pastry bag fitted with a ½-inch plain pastry tip, pastry bag fitted with a ¼-inch open tip, candy thermometer, pastry brush, template

For the lemon sparkle sugar
½ cup (300 grams) sparkling sugar

1 drop liquid yellow food coloring

For the macarons
1 recipe French Macarons (pages 40 to 42)

¼ teaspoon (1 gram) liquid yellow food coloring

For the filling
2 cups (360 grams) Italian Meringue Buttercream (pages 32 and 33), softened

1 cup (200 grams) Lemon Cream (pages 30 and 31), at room temperature

These light yellow macarons have a surprise pizazz of lemon in the center, ensuring their citrusy notes are sung soprano. Although macarons are traditionally sandwiched and cured overnight, another way to eat them, in dainty fashion, is to dip the single shells in lemon cream just before taking a bite.

Method

1 In a small bowl, combine the sparkle sugar with the yellow food coloring, then mix together with your hands (you may want to use rubber gloves for this part) until the sugar is uniform in color. Set aside to dry.

2 Prepare the French Macaron recipe, adding the food coloring during step 4. After the macarons have been piped, sprinkle them lightly with the colored sugar before they are set aside to dry. Continue as directed until the macarons are ready for assembly.

3 To assemble, sort the macaron shells, arranging them into compatible sizes. Turn half of the shells over, revealing their flat side up, where you will pipe the filling.

4 In a medium bowl, combine the buttercream and half of the lemon cream. Whisk until the ingredients are smooth and creamy. Fit a pastry bag with a ½-inch tip and fill it two-thirds full with the lemon buttercream filling. Pipe a generous amount of filling onto the upturned shells. Fill the pastry bag fitted with the ¼-inch open tip with the lemon cream. Pipe a small dollop on the center of each buttercream mound. Place the remaining shells on top, then lightly press down to sandwich the two shells together.

5 Place the macarons in an airtight container and refrigerate for 24 hours to "cure," then allow the macarons to sit out at room temperature for 1 hour before eating.

Coffee Macarons

Macarons au café

Makes 70 macarons

Special tools: pastry bag fitted with a ½-inch plain pastry tip, pastry bag fitted with a ¼-inch open tip, candy thermometer, pastry brush, template

For the macarons
1 recipe French Macarons (pages 40 to 42)

¼ teaspoon (1 gram) liquid brown food coloring

2 teaspoons (14 grams) coffee extract such as Trablit

For the filling
2 cups (360 grams) Italian Meringue Buttercream (pages 32 and 33), softened

2 teaspoons (14 grams) coffee extract, such as Trablit

Brimming with coffee flavor, these macarons are a decadent little confectionary pick-me-up. Using top-quality coffee extract will go a long way toward developing a truly great cup-of-coffee-flavor experience. Feel free to adjust the amount of extract, adding a bit more if you like your coffee strong. You can sprinkle these macarons with finely chopped almonds or a light dusting of cocoa powder or leave them plain. To double up on your afternoon inspiration, enjoy a macaron or two alongside a cup of coffee.

Method

1 Prepare the French Macaron recipe, adding the food coloring and coffee extract during step 4. Continue as directed until the macarons are ready for assembly.

2 To assemble, sort the macaron shells, arranging them into compatible sizes. Turn half of the shells over, revealing their flat side up, where you will pipe the filling.

3 In a medium bowl, combine the meringue buttercream and coffee extract. Whisk until the ingredients are smooth and creamy. Fill the pastry bag fitted with the ½-inch tip two-thirds full with the coffee buttercream filling. Pipe a generous amount of filling onto all of the upturned shells. Place the remaining shells on top, then lightly press down to sandwich the two shells together, forming a macaron.

4 Place the macarons in an airtight container and refrigerate for 24 hours to "cure," then allow the macarons to sit out at room temperature for 1 hour before eating.

Chocolate Chai Macarons

Macarons au chocolat et épices chaï

Makes about 50 shells,
enough for 25 macarons

Special tool: pastry bag fitted
with a ½-inch open pastry tip

1 recipe Chocolate Macarons
(pages 43 and 44)

2 tablespoons (14 grams)
cocoa powder or ½ cup
(75 grams) cocoa nibs
(optional)

1 recipe Chocolate Chai
Ganache (page 37), chilled,
then softened to room
temperature

The blending of chocolate with spice travels back to the when the Mayans would grind chiles into their chocolate and drink it unsweetened as a health tonic. Over time, chocolate made its way north, with the addition of sugar turning chocolate into a luxury item. Chai spice adds an infusion of mysterious depth to the rich chocolate ganache, and when sandwiched between ethereal macaron shells it delivers a descent into sheer deliciousness. The ganache itself can also be spread between layers of Hazelnut Dacquoise (pages 221 to 223), or you can eat it in its pure form as little chocolate-spiced truffles! My inspiration for this macaron came from my dear friend Neil Harley, who owns the company Chai Wallah and makes the best chai spice mix I've had (see Sources, pages 14 and 15).

Method

1 Prepare the Chocolate Macaron recipe as instructed. After the macarons have been piped, sift the tops with a very light dusting of cocoa powder or sprinkle them with cocoa nibs before they are set aside to dry. Continue as directed until the macarons are ready for assembly.

2 To assemble, sort the macaron shells, arranging them into matching sizes. Turn half of the shells over, revealing their flat side up, where you will pipe the filling.

3 In a medium bowl, whisk the chocolate chai ganache until it is smooth and creamy. Fit a pastry bag with a ½-inch tip, then fill the bag two-thirds full with ganache. Pipe a generous amount of filling onto each turned-up shell, then place the remaining shells on top and lightly press down to sandwich the shells together.

4 Place the macarons in an airtight container and refrigerate for 24 hours to "cure" before eating. Allow the macarons to sit out at room temperature for 1 hour before eating.

Chocolate Raspberry Macarons

Macarons aux framboises et chocolat

Makes about 50 shells, enough for 25 macarons, or 144 shells, enough for 72 macarons

---

Special tool: pastry bag fitted with a ½-inch plain pastry tip

1 recipe Chocolate Macarons (pages 43 and 44) or French Macarons (pages 40 to 42)

Unsweetened cocoa powder for dusting

1 recipe Dark Chocolate Ganache (page 36)

75 fresh raspberries

Chocolate and raspberry are matched for a moment of heaven on earth. Fresh raspberries burst into creamy ganache in this refreshing macaron variation. Fresh fruit is the star of the show, so using the highest quality raspberries—fresh, local, and organic—will make these macarons really shine. These macarons also welcome other buttercream fillings such as pistachio, raspberry, or hazelnut. The chocolate or French macaron recipe will work equally well for these luscious treats.

Method

1 Prepare the Chocolate Macaron or French Macaron recipe as instructed. After the macarons have been piped, sift the tops with a very light dusting of cocoa powder before they are set aside to dry. Continue as directed until the macarons are ready for assembly.

2 To assemble, sort the macaron shells, arranging them into matching sizes. Turn half of the shells over, revealing their flat side up, where you will pipe the filling.

3 Fill the pastry bag fitted with a ½-inch tip two-thirds full with ganache. In a medium bowl, whisk the chocolate ganache just until it is smooth and creamy. Do not whisk it too long, or you will begin to whip the cream and the ganache will lighten in color and begin to stiffen.

4 Pipe a small amount of ganache, approximately ½ teaspoon, onto the center of a turned-up shell, then place three raspberries on the outside edge of the shell, adhering the berries to the ganache. Next, pipe a dollop of ganache in the top center of the raspberries, set another shell on top, then lightly press down to adhere the top shell. Pipe a small ball of ganache in between each raspberry. Repeat until all the shells are matched up.

5 Place the macarons in an airtight container and refrigerate for 24 hours to "cure" before eating. Allow the macarons to sit out at room temperature for 1 hour before serving.

Giant Meringues

Meringue géantes

Makes about 12

---

8 large egg whites
(255 grams), at room
temperature

2½ cups (500 grams)
granulated sugar

2 teaspoons (10 grams)
white vinegar

2 teaspoons (4 grams)
cornstarch, sifted

¾ cup (100 grams)
candied coconut chips
(see Sources, pages 14 and 15)

½ cup (95 grams) mini
chocolate chips or finely
chopped chocolate

½ cup (75 grams)
raw coconut flakes

If you could eat a cloud, I imagine it would be like one of these giant, ethereal confections. Light and airy, these puffy meringues have a firm external shell that collapses into its soft center while wondrously melting in your mouth. The addition of white vinegar and cornstarch help stabilize the whites to prevent collapsing and contributes to the creamy marshmallow-like middle. Candied coconut chips and mini chocolate chips embellish the meringues; you can also enhance these wondrous treats with coffee extract, spices, or chocolate shavings, or sprinkle them with toasted, sliced almonds. Or to keep them pure, take inspiration from the Italian Pavlova: shape the meringues into leveled mounds, bake, cool, and finish with Chantilly cream and fresh fruit.

Method

1 Line two 12-by-17-inch baking sheets with parchment paper and set aside.

2 Pour the egg whites into the bowl of a stand mixer fitted with the whisk attachment. Turn the mixer to high speed and whip the egg whites until they begin to hold soft peaks. Keep the mixer running at high speed and begin adding the sugar, 1 tablespoon at a time, in a continuous motion. Add the vinegar and whip for 30 seconds. Add the cornstarch and whip on high speed until the meringues hold stiff peaks.

3 Using a rubber spatula, gently fold the candied coconut and mini chocolate chips into the meringue.

4 Preheat the oven to 220°F (105°C).

5 Using a large ice cream scoop or two large spoons, scoop large mounds of meringue onto the parchment paper–lined baking sheets, distributing six mounds per baking sheet.

The meringues will be approximately 4 inches wide by 4 inches tall. Their shape will be irregular, and you can play around using the spoons to make irregular peaks here and there. Sprinkle the meringues lightly with the coconut flakes.

6 Bake the meringues for 1 hour. Do not open the oven while they are baking. Turn the oven off and leave the meringues in the oven for at least 2 hours or overnight. Do not open the oven until it is completely cool. The meringues are best enjoyed within 24 hours but will keep in a covered container for up to 2 days.

Hazelnut Chocolate Dacquoise

Dacquoise noisette chocolat

Makes four 8-inch discs

Special tools: 2 pastry bags, each fitted with a ½-inch open tip, pastry bag fitted with a medium star tip

For the meringue discs

½ cup (50 grams) almond flour

⅓ cup (40 grams) hazelnut flour

¾ cup (150 grams) granulated sugar

5 large egg whites (165 grams), at room temperature

¾ cup (100 grams) blanched hazelnuts, split in half

Confectioners' sugar for dusting

For the filling

1½ cups (190 grams) Dark Chocolate Ganache (page 36), softened to room temperature

1½ cups (270 grams) French Buttercream (pages 34 and 35) or Italian Meringue Buttercream (pages 32 and 33), at room temperature

¼ cup (120 grams) hazelnut paste (see Sources, pages 14 and 15), at room temperature

A member of the nutty meringue family, dacquoise is assembled as a sandwiched pastry or is layered in cakes, adding textural interest and flavor complexity. These spiral discs are studded with nuts and later filled with dark chocolate ganache and tantalizing hazelnut buttercream peeking through the sides. Dacquoise meringues start out crunchy, then a soft, moist filling is added, and they're chilled overnight to transform. The result is a magnificent crisp, crunchy meringue pastry that collapses into the melting bliss of its indulgent fillings. Feel free to make smaller versions of the dacquoise; decrease the baking time and check to make sure the meringue discs are baked until crisp and firm to the touch.

Method

1   Create a stencil by tracing the outline of two 8-inch-diameter circles onto two pieces of 12-by-17-inch parchment paper. Invert the parchment paper templates and place them on two 12-by-17-inch baking sheets.

2   In a food processor fitted with a metal blade, combine the almond flour, hazelnut flour, and ¼ cup (50 grams) of the granulated sugar, then process until the mixture is very fine. Press the mixture through a medium-mesh sieve into a bowl, then reprocess any remaining large bits and press them through the sieve. Repeat until all of the mixture has been pressed through the sieve.

3   In a stand mixer fitted with the whisk attachment, whip the egg whites on medium speed until they turn frothy and begin to lighten in color. Increase the speed to medium–high and slowly add the remaining ½ cup (100 grams) sugar. Turn the mixer to high speed and whip until the whites hold stiff, glossy peaks.

4 Remove the bowl from the mixer and sprinkle one-third of the flour and sugar mixture on top, then gently fold it into the meringue. Add the remaining flour-sugar mixture and continue folding until the meringue is visually uniform in texture. Do not overmix or you will deflate the meringues.

5 Fill one of the pastry bags fitted with the ½-inch tip two-thirds full with batter. Beginning in the center of the circle, pipe a spiral disc with the edges touching onto the parchment paper, forming a solid disc. Use the template as a guide to keep the discs uniform in size.

6 Randomly scatter the hazelnut pieces over the top of each disc, then dust the top of each meringue lightly with confectioners' sugar. Allow the discs to sit for 10 minutes, then lightly dust the meringue tops a second time with confectioners' sugar and let them rest 10 more minutes.

7 Preheat the oven to 325°F (165°C).

8 Bake the meringue discs for 35 to 45 minutes, until they are crisp and firm to the touch. Carefully lift a disc to check the bottom to be sure they are dry. Place the baking sheet on a cooling rack to cool completely before assembly.

9 In a medium bowl, briefly whisk the dark chocolate ganache until it is smooth and creamy in consistency. In the bowl of a stand mixer fitted with the whisk attachment, combine the buttercream with the hazelnut paste and whip on high speed until they are homogenous.

10 Fill the second pastry bag fitted with the ½-inch open tip with the ganache. Fill the pastry bag fitted with the medium star tip with the buttercream. Place half of the meringue discs, nut side up, on a baking sheet. Pipe twelve ¾-inch balls of ganache, equally spaced at the edge of the disc. Pipe a shell shape between each ball of ganache, drawing the shell toward the center of the disc. Pipe a single large ball of ganache in the center. Gently but firmly set the second disc on top, nut side up, then press down lightly to adhere it to the filling. You should be able to see the design of the ganache balls and shell shapes at the edge of the dacquoise.

11 Refrigerate the dacquoise in a covered container overnight or up to 2 days; it can also be frozen for up to 1 month. Allow the dacquoise to rest overnight before serving at room temperature.

Concorde

Concorde

Makes one 8-inch cake

Special tools: pastry bag fitted with a ½-inch plain tip, pastry bag fitted with a ¼-inch plain tip

1½ cups plus 3 tablespoons (180 grams) confectioners' sugar

6 tablespoons (42 grams) cocoa powder

8 large egg whites (265 grams), at room temperature

1 cup (200 grams) granulated sugar

1 teaspoon (2 grams) cocoa powder, for dusting the rods

1 recipe Honey Chocolate Mousse (page 39)

In 1969, Air France made history with its first flight of the Concorde. That same year, famous French pastry chef Gaston Lenôtre created his Concorde, a chocolate cake consisting of meringue discs layered with chocolate mousse and garnished with rods of cocoa meringue, fashioning an abstract pastry sensation. When adding the cocoa rods, there is no correct way to finish this cake—just have fun and allow it to reveal itself to you!

Method

1 Preheat the oven to 250°F (120°C).

2 Make a template by drawing 8-inch circles on three pieces of parchment paper. Turn the papers upside down and place them on three separate baking sheets.

3 Sift the confectioners' sugar and cocoa powder into a medium bowl and set aside.

4 Pour the egg whites into the bowl of a stand mixer fitted with the whisk attachment. Turn the mixer to medium speed and whip until the egg whites become frothy and begin to foam, then increase the mixer speed to high and whip until the whites hold soft peaks. Continue to whip on high speed and add the sugar in a slow, steady stream, whipping until the whites are glossy and hold firm peaks.

5 Using a large silicone spatula, gently, but swiftly fold the confectioners' sugar and cocoa mixture into the egg whites. The meringue will begin to lose volume, so you want to work quickly.

6 Fill the pastry bag fitted with the ½-inch tip with meringue. Beginning at the center of each circle, pipe a spiral, with the edges touching, forming a solid disc. The discs should be approximately ⅓ inch thick; if any areas are thicker or thinner, use a small metal spatula to smooth the discs even, being careful not to deflate the meringue. Refill the pastry bag as needed to finish piping the three meringue discs.

7 Fill the pastry bag fitted with the ¼-inch tip with the meringue. Pipe as many long, thin, straight rods of meringue as you can fit on the remaining space on the three baking sheets. Refill the pastry bag as needed, piping all the remaining meringue in this manner. Lightly sift the cocoa powder over the rods, giving them a speckled appearance.

8 Bake the meringues for 1½ hours, then turn the oven off and leave them to continue to dry for at least 2 more hours or overnight. Cool the meringues completely before removing them from the parchment paper. The meringues will keep, covered, in a cool, dry place for up to 5 days before assembly.

9 When you are ready to assemble the cake, smear a dollop of the mousse on a cake plate and adhere one meringue disc over the mousse. Cover the disc with one-third of the mousse, smoothing the surface level with a metal spatula. Do not overwork the mousse or it will become grainy. Settle the second disc on top, then apply one-third of the mousse. Place the final disc on top, jiggling it to settle firmly. Cover the top and sides of the meringue discs with the remaining mousse and give it a smooth finish with the metal spatula. Freeze the cake for 2 hours before final assembly.

10 Cut the meringue rods into ½-inch lengths by sawing them with a serrated knife. Some of them will break unevenly, which is okay, as it gives added textural interest to the finished presentation. Remove the cake from the freezer and use a chef's torch or a blow-dryer to warm the top and sides of the cake. Press the meringue rods into the cake in an abstract pattern of your choice. Return the cake to the freezer and allow it to sit overnight before serving. The cake can be wrapped well and frozen for up to 1 week. Before serving, defrost the cake in the refrigerator overnight.

Chocolate Strawberry Meringues

Meringues aux fraises et chocolat

Makes about 12

Special tools: pastry bag fitted with a large star tip, pastry bag fitted with a medium star tip, template

For the French meringues

3 large egg whites (100 grams), at room temperature

⅛ teaspoon (1 gram) sea salt

⅔ cup plus 1 teaspoon (135 grams) granulated sugar

1 teaspoon (5 grams) pure vanilla extract

6 tablespoons (65 grams) confectioners' sugar, sifted

Pink or red food coloring

For the chocolate strawberry ganache

1 cup (170 grams) fresh strawberries

½ recipe Dark Chocolate Ganache (page 36), softened

Similar to the Swiss meringue ratio of two parts sugar, one part egg white, the high sugar content in French meringues is necessary to create hard-shelled meringues. For a softer meringue, refrigerate the finished sandwiched meringues overnight, which will make them absorb moisture and become more tender, or reduce the granulated sugar in this recipe by 2 tablespoons. The meringues are light and versatile and pop with color: stripe them with different colors, fill them with any number of flavored creams and ganaches, and pipe them in various shapes. Try adding fresh strawberry slices on top of the ganache filling, or keep the meringues pure white, layer them with Chantilly cream, and drizzle them with chocolate. These spiraled French meringues are a fun recipe to make with the kids.

Method

Make the French meringues

1 Preheat the oven to 250°F (120°C).

2 Combine the egg whites and salt in the bowl of a stand mixer fitted with the whisk attachment. Whip on medium-high speed for 30 seconds.

3 Increase the mixer to high speed, add one-third of the granulated sugar in a slow, steady stream, and whip for 2 minutes. Continue whipping on high speed while gradually pouring the remaining granulated sugar into the egg whites. Once all the granulated sugar has been added, continue whipping on high speed for 3 minutes, or until the meringue becomes stiff and shiny.

4 Remove the bowl from the mixer, scrape off the whisk, and transfer the meringue to a larger bowl to accommodate the next step. Add the vanilla and the confectioners' sugar all at

once, then fold it in with a large silicone spatula. Be certain to reach to the bottom of the bowl and fold as efficiently as possible. You want to incorporate the ingredients while preserving the volume of the meringue. Be careful to not overmix or the meringue may become too stiff and crack when baked.

5 Preheat the oven to 250°F (120°C).

6 Create a template by tracing the outline of a 3-inch round cookie cutter; trace 12 circles onto a 12-by-17-inch piece of parchment paper. Set the template in the bottom of a 12-by-17-inch baking sheet and set a new piece of parchment paper on top.

7 Fit a pastry bag with the large star tip. Squeeze a thin stripe of food coloring from the inside bottom, near the base of the tip, upward, halfway up the inside of the pastry bag. Repeat with four additional stripes of food coloring. Fill the pastry bag two-thirds full with the French meringue, then pipe flat rosette spirals on top of the parchment paper, following the guidelines of the template below. Continue in this manner until all the meringue has been piped from the pastry bag, repeating the process of striping the pastry bag with the food coloring as necessary.

8 Bake the meringues for 1 hour, or until crisp. The meringues should not brown; if they begin to show color, lower the temperature of the oven by 10 degrees. Remove from the oven and set the pan on a cooling rack to completely cool.

Make the chocolate strawberry ganache and assemble the meringues

1 Wash and stem the strawberries, then puree them in a food processor. Pour the mixture through a medium-mesh sieve.

2 Whisk the berry puree into the soft chocolate ganache until combined.

3 Fit a pastry bag with a medium star tip and fill two-thirds full with the chocolate strawberry ganache. Pipe a generous amount of filling onto the bottom of one meringue spiral, then top with another, lightly pressing the two halves together to form a sandwiched meringue cookie.

CHAPTER SEVEN

Cream Puff Pastries

Cream Puff Pastries

Les choux

Cream puff–type pastries are made with a dough called *pâte à choux* and are piped from a pastry bag into various shapes and sizes. When pâte à choux is baked, the pastry rises and releases steam, creating a hollow center for the filling.

Crackle Top Cream Puffs, filled with a bright berry cream, start off the chapter with their merry presence. The Nuns, a double-decker cream puff with an elevating pistachio flavor and elaborate finish, follow. Oblong-shaped Éclairs are made in the classic style here with pastry cream and a chocolate glaze. *Paris–Brest*, a wheel-shaped cream puff pastry, showcases a praline filling. We'll sizzle things up at the end with the *Beignets soufflé*, a light fried pastry that is quick to make and delightful to watch as it expands and transforms into a puffy golden delight. Get ready to make some magic in your kitchen with these dreamy creamy puff pastries.

Crackle Top Cream Puffs

Choux au craquelin

Makes about 36 medium
puffs

Special tools: 1½-inch-
diameter spherical silicone
molds, 2 pastry bags, each
fitted with a ½-inch open
tip, 1¼-inch-diameter round
cutter, pastry brush

For the crackle tops
½ cup plus 1 tablespoon
(120 grams) brown sugar

⅓ cup (70 grams)
unsalted butter, softened

½ cup plus 2 tablespoons
(100 grams) Steve's Gluten
Free Cake Flour
(see pages 1 and 2)

¼ cup (20 grams)
almond flour

⅛ teaspoon (1 gram) sea salt

For the dough
1 recipe Cream Puff Pastry
Dough (pages 51 and 52)

Egg Wash (page 19)

(continued on page 235)

Cream puffs are small round pastries that can be made sweet or savory, depending on the choice of filling. *Choux à la crème* is a classic sweet version filled with lightly sweetened whipped cream. Here, a modern variation of the cream puff showcases a crackled crown that gives it a contrasting texture. The top is made with a cut-out cookie dough that's set onto the choux dough before baking. The cookie melts onto the puff, draping it with a crackly streusel-like appearance, while the filling reveals a bright berry cream peeking out from inside. Try filling them with equal parts lemon cream and whipped cream lightly folded together or Honey Chocolate Mousse (page 39). Let your pastry wanderlust take you into the new realm of this little *choux* temptress, the Crackle Top Cream Puff.

Method

Make the crackle tops

1 Combine the brown sugar and butter in the bowl of a stand mixer fitted with the paddle attachment. Mix on medium speed until the ingredients combine. Add the gluten-free flour, almond flour, and salt, then mix on medium-low speed until the ingredients appear homogenous. Using a silicone spatula, scrape the bowl and paddle as necessary. The mixture will remain crumbly and will not gather into a solid mass.

2 Transfer the mixture to a 1-gallon freezer bag, then use your hands to squeeze and flatten the mixture. With a rolling pin, continue to flatten the dough until it is ⅛ inch thick. Set the dough onto a baking sheet and freeze for 15 minutes. Set a 12-by-17-inch piece of parchment paper onto your work surface, then place another piece of plastic wrap of the same size on top of the parchment paper. Cut and remove half of

For the berry cream filling

1 cup (about 170 grams) fresh raspberries or strawberries (or a combination of both)

1 cup (250 grams) Pastry Cream (pages 26 and 27)

1 cup (225 grams) heavy cream

18 whole raspberries, halved

the dough from the bag, then put the remaining half of the dough back in the freezer. Place the dough on top of the plastic wrap and cover it with a second piece of plastic wrap. Use a rolling pin to roll the dough out between the sheets of plastic wrap. Slide the parchment paper with the plastic wrapped dough onto the top of a baking sheet, then place it in the freezer. Continue in this manner until the dough is 1/16 inch thick, setting the dough back into the freezer when it becomes too soft to roll. During the rolling process the dough will crack and develop small holes. Patch the dough by pressing it back together with your fingers over the top of the plastic wrap. The edges of the dough will remain crumbly, but this is okay; when you cut the tops with a cutter, you will avoid the edges. When the dough reaches the correct thickness, freeze it completely before cutting. The dough may be frozen for up to 1 month.

3 When you are ready to cut the crackle tops, remove the dough from the freezer. Unwrap the dough carefully, as it is fragile. Using a 1½-inch-diameter round cutter, cut as many rounds as possible from the dough. Gather the dough scraps and repeat the earlier rolling process or freeze for later use. Set the frozen rounds onto a baking sheet. You can also put them into a container and keep in the freezer until ready to apply.

Make the cream puffs

1 Set the spherical molds onto a baking sheet.

2 Transfer the cream puff pastry dough to a pastry bag fitted with the ½-inch open tip, then pipe the dough into the molds, filling each cavity near full to the top. If the tops are uneven, moisten the tip of your finger with water and gently smooth the dough flat. Cover the molds with plastic wrap and freeze for 1 hour, or until they are firm enough to easily unmold. The dough may be frozen for up to 1 month; unmold the frozen rounds, wrap them, and store them in the freezer.

3 When you are ready to bake the cream puffs, preheat the oven to 375°F (190°C). Line two baking sheets with parchment paper or silicone baking mats.

4 Unmold the frozen cream puffs and arrange them, flat side down, on the baking sheets, allowing 1½ inches between each puff. Using a pastry brush, lightly apply egg wash to each round, then set one frozen crackle cookie atop each puff.

5 Place the baking sheets in the oven and immediately lower the oven temperature to 350°F (175°C). Bake the puffs for 25 to 35 minutes, until golden brown. Lift one puff off the baking sheet and check the bottom to ensure adequate browning. The puffs should feel firm to the touch. Bake the puffs darker, rather than lighter, because this will help create the hollow center for the filling. When the puffs are finished baking, set them on a cooling rack to cool completely before filling.

Make the filling and assemble

1 When you are ready to finish the puffs, slice the top third off each round and set aside the crackle top.

2 Place 1 cup of berries into the bowl of a food processor and pulse until smooth. Press the mixture through a medium-mesh sieve and discard the seeds.

3 With a hand whisk, whip the pastry cream until smooth. Add the berry puree, then whip until incorporated.

4 In the bowl of a stand mixer fitted with the whisk attachment, whip the cream until it holds soft peaks. Add the whipped cream to the pastry berry mixture and gently fold them together.

5 Fill a pastry bag fitted with the ½-inch open tip and pipe mounds of the cream into the bottom shell of each puff, piling it upward to about 1 inch above the rim. Top each puff with its crackle lid, allowing the pink berry cream to remain visible, then finish by setting a raspberry half on top. Serve immediately.

Pistachio Nuns

Religieuses à la pistache

Makes 16

Special tools: 1-inch spherical silicone mold, 1½-inch spherical silicone mold, pastry bag fitted with a ½-inch open tip, pastry bag fitted with a small star pastry tip, ¾-inch round cutter, 1½-inch round cutter

Crackle tops
(pages 233 to 235)

For the dough
1 recipe Cream Puff Pastry Dough (pages 51 and 52)

Egg Wash (page 19)

For the filling
½ cup (120 grams) pistachio paste, softened to room temperature

2 cups (500 grams) Pastry Cream (pages 26 and 27)

2 cups (450 grams) heavy cream

(continued on page 239)

A *religieuse* is a nun, and a divinely sinful one at that! Created in the mid-1800s by a French *pâtissier,* this pastry was made to resemble a nun in her habit. It's a double cream puff made modern crackle-top style—one large puff and one small puff, filled with ethereal pistachio cream, dipped in royal icing, decorated with a buttercream teardrop collar, and topped with a rosette swirl. Temporal by nature, these cream-filled nuns are a playful option to serve when entertaining. Try filling them with chocolate mousse, raspberry cream, a combination of both, or any number of other filling combinations you might like.

Method

Make the crackle tops

1 Make the crackle top dough through step 2. When you are ready to cut the crackle tops, remove the dough from the freezer. Unwrap the dough carefully, because the dough is fragile. Using the ¾-inch round cutter and the 1½-inch round cutter, cut an equal number of rounds of each size from the dough. Gather the dough scraps and repeat the earlier rolling process or freeze for later use.

2 Set the frozen cut cookie rounds onto a baking sheet or into a container and keep in the freezer until ready to apply.

Make the cream puffs

1 Set the spherical molds onto two separate baking sheets.

2 Transfer the cream puff pastry dough to a pastry bag fitted with an open tip, then pipe the dough into the molds, filling each cavity to the top. Fill an equal number of each size of the spherical molds. If the tops are uneven, moisten the tip of your finger with water and gently smooth the dough flat. Cover the molds with plastic wrap and freeze for 2 hours, or

For the pistachio buttercream

2 cups (360 grams) Italian Meringue Buttercream (pages 32 and 33), at room temperature

1 cup (120 grams) Pistachio Ganache (page 38), at room temperature

2 tablespoons (30 grams) pistachio paste, softened to room temperature

For the glaze

1 cup (100 grams) confectioners' sugar, sifted

2 tablespoons egg whites (70 grams)

A few drops of vanilla extract or water

16 whole pistachios, shelled

until they are firm enough to easily unmold. If you choose, at this point the dough can be unmolded, wrapped well, and frozen for up to 1 month.

3 When you are ready to bake the cream puffs, preheat the oven to 375°F (190°C). Line two baking sheets with parchment paper or silicone baking mats.

4 Unmold the frozen cream puffs and arrange them, flat side down, on the baking sheets, allowing 1½ inches between each puff. Keep the different size puffs on separate baking sheets, because they will have different baking times. Using a pastry brush, lightly apply egg wash to one puff at a time, then immediately set a frozen crackle cookie atop the puff. Place the smaller rounds onto the smaller puffs and the larger rounds onto the larger puffs. Continue in this way until all the puffs have been set with their crackle tops.

5 Place the baking sheets into the oven and immediately lower the oven temperature to 350°F (190°C). Bake the puffs for 25 to 35 minutes, until golden brown. Lift one puff off the baking sheet and check the bottom to ensure adequate browning. Bake the puffs darker, rather than lighter, because this will help create the hollow center for the filling. Remove from the oven and set them on a cooling rack to cool completely before filling.

Make the filling

1 When you are ready to finish the puffs, poke a ¼-inch hole in the bottom of each one using a small, round, open pastry tip or a chopstick.

2 In the bowl of a stand mixer fitted with the paddle attachment, beat the pistachio paste on medium speed until it is creamy and smooth. Add the pastry cream and beat on medium speed until the ingredients are completely blended. There should be no remaining small bits of pistachio paste visible. Transfer the pastry cream mixture into a separate large bowl.

3 In the bowl of a stand mixer fitted with the whisk attachment, whip the cream until it holds medium soft peaks. Scrape the cream into the pistachio pastry cream mixture, then fold them together using a silicone spatula.

4 Fill a pastry bag fitted with a ¼-inch open tip with the cream mixture, then pipe it into the bottom of each puff, filling until it begins to subtly expand in your hand. A little cream may push back out from the hole; scrape it off against the edge of the bowl and continue on with the next puff until you have filled all of both size puffs.

Make the pistachio buttercream
1 Whisk the buttercream, pistachio ganache, and pistachio paste together until well blended and completely homogeneous.

Make the glaze
1 Sift the confectioners' sugar into a medium bowl. Using a wooden spoon, stir in the egg whites and beat the mixture until it becomes stiff and white.

2 Thin the paste into a glaze by adding 1 to 2 drops of vanilla extract or water and stirring until the glaze is thick enough to coat the tops of the puffs but not runny. Add more liquid as necessary, but do so gradually. If the glaze becomes too thin, add additional sifted confectioners' sugar.

Assemble the pastries
1 Dip one large crackle top puff into the glaze. Immediately dip a smaller crackle top into the glaze and set it on top of the larger one. Continue until all the cream puffs have been dipped and stacked to become double cream puffs.

2 Fit a pastry bag with a small star tip and fill it two-thirds full with the pistachio buttercream. Pipe upward elongated teardrops around the joint where the two cream puffs meet. This aspect of the pastry is considered the collar of the nun. Finish by piping a rosette on top and garnishing with a whole pistachio. Serve immediately. You can store them in a plastic container in the refrigerator overnight.

Éclairs

Éclairs

Makes 16

Special tools: pastry bag fitted with a #847 star tip, pastry bag fitted with a large star tip

1 recipe Cream Puff Pastry Dough (pages 51 and 52)

1 recipe Pastry Cream (pages 26 and 27)

1 cup (125 grams) Dark Chocolate Ganache (page 36), melted

Chocolate shavings

The meaning of the word éclair is "flash of lightning," and this pastry's shape is formed to resemble a bolt. Another interpretation is for the style in which these popular pastries are eaten—in a flash!

Traditionally éclairs are filled with vanilla pastry cream and glazed with chocolate, but as with all cream puff pastries, the options for fillings are endless; you can experiment with flavors ranging from pistachio to coffee, chocolate, coconut, and berry. You can also add a layer of chocolate, caramel, or fruit inside the éclairs. This classic version happens to be one of my father's favorites, and I have fond memories of him slowly snacking on one, stretching out the moments to enjoy the creamy filling long after mine was gone.

Method

1 Line two baking sheets with parchment paper or silicone mats. Preheat the oven to 400°F (205°C).

2 Transfer the cream puff pastry dough to a pastry bag fitted with the #847 star tip, then pipe 1-by-5-inch "fingers," leaving 2½ inches between each one.

3 Place the baking sheets into the oven and immediately lower the oven temperature to 350°F (175°C). Bake the éclair shells for 25 to 35 minutes, until golden brown. Do not open the oven during baking, as doing so could cause the eclairs to fall. Check for doneness by lifting one éclair and inspecting the bottom to ensure adequate browning. Bake the éclairs darker rather than lighter, as this will help create the hollow center for the filling. Remove the éclairs to a cooling rack to cool completely before filling.

4 When you are ready to finish the éclairs, slice the top third off each one and set it next to its bottom half.

5 In the bowl of a stand mixer fitted with the paddle attachment, beat the pastry cream on medium speed until it has a smooth, creamy consistency.

6 Fit a pastry bag with a large star tip and fill it two-thirds full with pastry cream. Pipe an undulating shell pattern into the bottom of the éclair shell, allowing the pastry cream to peek out of the edge of the shell.

7 Using your finger or a small metal spatula, spread melted chocolate ganache over the éclair top. Place the top over the custard-filled bottom shell, then sprinkle with chocolate shavings. Serve immediately or store in a plastic container in the refrigerator overnight.

Paris Brest

Paris–Brest

Makes 12 pastries

Special tools: pastry bag fitted with a #867 large star tip, 3½-inch round cutter, pastry brush

For the Paris Brest wheels

1 recipe Cream Puff Pastry Dough (pages 51 and 52)

Egg Wash (page 19)

½ cup (40 grams) almonds, sliced or chopped

½ cup (70 grams) pearl sugar (optional)

For the hazelnut praline cream filling

⅓ cup hazelnut praline paste (see Sources, pages 14 and 15), at room temperature

2 cups (500 grams) Pastry Cream (pages 26 and 27)

1½ cups (270 grams) Italian Meringue Buttercream (pages 32 and 33), softened to room temperature

Confectioners' sugar for dusting

Created in 1891, this cream puff pastry is named in honor of the bicycle race from Paris to Brest, France, with its pastry ring shape fashioned to resemble a bicycle tire. The pastry is traditionally sprinkled with sliced almonds and filled with praline cream. Here the pastry is finished with chopped almonds and pearl sugar and filled with an extravagant hazelnut cream: a blend of vanilla-infused pastry cream, hazelnut praline paste, and Italian meringue buttercream. This playful pastry ring is a welcome platform to enjoy other flavor combinations; try it with Honey Chocolate Mousse (page 39) and fresh raspberries, or lighten it up with lemon whipped cream and blueberries.

Method

Make the wheels

1 Make a template: using a fine tip marker, trace the 3½-inch round cutter to draw six rings onto a 12-by-17-inch piece of parchment paper, spacing each ring about 2 inches apart.

2 Set the template on a baking sheet and cover it with a piece of parchment paper or silicone baking mat.

3 Preheat the oven to 400°F (205°C).

4 Transfer the cream puff pastry dough to a pastry bag fitted with the #867 star tip, then pipe the dough around each template guide, slightly overlapping the dough at the end of each ring. Brush each dough ring lightly with egg wash, then sprinkle with chopped almonds and pearl sugar, if using.

5 Place the baking sheets into the oven and immediately lower the oven temperature to 350°F (175°C). Bake the rings for 25 to 35 minutes, until golden brown. Check for doneness by lifting a baked ring to ensure adequate browning on the bottom of the pastry. Bake the dough darker, rather than lighter, as this will help create the hollow center for the filling. Remove the baking sheet to a cooling rack to cool completely before filling. When the pastries have cooled, use a sharp serrated knife to horizontally slice off the top third of each ring, creating a top and a bottom.

Make the hazelnut praline cream filling

1 In the bowl of a stand mixer fitted with the paddle attachment, beat the praline paste on medium speed until smooth. Add the pastry cream and beat on medium speed until the ingredients are creamy and well blended. Remove the paddle and replace it with the whisk attachment. Add the softened buttercream and whip until the ingredients are blended.

2 Fit a pastry bag with a large star tip. Fill the bag two-thirds full with hazelnut praline cream. On the bottom pastry ring, pipe a spiral design on the inside edge and a second spiral around the outside edge, or pipe a design of your choice. Dust the pastry tops with confectioners' sugar, then set them on top of the filled bottoms, creating a closed pastry with the filling peeking through the sides. Serve immediately or refrigerate for up to 24 hours; remove from the refrigerator 1 hour before eating.

Beignets

Beignets de soufflé

Makes about 20

Special tools: 1½-inch ice cream scoop or spoons, deep-fry thermometer, slotted spoon, deep fryer or large, heavy saucepan

For the orange glaze

1 cup (100 grams) confectioners' sugar

2 teaspoons (12 grams) orange juice

Cold water as needed

For the batter

½ cup (115 grams) whole milk

½ cup (115 grams) water

6 tablespoons (85 grams) cold unsalted butter, cut into small pieces

2 tablespoons (30 grams) granulated sugar

½ teaspoon (4 grams) sea salt

1 cup plus 2 tablespoons (180 grams) Steve's Gluten Free Cake Flour (see pages 1 and 2)

1 tablespoon (5 grams) chia powder

(continued on page 249)

Sweet, ethereal, and easy to make, these baby beignets made with a pâte à choux dough variation retain a lightness of consistency that is unexpected from a fried pastry. Handle them gently while they are in the fryer and you will be rewarded with their unassuming charm. These little golden globes develop a delicately crisp exterior and remain soufflé-like and soft inside. And when you roll them in the tangy orange glaze, they will pop with sweet, zesty citrus. *Beignet* translates to "bump" and is synonymous with the fritter, or deep-fried pastry. Alternately, you can pipe the beignet dough into long, serrated cruller shapes (as seen in the photo) using a large French star tip and finish them with a dusting of cinnamon sugar or confectioners' sugar. Beignets generally are best enjoyed while fresh or still warm.

Method

Make the glaze

1 Sift the confectioners' sugar into a small bowl. Slowly add the orange juice and a few drops of water and stir until the mixture becomes smooth. Add additional water a few drops at a time until you reach the desired consistency. You want the glaze to be fluid but not too runny. Adjust the consistency by adding more confectioners' sugar to make a stiffer glaze or more water for a thinner glaze.

Make the beignet batter

1 In a medium saucepan, combine the milk, water, butter, sugar, and salt and bring to a boil over medium-high heat.

2 While the milk mixture is heating, use a hand whisk to blend together the flour, chia powder, and baking powder.

3 When the milk mixture comes to a boil, add the flour mixture all at once. Using a wooden spoon, stir vigorously

1 teaspoon (4 grams)
baking powder

3 large eggs (165 grams),
at room temperature

1 large egg white (33 grams),
at room temperature

1 tablespoon (16 grams)
orange blossom water

Zest from 1 large orange
or 1 teaspoon (6 grams)
orange oil

For frying
About 2 quarts (1800 grams)
safflower oil

until the dough comes together and a slight film forms on the bottom of the pan. Continue stirring until the dough forms a homogenous mass.

4 Transfer the dough into the bowl of a stand mixer fitted with the paddle attachment. Turn the mixer to medium speed, then add the eggs, one at a time, beating to incorporate each addition before adding the next. Add the egg white and beat on high speed for 1 minute. Scrape the bottom and sides of the bowl and beat again briefly. Add the orange blossom water and orange zest and beat for 30 seconds. Turn the mixer off and scrape the sides and bottom of the bowl with a silicone spatula, then continue mixing on high speed for 1 to 2 minutes, until the dough comes together in a soft, smooth mass.

Fry the beignets

1 Pour safflower oil to a depth of 3 to 4 inches into a deep fryer or large, heavy saucepan over medium heat until the oil reaches 350°F (175°C). It is important to keep the oil at 350°F; if the temperature is too low, the beignets will absorb oil, and if the oil is too hot, the beignets will brown before cooking through to the center.

2 While the oil is heating, set out a baking sheet and line it with a few layers of paper towels. This is where you will set the beignets as they come out of the hot oil.

3 Scrape the dough into the ice cream scoop and level it against the edge of the bowl. Carefully release the dough into the hot oil. Repeat this process, adding four or five more beignets. Do not overcrowd the beignets, as they need room to fry evenly and they will expand to nearly three times their original size. Soon after you have added the beignets to the oil, check to ensure they are floating, not sitting on the bottom. If they have sunk to the bottom, use a long metal spatula to gently pry them loose. Use a slotted spoon to gently turn the beignets so they cook and brown evenly.

About halfway through cooking, a fissure or split will appear; this is normal. Continue to cook for a total of 6 to 8 minutes, until the beignets are golden brown.

4 Remove the beignets from the oil with a slotted spoon and place them on the lined baking sheet to drain and cool for 10 minutes. Gently roll the warm beignets in the orange glaze and set aside on a cooling rack for 5 minutes to set up. Stir or adjust the thickness of the glaze as needed. Serve immediately; beignet soufflés are best eaten soon after they are prepared.

Sweet Beginnings

I was raised on fresh air and doughnuts. My great love of baking began when, as a very young child, I stood clinging to the leg of the kitchen table peering up at the undersides of small bowls filled with cinnamon and sugar: the final flourish for my father's cherished doughnut recipe. Five eager children surrounded the table, while Dad towered over the earthy brown deep fryer that sat high on an adjacent counter. When Mom worked the night shift, Dad made his sweet fried snacks, providing entertainment for the evening and filling the house with the familiar, mouthwatering aromas from his childhood. The scene was sensational as I took in the larger-than-life sights, sounds, and scents of my father's doughnut production. His large hands would toss clouds of flour onto the dark wooden cutting board, and using a red-handled rolling pin, he would lay flat the soft dough. Dad's experienced hands cupped the one and only doughnut cutter, swiftly shaping the doughnuts with deft cuts. The rings and holes would then fall fast into the wicked hot oil, sending a sweet spiciness to our nostrils while our little mouths began to water. When the doughnuts were ready, Dad would lift them out of the fryer and place them on brown paper bags to drain and cool for a few long moments. Finally, the warm doughnuts were tossed into the cinnamon sugar, and we would joyfully pop the small rounds into our hungry mouths, sugar lingering against our lips and fingers.

CHAPTER EIGHT

Brioche

Brioche

Les brioches

Light, tender, golden buttery brioche is a wonderfully versatile yeast dough made with ample eggs and butter. Brioche sits in a category all its own—neither bread nor pastry, but rather a unique union of each. Ideally, brioche is eaten warm from the oven as exquisite breakfast fare or lightly toasted until crisp and delicate. You can also shape brioche into loaves to slice for luncheon bread, or transform it into a lavish dessert.

The chapter begins with Sugared Brioche, which are made in traditional fluted molds and sprinkled with a touch of pearl sugar; you can opt to go savory and switch out the sugar for a light sprinkle of Maldon sea salt. The grab-and-go Chocolate Brioche Sticks make a sweet companion alongside your morning cup of motivation. Brioche Alsace is made ring style with snail-shaped buns and scattered with rum raisins and pecans. Stepping into desserts, Dancing Brioche Buns are resplendent Kirsch-soaked, cream-filled pastries fashioned with meringue, and then we move on to Brioche Saint Tropez, the pastry named after the paradise of the French Riviera, where the dessert gained acclaim. Pull the pure butter from the refrigerator and settle in for what could become the next pastry (or is it bread?) love of your life.

Sugared Brioche

Brioche sucrée

Makes 12

Special tools: 12 fluted brioche molds 3¼ inches across the top, pastry brush

Nonstick cooking spray

1 recipe Brioche Dough (pages 53 and 54)

Gluten-free flour for dusting

Egg Wash (page 19)

¼ cup (50 grams) pearl sugar

Made in the traditional flared, fluted molds, these buns are buttery, light, and perfect slightly warmed or toasted for a morning snack. A light sprinkling of pearl sugar adds texture, visual appeal, and a smidge of sweetness. You can also bake this recipe in a medium loaf pan. Slicing the bread just may lead to dangerously fantastic brioche French toast that calls for the best butter you can find and real maple syrup.

Method

1 Spray the fluted molds with cooking spray, then set them onto a baking sheet.

2 Remove the dough from the refrigerator and scrape it out of the bowl onto a lightly dusted work surface. Using a bench cutter or knife, score and weigh 12 portions at 45 grams each. Roll each portion into a smooth ball, cupping the dough in the palm of your hand and pressing it lightly but firmly as you make a circular motion against the lightly floured work surface. You want the dough to be just tacky enough to roll easily but not too sticky. Add small amounts of flour as needed. When each ball is smooth and uniform, set it into the fluted mold.

3 Preheat the oven to 350°F (175°C).

4 Using a small, soft pastry brush, apply a light coating of egg wash to the brioche, being careful to avoid pooling in the fluted edges. Set the brioche aside to rise for 1 to 2 hours, until they have increased in volume and reach the top of the molds. Apply a second light coating of egg wash, then sprinkle the tops with the pearl sugar.

5 Place the brioche in the oven and bake for about 15 minutes, until the tops are browned. Place the baking sheet on a cooling rack to cool for 5 minutes, then release the brioche by rapping the edge of the mold onto the baking sheet. The brioche is best enjoyed fresh from the oven, slightly cooled. Store the brioche wrapped well in plastic for up to 3 days.

Chocolate Brioche Sticks

Bâtonnets de brioche au chocolat

Makes 18

Special tool: pastry brush

Gluten-free flour for dusting

1 recipe Brioche Dough
(pages 53 and 54)

1½ cups (380 grams)
Pastry Cream (pages 26 and 27)

Egg Wash (page 19)

1 cup (95 grams)
mini chocolate chips

¼ cup (50 grams)
dark chocolate, melted

An agreeable breakfast indulgence or afternoon snack, these brioche sticks are spread with a layer of pastry cream, or you could substitute Almond Cream (page 23) or Frangipane (pages 24 and 25), and generously sprinkled with tiny chocolate chips. Turn up the flavor by sprinkling the pastry cream with cinnamon and adding a handful of toasted nuts. Drizzle the baked pastries with melted chocolate for a final irresistible treat.

Method

1 Line two 12-by-17-inch baking sheets with parchment paper or silicone mats.

2 Lightly dust your work surface with flour and turn the dough out of the bowl. The dough will be sticky and loose, so you will need to work proficiently. Keep your hands floured as necessary to prevent sticking. Roll the dough out to form a 12-by-18-inch rectangle, with the short side vertical. Brush off any excess flour.

3 In the bowl of a stand mixer fitted with the paddle attachment, beat the pastry cream until it is smooth, then use a metal spatula to spread the cream in an even layer over the brioche dough, leaving ½ inch along the bottom edge clean. Use a pastry brush to apply the egg wash to the clean bottom edge.

4 Sprinkle the chocolate chips over the pastry cream, then fold the rectangle in half, bringing the top over to meet the bottom edge. Use a sharp chef's knife to cut eighteen 1-inch-thick slices. Gently lift and set nine slices onto each baking sheet, allowing 1 inch between each slice. Using a pastry brush, apply a light egg wash to the top of each stick. Set aside to rise for 60 to 90 minutes.

5 Preheat the oven to 350°F (175°C).

6 Place the chocolate brioche sticks in the oven and bake for 20 minutes, or until golden brown and firm to the touch. Remove from the oven and set the pans on a cooling rack to cool for 20 minutes, then drizzle with melted chocolate, and serve. Store wrapped in plastic and refrigerated for up to 3 days. Reheat at 350°F (175°C) for 10 minutes before eating.

Brioche Alsace

Brioche "Chinois" alsacienne

Makes one 10-inch cake

Special tools: 10-inch cake pan or springform pan, pastry brush

For the buns
Nonstick cooking spray

½ cup (85 grams) raisins

1 cup (230 grams) water

¼ cup (64 grams) dark rum

2 cups (500 grams) Almond Cream (page 23), at room temperature

Gluten-free flour for dusting

1 recipe Brioche Dough (pages 53 and 54)

Egg Wash (page 19)

2 teaspoons (4 grams) ground cinnamon

½ cup (58 grams) pecan pieces

For the icing
¾ cup (75 grams) confectioners' sugar

2 teaspoons (12 grams) orange juice

Cold water as needed

A cinnamon breakfast-style ring cake with individual portions pulled from the whole creates the breaking of sweet bread, in this case, rich brioche buns. The dough is amply spread and rolled up with almond cream, or substitute Frangipane (pages 24 and 25), cinnamon, rum raisins, and pecans, and then settled into a cake pan. The ring is then baked and finished with a sweet sugar glaze while still hot.

Method
Make the buns
1 Spray the springform pan with cooking spray and line it with a parchment circle.

2 Next, make the rum raisins. Place the raisins in a small, heatproof bowl. In a small saucepan, bring 1 cup (230 grams) of water to a boil over high heat. Remove the pan from the heat and pour the water over the raisins, just enough to cover. Allow the raisins to sit for 15 minutes, then drain them with a metal strainer and discard the liquid. In a small bowl, combine the raisins and the rum and set the bowl aside for 15 minutes.

3 Strain the raisins from the rum, capturing the rum in a bowl. Add the rum to the almond cream and whisk until the mixture is smooth.

4 Lightly dust your work surface with flour, remove the brioche dough from the refrigerator, and scrape it out of the bowl and onto the work surface. The dough will be sticky, so keep your hands floured, but use extra flour only as necessary. Roll the dough out to a 12-by-14-inch rectangle that's about ½ inch thick, with the short side vertical. Brush any excess flour from the dough.

5 Spread the almond cream in an even layer over the brioche dough, leaving ½ inch along the bottom edge clean. Brush the bottom edge with egg wash.

6 Sprinkle the cinnamon across the top of the almond cream, then evenly distribute the raisins and pecans over the cinnamon-dusted almond cream. Starting with the top edge, give the dough a ½ inch fold over, then continue to roll the dough into a tight log shape. With the seam side down, use a chef's knife to cut nine 1½-inch-thick slices from the dough log. Set eight slices spaced around the inside edge of the pan and one in the center. Using a pastry brush, apply a light egg wash to the top of the buns. Set aside to rise for 60 to 90 minutes.

7 Preheat the oven to 350°F (175°C).

8 Place the brioche buns in the oven and bake for 25 to 35 minutes, until golden brown and firm to the touch.

Make the icing
1 Sift the confectioners' sugar into a small bowl. Slowly add the orange juice and a few drops of water, then stir until the mixture becomes smooth and fluid but not runny. Add additional water a few drops at a time until you reach the desired consistency. Adjust the consistency by adding more confectioners' sugar to make a stiffer glaze or more water for a thinner glaze.

To finish
1 Remove the pan from the oven and set it on a cooling rack. While the buns are hot from the oven, use a pastry brush to glaze the top of the buns with the icing. Allow the buns to cool for 15 minutes, then serve immediately.

2 You can wrap the buns in plastic and store them for 2 to 3 days at room temperature. Reheat at 350°F (175°C) for 5 minutes before eating.

Dancing Brioche Buns

Brioche polonaise

Makes 12 to 15

Special tools: 2½-inch-diameter round silicone molds, pastry brush, culinary or chef's torch, pastry bag with a ½-inch open tip

For the kirsch syrup

2 cups (575 grams) Simple Syrup (page 20), at room temperature

6 tablespoons (96 grams) kirsch

For the dough

1 recipe Brioche Dough (pages 53 and 54), made through step 3

Egg Wash (page 19)

For the cream filling

½ cup (112 grams) heavy cream

2 cups (500 grams) Pastry Cream (pages 26 and 27), chilled

½ cup (100 grams) candied orange peel, cut into ¼-inch pieces

1 tablespoon (16 grams) kirsch

For assembly

1 recipe Italian Meringue (page 29)

1½ cups (130 grams) sliced almonds

Notably referred to as "blessed bread" because it is frequently offered among faithful churchgoers, here brioche has historically transformed from bread to true cake. How this particular recipe came to be called Polish Brioche remains uncertain, but its lively features have earned its description as a dancing dessert. Kirsch-soaked brioche filled with pastry cream, speckled with candied fruit, sculpted magnificent with meringue, sprinkled with sliced almonds, and torched golden—truly a mystical pastry encounter that could have you swaying to the sweet tune of dancing brioche buns. For these buns you'll make the Brioche recipe through step 3, where the dough is at batter consistency.

Method

Make the syrup

1 In a medium bowl, whisk together the simple syrup and kirsch. Set aside.

Bake the brioche

1 Fit a pastry bag with a ½-inch open tip, then fill the bag two-thirds full with brioche dough. Fill the silicone molds halfway with batter, place them on a baking sheet, then set them into the refrigerator to rest for 2 hours.

2 Remove them from the refrigerator and set aside to rise for 1 to 2 hours, until they have doubled in volume and reach the top of the molds. Gently apply a light coating of egg wash.

3 Preheat the oven to 350°F (175°C).

4 Place the brioche in the oven and bake for 20 minutes, or until the tops are browned. Place the baking sheet on a cooling rack to cool for 5 minutes, then release the brioche by inverting the silicone molds onto the rack. Allow them to cool completely before assembly.

Make the cream filling

1 In the bowl of a stand mixer fitted with the whisk attachment, whip the heavy cream on high speed until it forms soft peaks, then transfer it to another bowl. Add the chilled pastry cream to the bowl of a stand mixer fitted with the paddle attachment and beat on medium speed until smooth, about 30 seconds. Add the candied orange peel and kirsch and beat briefly, just until blended.

2 Using a silicone spatula, fold the whipped cream into the pastry cream mixture until just combined. Place the cream filling into the refrigerator while you prepare the brioche for assembly.

Assemble the brioche pastries

1 Using a serrated knife, cut the brioche crosswise into three slices. Use a pastry brush to generously coat each layer with the kirsch syrup, beginning with the flat bottom layer.

2 Using a small metal spatula, spread a ¼-inch-thick layer of the cream filling onto each brioche layer, reassembling the brioche as you go. Set on the top layer, then brush with syrup. Cover with plastic wrap and set the filled brioches into the freezer for 30 minutes. While the brioche is in the freezer, prepare the Italian meringue.

3 Remove the brioche from the freezer, then use a metal spatula to coat each frozen brioche evenly with the Italian meringue. Set the meringues onto a cooling rack and sprinkle them lightly with sliced almonds. Finish the meringues by toasting them with a culinary torch. Alternately, place the meringues beneath a broiler; keep a close watch on them so they do not brown too much. Serve immediately.

Brioche Saint Tropez

Tarte tropézienne

Makes one 10-inch cake

Special tools: 10-inch metal ring mold, pastry brush

1 recipe Brioche Dough (pages 53 and 54)

Egg Wash (page 19)

1 cup (180 grams) Streusel (page 22)

For the syrup
¾ cup (215 grams) Simple Syrup (page 20)

½ vanilla bean, split and scraped

1 tablespoon (16 grams) kirsch

For the cream filling
1 cup (250 grams) Pastry Cream (pages 26 and 27), at room temperature

1¾ cups (315 grams) Italian Meringue Buttercream (pages 32 and 33), at room temperature

1½ tablespoons (24 grams) kirsch

1½ tablespoons (24 grams) orange blossom water

1¼ cups (280 grams) heavy cream

A cake more than a tart, Brioche Saint Tropez originates from Provence-Alpes-Côte d'Azur, a resort region in southeastern France. The cake is composed of two layers of brioche moistened with vanilla bean syrup and spread with a thick layer of ethereal cream. A crunchy streusel topping adds textural contrast to the cake, while the complex creamy filling is scented with the tropical flavors of cherry kirsch and orange blossom. Prepare the cake a few hours before you plan to serve it, then kick up your feet and follow your imagination to the French Riviera.

Method

Make the brioche

1 Line a 12-by-17-inch baking sheet with parchment paper, then set a 10-by-3-inch metal ring mold onto it.

2 Lightly dust your work surface with flour, remove the brioche dough from the refrigerator, and scrape it out of the bowl and onto the work surface. The dough will be sticky, so keep your hands floured, but use extra flour only as necessary. Deflate the dough, then use your hands to form it into a round, flat disc; roll it to just under 10 inches in diameter. Brush off any excess flour from both sides, then set the dough into the metal ring mold, pressing with your fingers to distribute the dough evenly into the ring.

3 Using a pastry brush, glaze the top of the brioche with egg wash. Cover the brioche ring with plastic wrap and set it aside to rise in a warm place for about 1 hour, until it doubles in size.

4 Preheat the oven to 350°F (175°C).

5 Give the brioche a final egg wash, then sprinkle the top with the streusel. Bake the brioche for 20 to 30 minutes, until it is light golden brown on the top and firm to the touch in the

center. Remove the baking sheet from the oven, set it on a cooling rack, and allow the brioche to cool for 10 minutes.

6 Slide a flat metal spatula under the brioche and around the inside edge of the ring. Lift off the ring mold, then remove the brioche from the parchment paper and set it on a cooling rack to cool completely before proceeding.

Make the syrup

1 Combine the simple syrup and vanilla bean seeds and pod in a small saucepan and bring to a boil over medium-high heat Remove from the heat and allow the syrup to cool completely, then remove the vanilla bean pod.

2 Add the kirsch and stir to combine.

Make the cream filling

1 In the bowl of a stand mixer fitted with the paddle attachment, beat the pastry cream until it's smooth and creamy, about 30 seconds. Remove the paddle and fit the mixer with the whisk attachment. Add the softened buttercream and whisk on medium speed to combine the ingredients, about 1 minute. Add the kirsch and orange blossom water and whip briefly to combine. Transfer the mixture to a large bowl and set aside.

2 Pour the heavy cream into the bowl of a stand mixer fitted with the whisk attachment and whip on high speed until the cream reaches soft peaks. Gently fold the whipped cream into the buttercream mixture, being careful to not overmix, or the cream could become grainy.

Assemble the cake

1 Remove the brioche cake from its ring by sliding a small metal spatula along the inside edge of the ring. Using a serrated knife, slice the brioche in half horizontally. Set the metal cake ring onto a serving plate, then put the bottom brioche layer inside the cake ring. Using a pastry brush, generously brush the bottom layer with the syrup.

2 Scrape the cream filling out of the bowl and onto the bottom layer of brioche, then use an offset metal spatula to spread the filling into an even layer.

3 Flip the top brioche cake upside down and quickly brush a light soaking of syrup on its underside. Flip the cake over and set it on top of the cream layer. Using your hands, press down gently but firmly to ensure that the brioche is set against the cream filling. Cover the cake and refrigerate for 2 hours before unmolding.

4 To unmold, run a small, flat metal spatula around the inside edge of the ring. Slowly lift the ring off the cake. Serve the cake immediately. To store, cover the cake in plastic wrap and refrigerate for up to 24 hours.

CHAPTER NINE

Flaky Pastries

Flaky Pastries

Les feuilletée

Crispy. Flaky. Two of the most elusive words in the world of gluten-free baking. This chapter brings them back. All of these recipes are made with laminated dough, so grab your rolling pin and pure unsalted butter. We start with yeasted flaky pastries, so the buttery scent of croissants can fill your kitchen. Perhaps you'll set a few aside to make almond croissants, a twice baked nut crispy pastry made from leftover croissants. A new croissant sensation included is Breton Butter Cake, a rustic-looking pastry made with caramelized croissant dough. Move on to puff pastry, where you'll find a French version of our American turnovers, imaginatively called Apple Slippers. Skip over to puff pastry cookies with much loved *Palmiers* and Arlettes, an abstract, oval, wafer-like cookie scented with cinnamon. *Sacristains*, twisted pastry embedded with sparkle sugar and almonds, are a favorite for teatime. And Straws are an uncommon crispy jammy sandwiched cookie. Stack up the pastry layers for scrumptious Napoleons filled with smooth vanilla bean pastry cream. Rounding out the selection is *Pithivier*, a traditional pastry etched with a sunburst design—made with two circles of dough and filled with aromatic frangipane. Fetchingly pretty, the Pear and Berry Pastries are stylish and await your full attention. Put the kettle on and reach for the realms of flaky pastry!

Croissants

Croissants

Makes about 16

Special tool: pastry brush

Gluten-free flour for dusting

1 recipe Croissant Dough
(2 pieces; pages 58 to 61)

Egg Wash (page 19)

This recipe rewards you with the satisfying, yeasty, buttery taste known only to croissants. Gluten-free croissants are dissimilar to standard wheat croissants in that the absence of gluten prevents the dough from stretching to develop the classic flaky layers in traditional croissants. However, at the end of the day, these croissants will be reminiscent of lovely crescent rolls with their soft interior and gentle crust formation.

The dough is finicky, as is all laminated dough, whether gluten-free or wheat-based, so treat it with care and follow a few cardinal rules. One is to make sure the butter block and dough are at similar textures; if the butter is too cold, it will break in the dough and make the lamination difficult. Note that gluten-free dough tends to crack; gently press it back together with your fingers as necessary. This gluten-free croissant dough is given an overnight rest to help develop its flavor before the lamination process begins.

Method

1 Lightly dust your work surface with flour. Roll out one piece of dough into an 8-by-16-inch rectangle that's ¼ inch thick. Brush away any excess flour from both sides of the dough. Cut the dough into 2½-by-8-inch triangles. Roll the croissants up into crescent shapes, tuck their tails beneath them, and place onto parchment paper–lined baking sheets. Using a pastry brush, give the croissants a light egg wash, then set them aside in a warm place to rise for 1 to 2 hours, until they are puffy and the layers show separation. Repeat with the second piece of croissant dough.

2 Preheat the oven to 425° (220°C).

3 Place the croissants in the oven and bake for 15 to 20 minutes, until golden brown and firm to the touch on their lower back side.

4 Remove the pan from the oven and set it on a cooling rack for 10 minutes before serving. When the croissants have cooled completely, wrap them in plastic and store at room temperature for up to 2 days. Rewarm them at 350°F (175°C) for 5 minutes to regain their crispness.

Almond Croissants

Croissants aux amandes

Makes 6

Special tool: pastry brush

6 plain baked croissants
(pages 273 to 275)

For the rum syrup
1 cup (285 grams)
Simple Syrup (page 20)

1 tablespoon (16 grams)
dark rum

For the almond cream
½ cup (115 grams) unsalted
butter, at room temperature

¾ cup (150 grams)
granulated sugar

1½ cups (150 grams)
almond flour

½ cup (125 grams) cold Pastry
Cream (pages 26 and 27)

1 large egg (55 grams)

½ teaspoon (3 grams)
almond extract

½ cup (80 grams) gluten-free
flour blend (see pages 1 to 3)

2 cups (168 grams)
sliced natural almonds

Confectioners' sugar for
dusting

Originally made from leftover croissants, these pastries are good enough to warrant a special batch of plain croissants explicitly to transform into these rich, buttery almond pastries. Split the croissants lengthwise, brush with dark rum syrup, spread with almond cream, sandwich, slather the outside with almond cream, then roll in sliced almonds. Bake them until golden brown, dust with a touch of confectioners' sugar, and immerse yourself in the French world of an impossibly delicious twice-baked breakfast pastry.

Method

1 Line a 12-by-17-inch baking sheet with parchment paper or a silicone mat.

2 To make the rum syrup, in a small bowl, stir together the simple syrup and rum.

3 To make the almond cream, in the bowl of a stand mixer fitted with the paddle attachment, combine the butter, sugar, almond flour, and pastry cream and blend on medium speed for 1 minute. Add the egg and almond extract and mix to combine. Add the gluten-free flour and mix on low speed; gradually increase to medium speed and beat for 1 minute. Using a silicone spatula, scrape down the sides and bottom of the bowl and finish mixing by hand as needed.

4 Preheat the oven to 425°F (220°C).

5 Using a serrated knife, slice each croissant in half lengthwise. With a pastry brush, apply a generous swipe of rum syrup to the inside top and bottom of the croissants. Using a metal spatula, spread 1 tablespoon of almond cream

across the bottom half of each croissant, then sandwich with its top. Next, liberally coat the top and sides (leave the bottom as is) of the croissant with almond cream. Generously sprinkle the croissants with sliced almonds, then place them onto the baking sheet.

6 Bake the almond croissants for 20 to 30 minutes, until they are golden brown. Remove from the oven and set the baking sheet on a cooling rack for 20 minutes, then give the croissants a light sprinkle of confectioners' sugar. Serve immediately. The croissants can be wrapped in plastic and stored for 24 hours at room temperature.

Breton Butter Cake

Kouign-amann

Makes 8

Special tools: jumbo muffin pans or eight 3½-inch metal tart rings or pans set onto a parchment paper– or silicone mat–lined baking sheet

½ recipe Croissant Dough (pages 58 to 61), completed to three turns only

¾ cup (150 grams) granulated sugar

Caramelized croissant dough suitably defines this fabulous breakfast pastry that has recently gained popularity in the United States. The unusual name, *Kouign-amann*, translates to "butter cake." It is a specialty of Brittany, where it originated in the mid-1800s. The cake itself is made through croissant dough lamination with its final turn receiving a generous sprinkling of sugar—try vanilla sugar to add another dimension of flavor. Biting into a Breton butter cake is a unique, buttery, crisp pastry revelation that's open to variation. My favorite is to scoop a teaspoon of black currant jam into the center of the pastry just before baking. The fruity depth of currant flavor meeting the higher sweet notes of the Kouign-amann may find you singing its praises.

Method

1 Complete three turns of the croissant dough. On the fourth turn, sprinkle the dough liberally with sugar on both sides. Roll the dough out, make the final turn and give the dough another three-fold, cover with plastic wrap, and refrigerate for 1 hour.

2 Remove the dough from the refrigerator, then roll it out onto a large piece of plastic wrap or parchment paper. The dough will be moist from the sugar, so use additional sugar as necessary to keep the dough from sticking. Roll the dough into a 16-by-16-inch square that's ⅛ to ¼ inch thick.

3 Cut the dough into 4-inch squares, resulting in eight squares. Fold the four corners into the center of each square, then make a second fold of the four corners half way into the center. The pastries may crack and look a bit roughly formed; this is okay. Place the pastries into their pans, then set aside in a warm spot to rise for 1 to 2 hours, until the dough is puffy and has nearly doubled in volume.

4 Preheat the oven to 450°F (230°C).

5 When the Kouign-amann have nearly doubled in volume, place them in the oven, lower the temperature to 425°F (220°C), and bake for 25 to 30 minutes, until the pastries turn a deep golden brown. Set the baking sheet onto a cooling rack to cool for 15 minutes.

6 Release the Kouign-amann from the pans by rapping them against the cooling rack. If necessary, use the tip of a paring knife to help free them. Serve immediately, or wrap in plastic and store for 24 hours at room temperature. Rewarm the pastries in a 350°F (175°C) oven for 5 minutes before eating.

Apple Slippers

Chaussons aux pommes

Makes 6

Special tools: 6-inch round cutter, sharp-tipped paring knife, small pastry brush

1 tablespoon (15 grams) unsalted butter

1 pound (455 grams) baking apples, peeled, cored, and cut into ½-inch pieces

½ vanilla bean, split and seeds scraped

½ cup (100 grams) granulated sugar

1 tablespoon (18 grams) lemon juice

One and a half 11-by-16-inch Puff Pastry Dough sheets (pages 55 to 57), chilled

Egg Wash (page 19)

Legend says that in 1630 Sarthe Saint-Calais suffered from a terrible epidemic but was saved by a lady of the town who distributed apples and flour to the poor, who then made apple turnovers. Each September the town holds their traditional *Fête du Chausson aux Pommes* medieval festival in celebration of apple turnovers. Poetically named for their shape, these puff pastry slippers etched with a curvy leaf pattern are a cousin to our well-known apple turnovers, although more elaborate in appearance, texture, and flavor. The buttery pastry meeting the soft, sweet tanginess of the apples may inspire a visit to the orchard seeking apples for your next batch. When the slippers bake, they release juices that caramelize and are easiest to release from a silicone mat, but parchment paper will also work.

Method

1 In a medium saucepan, melt the butter over medium heat. Add the chopped apples, vanilla bean and seeds, sugar, and lemon juice. Bring the mixture to a simmer and cook over low heat for 5 to 10 minutes, stirring occasionally until the apples are softened but still retain their shape. Remove the pan from the heat and set aside to cool to room temperature.

2 Line a 12-by-17-inch baking sheet with parchment paper or a silicone mat.

3 Place the sheets of puff pastry dough onto a lightly floured piece of parchment paper, cover with plastic wrap, and allow to sit for 5 minutes. If at any point the dough becomes too soft to handle, you can refrigerate it for 10 minutes and then resume working with the dough where you left off. Conversely, if the dough is breaking, it may be too cold. If this is the case, allow the dough to sit out at room temperature for 10 minutes covered with plastic wrap until it is soft enough to handle without breaking.

4 Roll each piece of dough ¼ inch thick, then use a 6-inch round cutter to cut out six or seven puff pastry dough discs. Place the discs on the lined baking sheet and refrigerate for 15 minutes.

5 Remove the puff pastry discs from the refrigerator and use the blunt edge of a knife to lightly etch the top of each disc in half, without breaking the surface of the dough; you are making a delineation point, not cutting. You are now ready to cut a design into one half of the top of the dough. Using a sharp-tipped paring knife, make your cuts swift and concise, about ¹⁄₁₆ inch deep. Cut the design of a leaf-like pattern that includes the spine and veins and make your design large enough to fill one half of the space. Note: do not cut all the way through the dough. Cutting designs into puff pastry dough takes practice, so be patient. No matter how your cuts turn out, the end result will be delicious. When you are finished cutting your designs, refrigerate the dough for 15 minutes.

6 Remove the puff pastry discs from the refrigerator and turn each one over, revealing the plain side where the filling will go. The design should be at the top, facing down, and not visible. Brush the edge of the discs lightly with water. Spoon 3 tablespoons of apple filling into the center of each disc. Fold the top half of the disc over the apple filling to make a half circle shape, revealing the design. Adjust the location of the fold as necessary so the design is fully visible. Gently but firmly seal the edges of the dough together using your fingertips to press along the edges. Press the side of your cupped hand around the enclosed apples to seal the filling tightly inside. Flute the edge of the dough with your fingers or a knife. You should see the full pattern of your design on the top of the apple slipper. Let the apple slippers rest in the refrigerator for 30 minutes.

7 While the slippers are resting, preheat the oven to 425°F (220°C).

8 Lightly brush the slippers with egg wash and bake for 30 to 40 minutes, until the pastries have turned golden brown. Remove the baking sheet from the oven and place it on a cooling rack to cool for 20 minutes, then carefully peel the apple slippers off the silicone mat. The slippers are best eaten within 24 hours, or they may be wrapped in plastic and stored in the refrigerator for up to 2 days or frozen for up to 1 month.

Palm Leaves

Palmiers

Makes about 12

---

1 cup (200 grams)
vanilla sugar (page 287)
or plain granulated sugar

½ recipe Puff Pastry Dough
(pages 55 to 57), given five
turns

Egg Wash (page 19)

Probably the most popular French flaky pastry cookies, here in the United States palm leaves are also known as butterflies and elephant ears. When I was eighteen, I worked in a corner bakery in Provincetown, Massachusetts, where we sold a merry selection of pastries, including giant elephant ears that were carried happily away by small children. Once you are familiar with the technique of forming palmiers, you can easily scale their size up or down by rolling the dough into a longer or shorter rectangle. I like to make spiced palmiers with cinnamon-cardamom sugar.

Method

1 Line two 12-by-17-inch baking sheets with parchment paper or silicone baking mats.

2 Dust a large sheet of plastic wrap or parchment paper liberally with the vanilla sugar. Set the puff pastry onto the sugared surface and generously sprinkle the top of the dough with the vanilla sugar. Roll the pastry into a rectangle and give the dough its final turn with another three-fold. Wrap the dough in plastic and refrigerate for 30 minutes.

3 Return the dough to your work surface, setting it onto a piece of plastic wrap or parchment paper. Liberally sugar both sides of the dough, then roll out to a 12-by-16-inch rectangle that's about ⅜ inch thick. Trim the excess rough dough edges to makes the sheet even. Press your rolling pin down into the center of the long edge of the rectangle to make a slight indentation. Fold each side of the dough halfway into the center of this indentation, then make a second fold so the two sides meet in the center. There should be about ¼ inch of space remaining in the center. Using a pastry brush, apply a light coat of egg wash down the center band. Fold one side

over the center band to meet the far end of the other side. The dough should be equally folded on both sides. Use the rolling pin to gently flatten and press the dough together. One side should have a closed fold edge, and the other side should have two closed, folded edges.

4 Using a chef's knife, slice the dough into ¾-inch-thick slices and lay them flat onto the lined baking sheets. You should now be able to see the interfolded pattern. Space the slices about 3 inches apart, as they will expand when they bake. Place the baking sheets with the cookies into the freezer for 1 hour.

5 Preheat the oven to 425°F (220°C).

6 Place the baking sheets into the oven and reduce the oven temperature to 400°F (205°C). Bake the palmiers for 15 to 20 minutes, until they turn a deep golden caramel color. Set the baking sheet with the cookies on a cooling rack and allow them to cool to room temperature. Store the cookies wrapped in plastic at room temperature for up to 2 days.

Vanilla Sugar

Save your vanilla beans! After you have split and scraped their seeds, the vanilla bean pod can be used to create aromatic and flavorful vanilla sugar. Fill a quart-size glass jar two-thirds full with granulated sugar. If the vanilla bean has only been scraped, then settle the pod down into the sugar. If the vanilla bean was used for an infusion, rinse it thoroughly and set it aside to dry for a day, then add it to the glass jar with the sugar. After the sugar jar has accumulated a half dozen beans, let it sit at room temperature for a couple of weeks. Now your sugar is ready to grind! Pour the sugar and beans into a food processor fitted with a blade attachment and grind for 2 to 4 minutes, until the beans have broken into small pieces. Then sift the sugar over a bowl and discard the small, hard bits of bean remaining in the sieve. The sugar will appear speckled with the essence of the beans. Use your vanilla sugar to make butterfly wings, to sweeten whipped cream, or substitute it for granulated sugar in recipes where you want to boost the vanilla flavor.

Cinnamon Arlettes

Arlettes à la cannelle

Makes 14

Special tool: pastry brush

1 cup (200 grams) granulated sugar, plus more if needed

1 tablespoon (6 grams) ground cinnamon

One 10-by-16-inch Puff Pastry Dough sheet (pages 55 to 57)

Egg Wash (page 19)

Likely named after a French girl, Arlettes have a striking, dramatic appearance. Tall, oval, deep brown, and fragile, these puff pastry cookies draw attention with their unusual features. The cinnamon puff pastry is rolled up into a spiral, flattened exceptionally thin, and given the shape of an oval mirror. Delicate in texture, Arlettes can shatter easily, making lovely caramelized shards of cookies. The method for making Arlettes can be varied; one alternate version is to finish the final roll of puff pastry with cinnamon sugar and then proceed with the recipe. However you make them, Arlettes are simply mesmerizing, and their cinnamon sweet pastry is a distinct pleasure.

Method

1 Line a 12-by-17-inch baking sheet with parchment paper.

2 Whisk together the sugar and cinnamon in a small bowl and set it aside.

3 Lay a 12-by-24-inch piece of parchment paper on your work surface. Sprinkle one-third of the cinnamon sugar evenly into an approximately 11-by-17-inch rectangle on the parchment paper.

4 Set the puff pastry onto a separate piece of parchment paper, keeping it covered with plastic wrap so it does not dry out. Allow the dough to sit out for 5 minutes, or until it has softened enough to fold and shape without breaking.

5 Using a pastry brush, lightly brush one side of the puff pastry with the egg wash. Flip the puff pastry dough, egg wash side down, onto the parchment paper with the cinnamon sugar. Lightly brush the top of the dough with egg wash, then sprinkle one-third of the cinnamon sugar on top of the dough, distributing it evenly, smoothing it across the dough with your hands. Using a rolling pin, gently but firmly press the sugar into the dough. Flip the dough over and repeat the process of pressing the sugar into the dough. At this point, the objective is to press the sugar in, not roll the dough flatter. If the dough becomes too sticky to handle, lightly sprinkle additional sugar on both sides. Note: gluten-free puff pastry dough handles best when it is soft enough to shape, but not so warm that it becomes sticky. If at any point the dough becomes too soft to handle, you may refrigerate it for 15 minutes and then resume working with the dough where you left off.

6 Position the dough so the long end runs left to right. Beginning at the top, tuck the edge of the dough over, then begin to roll the dough toward you into a tight log. Slice the dough into fourteen pieces, each one approximately 1¼ inches thick.

7 Place a 12-by-12-inch piece of plastic wrap on your work surface. Generously sprinkle the plastic wrap with more cinnamon sugar. Place one of the puff pastry spirals upright (the spiral should be facing you) on top of the cinnamon sugar. With the heel of your hand, press the dough, slightly flattening it into a thick oval shape. Sprinkle more cinnamon sugar over the dough, then place a second piece of plastic wrap on top. With a rolling pin, gently press down on the center of the dough and begin to roll with steady, even pressure upward and downward. The shape of the spiral will begin to elongate and become a very flat, thin, long oval. The final dough shape will be 8 to 9 inches tall and 4 inches wide. If the edges of the dough begin to crack, carefully smooth them with your hands over the plastic wrap.

8 Transfer the oval onto a parchment paper–lined baking sheet. Gently remove the top layer of plastic wrap, then flip the dough over and remove the second piece of plastic wrap. If the plastic wrap sticks, chill the dough with the wrap still attached, then remove it. If you apply enough sugar on both sides of the dough before rolling it flat, the plastic wrap should easily peel off. Continue rolling each dough oval in the same method. Place three dough ovals on the parchment paper, cover with a second layer of parchment paper (or plastic wrap), and continue layering the ovals until you are finished rolling them out. Refrigerate the dough ovals for 30 minutes before baking.

9 Preheat the oven to 375°F (190°C).

10 To prepare the Arlettes for baking, you will essentially sandwich the dough ovals between two baking sheets. Place a piece of parchment paper on the top of an inverted 12-by-17-inch baking sheet. Place two dough ovals on top of the parchment paper, side by side. Cover the dough with a second piece of parchment paper, then lay a second baking sheet on top.

11 Bake the Arlettes for 10 minutes, or until the cookies have turned a dark golden brown. To check the cookies, carefully lift the upper pan to peek at their coloring. When the Arlettes are done, take them from the oven and remove the top baking sheet and parchment paper. Set the Arlettes on a cooling rack to cool completely and firm up before handling. Arlettes are best eaten on the same day they are baked.

Sacristains

Sacristains

Makes 16

Special tool: small pastry brush

One 10-by-16-inch, ¼-inch-thick Puff Pastry Dough sheet (see pages 55 to 57), chilled

Egg Wash (page 19)

½ cup (70 grams) raw almonds, finely chopped

¼ cup (50 grams) crystal or sparkling sugar

These corkscrew-shaped treats are named for the official—the sacristain—who oversees the sacristy in the Catholic church. Encrusted in chopped almonds and sparkling sugar, they are excellent alongside a cup of tea or coffee. Gluten-free puff pastry dough is finicky to work with; if at any point the dough becomes too soft to handle, you may refrigerate it for 15 minutes and then resume working with it where you left off. Alternately, the dough must be soft enough to twist without breaking, so it may need to rest at room temperature (covered, so it does not dry out) to reach a workable consistency.

Method

1 Line two 12-by-17-inch baking sheets with parchment paper.

2 Lay a 12-by-17-inch (or larger) piece of parchment paper on your work surface. Place the sheet of chilled puff pastry dough on the parchment paper. Lightly brush the egg wash evenly over the surface of the dough, then sprinkle half of the chopped almonds over the top. Sprinkle half of the sparkling sugar over the top of the dough. With a rolling pin, firmly press and roll lengthwise across the dough to embed the almonds and sugar into the surface. Flip the dough over and repeat these same steps, resulting in an almond and sugar-encrusted sheet of puff pastry.

3 Cut the rectangle into two halves, each 5 by 8 inches. Cut each rectangle into eight 1-inch strips that will be 5 inches long. Place the strips onto parchment paper–lined baking sheets, spacing them evenly. Take the end of each strip and twist the dough one half turn and continue for three twists on each strip, creating a corkscrew shape.

4 Refrigerate the puff pastry strips for 20 minutes and preheat the oven to 425°F (220°C).

5 Place the baking sheet into the oven and immediately reduce the temperature to 400°F (205°C). Bake for about 15 minutes, until the sacristains are golden brown. Set the baking sheet on a cooling rack to cool completely. Sacristains are best enjoyed the same day they are made, but they may be wrapped well in plastic and kept for up to 1 week. Place them in a 350°F (175°C) oven for 5 minutes to regain their crispiness.

Straws

Pailles

Makes 12

Special tool: pastry brush

One 10-by-16-inch, ¼-inch-thick sheet Puff Pastry Dough (see pages 55 to 57), chilled

Egg Wash (page 19)

½ cup (100 grams) granulated sugar

1 cup (340 grams) raspberry jam

Confectioners' sugar for dusting

The intriguing shape and construction of *pailles*—puff pastry sandwiched cookies oozing with jam—makes them alluring to the eye. A contrasting band of confectioners' sugar against the caramelized pastry gives a pretty finish to these crunchy, crumbly treats.

Remember that puff pastry is finicky; make sure the dough is soft enough before making your folds so it doesn't crack or break, and be sure to press the strips together firmly so they remain attached during baking. The parchment paper and metal cooling rack are there to ensure that the pastry pushes outward rather than upward during baking. Please yourself by filling the cookies with your favorite flavor of jam.

Method

1 Line two 12-by-17-inch baking sheets with parchment paper.

2 Lay a 12-by-17-inch (or larger) piece of parchment paper on your work surface. Place the sheet of chilled puff pastry dough on the parchment paper with the short side facing you. Lightly brush the egg wash evenly over the surface of the dough. Sprinkle half of the sugar over the top of the dough. Flip the dough over and repeat the egg wash and sugar application. Fold the dough in half (the long side of the rectangle). If the spine of the fold cracks, wait 5 minutes and try again. The pastry needs to be soft enough to manipulate into folds without breaking. Then fold the dough in half again, in the same direction. Slide the dough onto a parchment paper–lined baking sheet and set it in the freezer for 20 minutes.

3 Remove the dough from the freezer, set it onto a cutting surface, and allow it to sit for 10 minutes, or until the dough is

soft enough to cut easily. Position the long side of the dough parallel to your body. Using a ruler, score the dough into ¼-inch-wide strips. Slice all the strips with a sharp knife. Set one strip onto the parchment paper–lined baking sheet with the cut side facing up so you can see the folded layers. Place another strip next to it, and then another one, for a total of three strips pressed close together to form one large shape. Continue to assemble all the strips, then sprinkle the tops lightly with granulated sugar.

4 Preheat the oven to 425°F (220°C).

5 Cover the pastries with a piece of parchment paper, then top with a large metal cooling rack. Bake the pastries for 10 minutes, then remove the rack and the parchment paper. Using a wide metal spatula, flip the pastries over and continue to bake for about 10 minutes, until golden brown. Set the pastries onto a cooling rack to cool completely.

6 Sandwich the pastries with raspberry jam, then sift the edges lightly with confectioners' sugar. Serve immediately. Store the cookies wrapped in plastic for up to 2 days at room temperature.

Napoleons

Mille-feuille

Makes 7

One 12-by-16-inch sheet
Puff Pastry Dough
(pages 55 to 57)

1 recipe Pastry Cream
(pages 26 and 27)

¼ cup (50 grams)
dark chocolate, melted and
poured into a small zip-top
bag

Sugar Icing Glaze (page 21)

I had my first Napoleon when I was eight years old, after a family friend began transporting the stacked creamy constructions up to Vermont from New York City and selling them in his little corner store. My first experience of eating a Napoleon was a pastry pinnacle, consumed in complete silence as an entranced child.

Napoleons are made up of three layers of puff pastry that alternate with two layers of cream and are topped with confectioners' sugar or icing. You can finish your Napoleon in one whole rectangle or slice the pieces ahead of time and finish them individually. I find the second approach easier, as gluten-free puff pastry does not slice as readily as traditional wheat puff pastry. Yes, gluten-free puff pastry can be tricky, but this recipe will bring you back to the thrill of the Napoleon's high point with its puff pastry crunching into creaminess and mingling with its signature sweet icing.

When it comes to fillings and toppings, Napoleons are open to tremendous interpretation. Try your hand at filling them with piped balls of Honey Chocolate Mousse (page 39), Dark Chocolate Ganache (page 36), or Pistachio Buttercream (pages 237 and 240), or layering them with fresh fruit. Are you wondering how to eat one? However you please!

Method

1 Preheat the oven to 425°F (220°C).

2 Place the sheet of puff pastry onto a baking sheet lined with parchment paper. Bake the pastry for 30 to 40 minutes, until it is crisp and golden brown. Use a metal spatula to lift the pastry off the parchment to peek at the underside.

It should be golden brown when it is done. Remove the baking sheet from the oven, and set it onto a cooling rack.

3 Once the pastry has cooled, using a serrated knife, slowly saw the puff pastry sheet into three equal size rectangles, about 3 by 14 inches each. To assemble, place one puff pastry rectangle onto the back of a flat baking sheet. Spoon on 1½ cups of pastry cream, then use a small metal spatula to spread it across the puff pastry in an even layer, reaching to the corners. Add a second puff pastry rectangle on top of the pastry cream, then apply 1½ cups of pastry cream onto the new puff rectangle. Top the pastry cream with the third and final puff pastry rectangle. Using a small metal spatula, smooth and fill the horizontal spaces between the layers. Chill the pastry for 1 hour before glazing.

4 When you are ready to finish the pastry, fill the zip-top bag with the melted chocolate and snip a 1⁄16-inch tip off the corner of the bag, then carefully set it aside, ensuring that the chocolate does not leak out.

5 Heat the glaze to a neutral temperature (it should feel barely warm to the touch of your finger or lip), then add just enough water for the glaze to stay thick enough to spread but not runny. If it becomes too wet, add more confectioners' sugar, 1 teaspoon at a time, and mix to blend until you reach the desired consistency. You can also add more water or heat the glaze again to reach the correct temperature and consistency.

6 Pour the glaze over the top of the stacked puff pastry and quickly spread it across the top with a flat metal spatula. Pipe the melted chocolate in long horizontal stripes across the pastry, creating six stripes on the glaze. Moving quickly, pull a sharp paring knife through the top of the glaze at 1-inch intervals. Repeat this same step, with the paring knife inverted, so that you are pulling the chocolate into two different directions. Chill the Napoleon for 15 minutes, then remove from the refrigerator and use a paring knife to trim off the excess glaze.

7 With a serrated knife, cut the Napoleon into seven 2-inch slices. Hold the side of the Napoleon with one hand and deftly saw through the pastry with the other hand. It may be helpful to wipe off the knife between each cutting. Serve immediately or store in an airtight plastic container in the refrigerator for up to 24 hours.

Pear Berry Puff Pastries

Feuilletés aux poires et fruits rouges

Makes 2 dozen

Special tool: 4-inch fluted oval cutter or other large cutter

½ cup (100 grams) granulated sugar

1 recipe Puff Pastry Dough (pages 55 to 57)

1 cup (200 grams) Almond Cream (page 23)

2 large pears, peeled, cored, and cut into ⅛-inch-thick slices

1 cup (170 grams) fresh or frozen blueberries

½ cup (150 grams) Apricot Glaze (page 20), melted

Large, fluted, flaky pastries fanned with pears and dotted with blueberries are gorgeous to behold. I like to apply a swipe of almond cream beneath the fruit before baking to act as a moisture barrier and to add a bit of flavor. You could also substitute frangipane for the almond cream or omit it altogether. The dough can be cut into various shapes, larger or smaller—just remember to adjust the oven's baking time. Apricots, plums, mixed berries, or thinly sliced apples would be equally at home in this kindly pastry.

Method

1 Line a baking sheet with parchment paper or a silicone baking mat.

2 Lay a large piece of parchment paper onto your work surface and sprinkle lightly with sugar. Set the puff pastry onto the paper and roll it out to ¼ inch thick. Sprinkle the top with a thin coating of sugar. Cut out as many oval shapes as you can, setting them onto a parchment paper–lined baking sheet as you go. Place a piece of parchment paper between the layers of the cut-out ovals. When you have cut out as many shapes as possible, set the baking sheet in the refrigerator. Gather the scraps and gently press them together, wrap them in plastic, and refrigerate them for 30 minutes. Once they have chilled, re-roll them and cut out the remaining ovals.

3 Set the chilled ovals onto parchment paper–lined baking sheets, spacing them 1½ inches apart. Using a small offset metal spatula, smear a small amount (about 1 teaspoon) of almond cream onto the top of each oval. This will help act as a moisture barrier and add flavor. Fan three pear slices across the top of each oval. Next, sprinkle a few blueberries alongside the pears. Refrigerate the pastries while the oven heats up.

4 Preheat the oven to 425°F (220°C).

5 Bake the pastries for 20 to 30 minutes, until they turn golden brown. Use a metal spatula to lift an oval off the parchment to peek at the underside. It should be golden brown when it is done. Remove the baking sheet with the pastries from the oven and set the pan on a cooling rack. When the pastries are have cooled completely, use a pastry brush to apply a thin coat of apricot glaze on the fruit. Serve immediately, or store wrapped in plastic or in a plastic container in the refrigerator for 2 days.

Pithivier

Pithivier

Makes one 8-inch cake

Special tool: pastry brush

Two 10-by-10-inch, ¼-inch-thick Puff Pastry Dough sheets (pages 55 to 57), chilled

1 recipe Frangipane (pages 24 and 25)

Egg Wash (page 19)

This elegant yet simple flaky cake is traditionally served as a Twelfth Night cake in the Órleans region of France, where the town of Pithiviers is located. A pithivier—the pastry—is made by enclosing two large puff pastry circles that contain an almond cream or frangipane filling. The top is gracefully etched with a spiral sunburst design, and the pastry's edge is scalloped. Here the recipe calls for frangipane made with the bold flavor of pure almond paste.

Method

1 Line a 12-by-17-inch baking sheet with parchment paper or a silicone mat.

2 Place the sheets of puff pastry dough on a lightly floured piece of parchment paper, cover with plastic wrap, and allow to sit for 5 minutes. If at any point the dough becomes too soft to handle, you can refrigerate it for 10 minutes and then resume working with the dough where you left off. Conversely, if the dough is breaking, it may be too cold. If this is the case, allow the dough to sit out at room temperature for 10 minutes, covered with plastic wrap, until it is soft enough to handle without breaking.

3 Roll each piece of dough ¼ inch thick and cut out two 8-inch puff pastry dough discs. Place them on the parchment paper–lined baking sheet and refrigerate for 15 minutes.

4 Remove the puff pastry discs from the refrigerator and spoon the frangipane into a mound in the center of one of the discs. Leave the filling in a mound; once the top disc of dough is applied the filling will naturally spread. Wet your finger lightly with water and run it around the edge of the dough, then set the second pastry disc on top of the frangipane.

Do not press down on the top of the dough. Gently press the edges of the top and bottom discs together. You want a good seal so the filling does not leak out during baking.

5 You are now ready to cut a spiral design into the top of the dough. Using a sharp-tipped paring knife, make a 1⁄16-inch hole in the center of the pastry for steam to release during baking. From this point, draw out the spiral design. Make your cuts swift and concise, about 1⁄16 inch deep; be careful not to cut all the way through the dough. Cutting designs into puff pastry dough takes practice, so be patient. After the spiral has been drawn, use the knife to flute or scallop the outer edge. Refrigerate the dough for 15 minutes.

6 Preheat the oven to 425°F (220°C).

7 Using a pastry brush, apply a thin coating of egg wash to the pastry. Bake for 30 to 40 minutes, until the pastry is golden brown. Set the pan on a cooling rack to cool completely. Slice the cake and serve, or wrap it in plastic and store in the refrigerator for up to 1 week.

Playful *Petit Fours*

Little bite-size pastries—the name *petit four* refers to a small oven used to bake these diminutive confections that dates back to the 1800s. Apparently, the smaller items were baked after the larger pastries had been removed from the oven and the temperature had dropped. Petit fours has become a catchphrase for tiny, square-shaped confections, but there are numerous subcategories. *Petit Four Glacé* is a diverse group of pastries made with ganache, pastry cream, or buttercream, and then glazed. The Little Lemon Cakes (pages 159 and 160) would fall into this category. *Petit Four Sec* refers to ready-to-eat pastries directly after baking, such as small biscuits and cookies like tiny madeleines (pages 153 and 154) or financiers

(pages 155 to 157). *Petit Four Demi-Sec* refers to petit fours sec—a half-dry pastry portion that is combined with a cream, such as macarons (pages 40 to 42). *Petit Four Varitété* covers all other types that do not fall into a specific category, such as a savory petit four.

Many of the pastry recipes in this book are jubilant options for these petit four categories. For starters, you'll want to acquire tiny tart pans and molds. Then you can bake mini tigers, financiers, and madeleines. Also good for tiny treats are the pistachio baby cakes, lemon bites, tiny lemon or fresh fruit tarts, popper cream puffs, and miniature macarons. Just remember to adjust your baking times accordingly. These charming treats bring a big smile to children and adults and make for a lively, stylish presentation.

Ingredient	Cups/Tablespoons/Teaspoons	Ounces	Grams
Almonds, chopped	1 cup	5 ounces	140 grams
Baking powder	1 teaspoon	.13 ounce	4 grams
Baking soda	1 teaspoon	.21 ounce	6 grams
Butter	1 cup	8 ounces	225 grams
Chia powder	1 tablespoon	.16 ounce	4.5 grams
Cinnamon, ground	1 teaspoon	.07 ounce	2 grams
Cocoa powder	1 teaspoon	.08 ounces	2.5 grams
Coconut oil	1 tablespoon	.5 ounce	14 grams
Cornstarch	1 teaspoon	.11 ounce	3 grams
Cream, heavy	1 cup	8 ounces	230 grams
Cream of tartar	1 teaspoon	.11 ounce	3 grams
Flour, almond	1 cup	3.5 ounces	100 grams
Flour, gluten-free blend	1 cup	4.6 ounces	160 grams
Flour, potato	1 tablespoon	.42 ounces	12 grams
Hazelnuts, blanched and halved	1 cup	5 ounces	142 grams
Honey	1 tablespoon	.74 ounces	21 grams
Lemon zest	1 tablespoon	.17 ounce	6 grams
Milk, whole	1 cup	8 ounces	240 grams
Orange, zest	1 tablespoon	.17 ounce	6 grams
Sea salt	1 teaspoon	.25 ounce	7 grams
Sugar, brown, packed	1 cup	7 ounces	200 grams
Sugar, confectioners'	1 cup	3.5 ounces	100 grams
Sugar, granulated	1 cup	7 ounces	200 grams
Vanilla extract	1 teaspoon	.17 ounce	5 grams
Yeast, instant	1 tablespoon	.25 ounce	8 grams

Acknowledgments

Truly, this book springs from the creative talent, collaboration, and hard work of a great number of people. Writing a book is like a recipe within itself, an amalgamation of ingredients that are brought to the table by all participants, each one playing an essential role in the journey and final creation.

To my wonderful customers, thank you for showing up week after week to support my trade as a baker and for expressing your pleasures. Baking for you is a privilege and a joy.

My heartfelt thanks to the enormously talented Leda Scheintaub, cookbook author, book editor, recipe developer and tester extraordinaire, and soul sister. Your ample time and skill have made this book possible, and you have taught me with meticulous expertise, kindness, and patience. Thank you for believing in me and sharing your passion for culinary adventures. To Nash, for your warm smile, thoughtful input, and keeping me deliciously well fed from your Dosa Kitchen food truck to fire me up for writing.

To Marisa Bulzone, who gave so generously of her time to assist with my needs in understanding the minutiae of the publishing domain. You gave me a reality crash course that I seriously needed! Thank you for your exceptional consultation and substantial help.

After more than three decades, thank you for finding me again Jeffrey Hamelman. The timing was markedly serendipitous, and our correspondence and shared passion for baking has given me solid footing. Thank you for hiring me those long years ago, providing the opportunity to immerse myself into what was, at the time, a renaissance bakery in Brattleboro. You introduced me to an extraordinary new style of baking that forever changed my life, and I retain rich memories of those early mornings filled with the music of Mozart, the ritual jar of kimchi, and, ultimately, the experience of becoming a baker.

Fortune smiled on me to work directly with Charlie Ritzo, a gifted photographer who shot all the mouthwatering, uplifting photos for the book. Charlie traveled over the rainbow and back again to make this book a gorgeous one. Thank you for your patience, skill, and big heart, Charlie!

Margaret Shipman, you came along at the perfect moment to elevate the book cover design with great professionalism and style. Thank you for so graciously taking on the task and applying your design vision. To Maria Pugnetti, my appreciation for your sweet and earthy hand-drawn illustrations that appear as the "beginning" and endpapers in the book.

To Steve Rice, founder of Authentic Foods, thank you making that initial phone call and your generosity. And congratulations on creating a gluten-free, gum-free flour blend that can fool the traditionalists. Just see what you've made possible!

To my first bakery partner, Gabriel Capy, thank you for sharing your love and baking with me. Those years at The Bread Tree were arduous work that returned a thriving, beautiful bakery. We both have the sacred wounds to show it.

Merci beaucoup to the multi-linguistically talented Freeman-Graves family for graciously and expertly reviewing the French translations at the last minute, and for sharing and celebrating with food over the years.

Thank you to Skyhorse Publishing, in particular Abigail Ghering, for seeking me out at the farmers' market and urging me to submit my book proposal. And to my kind editor Brooke Rockwell, for her patience, good communication, and appreciation for my work.

To my extended family, Seth and Serena McGovern—my delightful Oregonian visit was a perfectly inspiring retreat that finally set my tracks firmly on the path to completing this book. Your generosity ultimately made it possible. Much gratitude and love to you both. Thanks and much love to Steve Procter, who held my heart for many years while I plunged back into the mixing bowl to find my place. Your encouragement and listening to my dreams urged me onward. Our earlier Procter-Austin family life gave me abundant opportunity to ply our festivities with a plethora of pastries. Rebecca McGovern, thank you for making chocolate truffles with me; that is a fond memory indeed. And Mark Procter, your rating system gave me cause to believe in myself.

As a child, I baked for my family as a way to give and receive love. Thank you Julie Walker for seeing and acknowledging this in me. Thank you, too, for my distant but remembered sisters in the Chicago area, Wini Nimrod and Janna Childs. You remain seated in my heart, and are woven through the pages of my life.

To Miriam Dror, for our shared hours and years of walking the beauty way. My gratitude for you deserves poetry. I know that without your love this book would never have come to pass. My deepest thanks to you Miriam.

To Anne and Tony Gengarelly and the poetry group—thank you for the exquisite evenings of contemplation, writing, and listening. I began this book in our circle, which gave me confidence to proceed.

A toast to the author's breakfast 101 with Michael Nethercott, mystery writer and kind-hearted friend. To Beth Neher for standing in my stead at market, and to Eliza Beardslee for your exemplary help preparing for the photo shoots, thank you both.

For the love of almond spice, Dutch-style, Ronnie Minnes, who has listened to me, and loved me, through all the scraps and scrapes and flying horses nearby.

To my friend David Schoales for sharing his stunning handmade cutting boards for the photo shoots. And to fellow author, friend, and baker, Kris McDermet, for loaning her lovely kitchen props.

Hugs and much love to my dear friend and chai wallah, Neil Harley, who keeps me blissfully plied with his delicious chai. Teatime has never been more ruckus or insightful, and you have been my brother for many lives.

To Lori Schreier, thank you for your support, encouragement, and unwavering faith in my book. And to Susan Dunning, a hearty acknowledgement for your discernment and realistic queries that help to keep me fiercely on track in the world of practical matters.

Once again, Paddy Brown, you found me, and thank you for loving me so sweetly.

Bold cheers and much love to my wild and colorful family, abundant with heart, humor, and heartbreak. Michael and Billy, I never thought we would still be on the planet; I am lucky to have you as my fearless brothers. Mom, you left too soon, but while you were here you made a mean stovetop cookie. Dad, you brought sweetness to the kitchen. I can still picture you in that damn La-Z-Boy chair calling out to me for warm cookies. Thank you for the life lessons, hailing from hell to heaven.

And, a good belly rub to my furry family, Honor and Gracie; you are the most patient creatures on this sweet sugar mountain. Thank you for coming into my life and our treasured, shared love for the natural world.

Index

About the Author

Born and raised in Vermont, Patricia began her lifetime love of baking in a busy family kitchen as a young child helping her father make doughnuts. At age seventeen, she became a croissant maker, and in the early 1980s, she worked as pastry chef assistant to Jeffrey Hamelman (award-winning Master Baker and now director of King Arthur Bakery) in Brattleboro, Vermont. From 1989 to 1996, she co-owned and operated the Bread Tree Bakery in Keene, New Hampshire, where she produced an extensive line of pastries and desserts.

In 2005, Patricia founded her cottage industry Wild Flour Vermont Bakery and became established at Vermont's premier farmers' market in Brattleboro, Vermont. She also works as a baking consultant and recipe developer and tester. Her most recent projects include recipe testing for world-renowned pastry chef Pierre Hermé's book *Pierre Hermé Macarons*, as well as dessert testing for the *MasterChef* series cookbooks. While Patricia follows a gluten-free diet, she continues to create both traditional and gluten-free French, European, and American-style pastries.